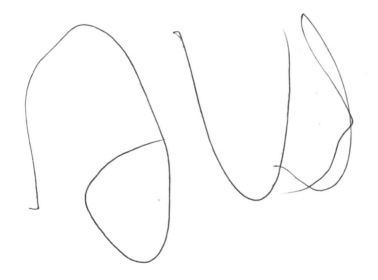

Tricks of Time

Tricks
of Time

Bergson,
Merleau-Ponty
and Ricoeur in Search of
Time, Self and Meaning

Mark S. Muldoon

Duquesne University Press
Pittsburgh, Pa.

Published in the United States of America by:
DUQUESNE UNIVERSITY PRESS
600 Forbes Avenue
Pittsburgh, Pennsylvania 15282

Library of Congress Cataloging-in-Publication Data

Muldoon, Mark.
    Tricks of time: Bergson, Merleau-Ponty and Ricoeur in search of time, self
and meaning/by Mark S. Muldoon.
        p. cm.
    Summary: "Invites readers into discussions of time, self and meaning under
the auspices of three thinkers: Henri Bergson, Maurice Merleau-Ponty and
Paul Ricoeur. The work of each thinker is highlighted to show how each 'dis-
rupts' 'clock time,' drawing out and reclaiming aspects of our humanity
neglected in mere chronology" — Provided by publisher.
    Includes bibliographical references and index.
    ISBN-13: 978-0-8207-0379-4 (hardcover: alk. paper)
    ISBN-10: 0-8207-0379-6 (hardcover: alk. paper)
    ISBN-13: 978-0-8207-0381-7 (pbk.: alk. paper)
    ISBN-10: 0-8207-0381-8 (pbk.: alk. paper)
    1. Time — Philosophy. 2. Merleau-Ponty, Maurice, 1908–1961. 3. Self. 4.
Meaning (Philosophy) 5. Bergson, Henri, 1859–1941. 6. Ricoeur, Paul. I.
Title.
    BD638.M75 2006
    115 — dc22

                            2006006252

Printed on acid-free paper.

To my parents and first teachers
Jack Henry Muldoon and Helen Agnes Hudecki

Contents

Abbreviations of Works Cited

Henri Bergson

TF   *Essai sur les données immédiates de la conscience.* Paris: Félix Alcan, 1889. Authorized translation by F. L. Pogson under the title *Time and Free Will.* London: George Allen & Unwin Ltd., 1971.

MM   *Matière et mémoire: essai sur la relation du corps avec l'esprit.* Paris, Félix Alcan, 1896. Authorized translation by N. Margret Paul and W. Scott Palmer under the title *Matter and Memory.* London: George Allen & Unwin Ltd., 1970.

CE   *L'Évolution créatrice.* Paris: Félix Alcan, 1907. Authorized translation by Arthur Mitchell under the title *Creative Evolution.* Lanham, Maryland: University Press of America, 1983.

ME   *L'Énergie spirituelle.* Paris: Félix Alcan, 1919. Authorized translation by H. Wildon Carr under the title *Mind-Energy.* New York: Henry Holt and Company, 1920.

TS   *Les Deux Sources de la morale et de la religion.* Paris: Félix Alcan, 1932. Authorized translation by R. Ashley Audra and C. Brereton under the title *The Two Sources of Morality and Religion.* London: Macmillan & Co. Ltd., 1935.

CM   *La Pensée et le mouvant.* Paris: Félix Alcan, 1934. Translated by M. L. Andison under the title *The Creative Mind.* New Jersey: Littlefield, Adams & Co., 1975.

Maurice Merleau-Ponty

SB   *La Structure de comportement.* Paris: Presses Universitaires de France, 1942. Translated by A. L. Fisher under the title *The Structure of Behavior.* Pittsburgh, PA: Duquesne University Press, 1985.

PP   *Phénoménologie de la perception.* Paris: Éditions Gallimard, 1945. Translated by Colin Smith under the title *Phenomenology of Perception.* London: Routledge and Kegan Paul, 1962.

PrP   "Le primat de la perception et ses conséquences philosophiques," in *Bulletin de la société française de philosophie* 49 (1947): 119–153. Translated by James M. Edie under the title *The Primacy of Perception and Other Essays.* Evanston, Illinois: Northwestern University Press, 1964.

SN   *Sens et non-sens.* Paris: Les Éditions Nagel, 1948. Translated by Hubert L. Dreyfus and Patricia Allen Dreyfus under the title *Sense and Non-Sense.* Evanston, Illinois: Northwestern University Press, 1964.

IPP   *Éloge de la Philosophie,* Paris: Libraire Gallimard, 1953. Translated by John Wild, James Edie, and John O'Neill under the title *In the Praise of Philosophy and Other Essays.* Evanston, Illinois: Northwestern University Press, 1988.

S   *Signes.* Paris: Éditions Gallimard, 1960. Translated by Richard C. McCleary under the title *Signs.* Evanston: Northwestern University Press, 1964.

VI   *Le Visible et l'invisible.* Paris: Éditions Gallimard, 1964. Translated by Alphonso Lingis under the title *The Visible and the Invisible.* Edited by Claude Lefort. Evanston, Illinois: Northwestern University Press, 1968.

Paul Ricoeur

HS   *Hermeneutics and the Human Sciences.* Edited by J. B. Thompson. New York: Cambridge University Press, 1981.

TN1   *Temps et récit I.* Paris: Éditions du Seuil, 1983. Translated by

Kathleen McLaughlin and David Pellauer under the title *Time and Narrative,* Vol. 1. Chicago: The University of Chicago Press, 1984.

TN2   *Temps et récit II.* Paris: Éditions du Seuil, 1984. Translated by Kathleen McLaughlin and David Pellauer under the title *Time and Narrative,* Vol. 2. Chicago: The University of Chicago Press, 1985.

TN3   *Temps et récit III.* Paris: Éditions du Seuil, 1985. Translated by Kathleen Blamey and David Pellauer under the title *Time and Narrative,* Vol. 3. Chicago: The University of Chicago Press, 1988.

FT   *From Text to Action: Essays in Hermeneutics II.* Translated by Kathleen Blamey and John B. Thompson. Evanston: Northwestern University Press, 1991.

RR   *A Ricoeur Reader: Imagination and Reflection.* Edited by Mario J. Valdés. Toronto: University of Toronto Press, 1991.

OA   *Soi-même comme un autre.* Paris: Éditions du Seuil, 1990. Translated by Kathleen Blamey under the title *Oneself as Another.* Chicago: The University of Chicago Press, 1992.

Introduction

Was not all sorrow in time, all self-torment and fear in time?
Were not all difficulties and evil in the world conquered as soon as one
conquered time, as soon as one dispelled time?
— Herman Hesse, *Siddhartha*

THE EXISTENTIAL PREAMBLE

Modern academic philosophy has often been criticized for losing
its original inspiration in struggling with first order questions that tor-
ment and haunt the human spirit, questions about why we exist and
how we should live confronted by the brevity of life and its seeming
meaninglessness.[1] Today, students of philosophy are no longer asked
to engage such large and poignant questions. Rather, they are instructed
to see philosophy as a set of competing discourses arguing over regional
problems such as personal identity, the nature of mind, moral theory.
Much time is spent teaching students the skills to construct discursive
arguments for or against certain positions held by eminent philosophers while more classical and dynamic confrontations with such elements as fate and destiny find little hearing save perhaps in a survey
course in ancient philosophy.

Missing is the encouragement and enticement to confront life head
on without compromise. Only on rare occasions might students be
invited to enter into the tempered pain of Pascal or the wild outrage
of Nietzsche. Perhaps the Russian existentialist Lev Shestov captured
best the spirit of philosophy's fiery confrontation with life and death
when he stated, "The task of philosophy is to tear itself loose from life

during life, if only in part. And even as man comes into the world wailing, or awakes with a cry from a torturing fever dream, so too the transition from life to death must clearly be accompanied by a senseless, desperate effort whose proper expression will also be a senseless, desperate cry or a wild sob. I think that many philosophers have known such an 'awakening' and have tried to tell it."[2] The problem of awakening takes us back to Plato's *Republic* and his open-eyed observation that for the better part of our lives we are asleep, embracing the shadows of a cave as if they were the reality of light. For some strange reason, hundreds of years of philosophical inquiry have not whetted our appetite for leaving the shadows. Perhaps they have only dulled it. As the title of one modern tome suggests, we cannot awake from "the dream of reason" in order to taste the bitter despair that chased the likes of Kierkegaard and overwhelmed Schopenhauer.[3] The price of being awoken from our slumber, and our enchantment with reason, is to become inquisitors of life, to demand a reckoning of our situation. The anxiety behind Kierkegaard's interrogation is almost palpable: "I stick my finger into existence — it smells of nothing. Where am I? What is this thing called the world? . . . Who is it that has lured me into the thing, and now leaves me here? Who am I? How did I come into the world? Why was I not consulted?"[4]

Feelings of entrapment, I believe, are endemic to the searching spirits who awake and demand an answer to the confines of their mortality against the alienating responses popular culture so easily offers. Modern academic minds have forgotten what guided the Greek mind, namely, that no awakenings, in this older philosophical sense that I have been alluding to, escape the hard bite of tragedy. While tragedy undoubtedly has many qualities and threads its way through innumerable human circumstances, both chosen and unchosen, there is a central font that fuels the tragic dimension in life. As Simone Weil aptly stated, "Time is the most profound and the most tragic subject which human beings can think about. One might even say: the only thing that is tragic. All the tragedies which we can imagine return in the end to the one and only tragedy: the passage of time. . . . It is the source of the feeling that existence is nothing."[5]

Whether in the form of epic poems, the reasoned conjectures of pre-Socratic thinkers, or the more systematic thought of philosophers since those times, the problem of time remains a central dilemma. For those whose eyes have left the shadows and its seductions, time exacts the greatest pain since the pathos of the fear of death is the greatest known to the human heart.[6]

The fight against the passage of time and the loss of all that is loved and cherished has inspired some of the greatest works of art to grace our culture. The problem of time is not a selfish one. Its examination, like a flood, rushes in with other demands of equal importance, namely, a disquiet about who we are, how we should live, and whether the quest for meaning is futile or not. To open the gate on time insists on questions that seem unrelated to it but are absolutely coreferential. It is the question of time, in all of its boldness, that forces the philosophical spirit to contend seemingly with everything at once.

I would neatly summarize this "everything at once" as the central problems of time, self, and meaning.

THE GENERAL PHILOSOPHICAL PROBLEM

Under rational scrutiny, the nature of time, the self, and meaning resist a definitive explication. In pursuing each theme with logical rigor, a number of controversial questions arise that are intrinsic to each theme. Debates still ensue, for example, as to whether time is an independent feature of reality or merely an aspect of our experience. This discussion is linked to questions of why time is directional with regard to the past and the future and whether or not time flows continuously or is composed of discrete moments.[7]

Similarly, the self has its own unique set of conundrums. On the surface, the self is an agent, the knower and the ultimate locus of the actions issuing from its body. However, the nature of consciousness and freedom raises the suspicion that there may be nonphysical aspects of the person not reducible to the body.[8]

Lastly, interest in the question of meaning has become exceptionally problematic. Since the rise of nihilism in the last century, the question of meaning has been backsliding not only from the existential critiques of Nietzsche, but also from the encroachment of postmodern discourses that espouse an antifoundationalism at every turn.[9]

In short, while the study of contemporary philosophy has honed its ability to rationally thematize aspects of time, self, and meaning, it remains humbled before the restless desire to thematize definitively any one of them in a totally intelligible manner. One of the reasons why philosophy has not been successful in rendering a full account of any of the three themes may lie in the assumptions behind its method of analysis.

Let us take for example the problem of the self. In the philosophical literature today there is no consensus as to how to approach the self in a consistent manner that would include both our "prephilosophical intuitions" about the self and our need to give it a "logically coherent account."

Until the eighteenth century, there was a general consensus about the nature of the self. It was understood as an inner, nonmaterial entity, accessible only to introspective consciousness. Unlike the constant change in the material world, the self was considered to be fixed, identified with an unchanging and immortal substance, that is, the soul. The first and perhaps still the most compelling argument against this traditional view of the self is found in David Hume's *A Treatise of Human Nature* (1739–40). It was Hume's claim that we have no access to a substantial and permanent locus of the self but only to a series of fleeting mental perceptions. Since no self could be found behind this "bundle of perceptions," he regarded it as a fiction.

Since Hume's time, the self-soul distinction has been replaced by a more materialistic self-body distinction that has spawned a myriad of competing arguments as to the nature of the self and how it persists through time, given the absence of a permanent substance that would underwrite it. These arguments include assertions that the self is a function of brain processes; that it is a fiction of logical, grammatical, or psychological parameters; that it is socially constructed; that it is the result of the narratives we produce; and that it doesn't really exist at all.

At the heart of the matter are competing intuitions about the self. One such set of deep intuitions is that the beliefs, values, desires, memories and other psychological features each person possesses make the person he or she is. The diversity, range, and uniqueness of such intuitions are the very stuff of subjective self-inquiry. They constitute the background against which the average person tacitly gauges his or her sense of self and whose loss or disruption would prevail in what is commonly called an "identity crisis." For the idealist, in a philosophical sense, access to such intuitions is direct and nonproblematic. For nonidealists, access to such intuitions is not direct and can only be seized upon from the interpretations of signs, symbols, and texts that objectify them.

Another set of intuitions concerning the self appeals to our rational inclinations. It is sometimes referred to as the "reidentification question."[10] In the absence of a permanent and unchanging substance, there is a logical necessity to give an account of what makes a person at time t_2 the same person as the person at time t_1. Analytical discussions abound as to whether personal identity should be defined by some version of the continuation of the body (the bodily continuity theory) or the continuation of a single psychological life (the psychological continuity theory). Analytic philosophers presume that the self and its existence over time (the reidentification problem) must fit the rigours of logical coherency. For forensic reasons, this is true. The necessity to reidentify an alleged criminal in a credible fashion some time after the criminal act is hardly arguable. But such coherency can only be attained if the self can be discussed from an ideally objective point of view. Theorists therefore strive to give a full account of "who I actually am" objectively while disavowing "who I think I am" intuitively as too subjective. It is this distinction between the need to give a logically coherent account of how the self persists over time and our deep and tacit intuitions about the nature of the self that generates the intractable problem of the self.

The difficulty is that neither set of intuitions can completely account for the other. Our deep intuitions about the self as morally responsible with its desires, aspirations, and regrets, for example, simply do not satisfy the demand for reidentification. In the meantime, the logical relations of identity that define the reidentification problem often overlook the fact that some sense of the self can be accessed in many ways. Not only can it be conceptualized and its logical relations of identity sought in terms of sameness (whether it is in terms of brain waves, fingerprints, DNA, memories, or other psychological features), but the self can also be narrated, imagined, remembered, and interpreted.

What defenders of either set of intuitions fail to appreciate is the fact that there is no monolithic question of personal identity. The question of identity arises in many different contexts, bearing different significance, and demanding different kinds of responses. To date, philosophy has not been able to find a general theory of self that would satisfy the demands of both sets of intuitions.

I believe the conflicts that flourish within the problem of the self arise with equal vehemence in the study of time. In thinking about time logically, we subvert and deemphasize the personal experience of time as a flow and passage. Once we isolate time as an independent feature of reality, we disengage it from the fabric of our own struggles with our mortality and the search for meaning in existence.[11] The time of science and time as measure simply do not satisfy our intuitions about the passage of time and its meaning. Similarly, dividing time between an A-series and a B-series, as McTaggart did, and arguing for the unreality of time does nothing to suppress the irresistible intuition that time is stronger than our logic and that death holds all the trump cards.[12]

In short, philosophically hypostatizing any one of these central themes like the self and time seems dangerous and undermines what the human mind and heart initially sought — a comprehensive understanding of existence in order to live better.

THE PRESENT STUDY

A better way to approach the themes of time, self, and meaning is to observe how they always seem to appear *together* in the actual act of philosophizing. The following work is an attempt to reveal how the notions of self and meaning in a philosophical system are dependent on the philosopher's fundamental assumption about time. A philosopher's belief in time as real or unreal, or as more psychological or objective, for example, will have direct consequences on how that philosopher defines self and meaning within a particular philosophical system.

One only has to think of Kant's appropriation of Newtonian physics and his struggle to fit some form of absolute time into his rationalist program. Where Kant demonstrates the persuasiveness of time in the function of cognitive reason, he suppresses the temporality of moral conscience and practical reason in order to save the integrity of the autonomous self. Consequently, Kant is forced to postulate the ground of moral freedom in a timeless noumenal self that is hard to reckon with the self of pure apperception in cognition and the self revealed in inner sense as the knower of the external world.[13] Kant is an exceptional example of how a philosopher's self-chosen concept of time underwrites and demarcates the lineaments of the self that will follow from it. No wonder one of his prime commentators concluded that Kant's "doctrine" of time "is the most vulnerable tenet in his whole system."[14]

To test the thesis that time, self, and meaning act as a dynamic configuration across various philosophical systems, I will look closely at a particularly compact period of philosophical history where this triad of themes appears over and over again, with time being the determining factor of self and meaning.

The historical snapshot that I find exceptionally instructive covers approximately a century of philosophical endeavour. It begins with the ideas of Henri Bergson (1859–1941), passes through the contributions of Maurice Merleau-Ponty (1908–1961), and ends with the thought of Paul Ricoeur (1913–2005). Bergson's famous *Essai sur les données immédiates de la conscience* appeared in French for the first time in 1889, while Merleau-Ponty published *Phénoménologie de la perception* in 1945. Ricoeur's English translation of *Temps et récit* appeared in 1988. Each of these thinkers was and is a recognized member of the French Continental tradition. Their successive chronology within that tradition is ideally posed to reveal their consistent confrontation with the triple thematic of time, self, and meaning as it ferments through three different eras of philosophical analysis and three different *points de départ*.

Bergson's ideas are often associated with but not identified with the French spiritualists and vitalists of the middle and late nineteenth century; Merleau-Ponty was central to French existential phenomenology during the 1940s and 1950s; Ricoeur's work is hermeneutical in nature and reflects one of the many conversations of late twentieth century postmodernism.

These three thinkers are important historically because their ideas embody in varying degrees some of the most important philosophical movements of the twentieth century.[15] First, each of these thinkers — albeit in his own unique fashion — decries the older "philosophy of representation" and emphasizes the unmediated presence of the human subject to the world. Hence, they moved French philosophy beyond the Kantian *Ding an sich* and the rational metaphysical tradition that it represented. Second, especially with regard to Merleau-Ponty and Ricoeur, there is the key emphasis on human finitude and the partiality of our knowledge of the world thanks to the overcoming of ontotheology by interpretation. Last, there is recognition of the semiological argument that a sign derives its meaning from other signs, not from its relation to an independent thing. The ultimate effect of this Saussurian advance was to open the door to the linguistic turn in contemporary philosophy and to question the reliability of any extralinguisitic reference to validate our assertions.

Bergson's designation of *durée réelle,* Merleau-Ponty's notion of temporality, and Ricoeur's "historical present" give rise to particular senses of self and meaning. For Bergson's notion of duration, there is the fundamental self and its freedom; for Merleau-Ponty, there is the ambiguity of identity and the contingency of meaning; and, for Ricoeur, narrated time is co-referential with narrative identity with the suggestion that meaning is refigured in light of the narrative function and reading.

In working my way through the three authors, I hope to show that self and meaning constellate around time. Each attempt to deepen our understanding of our temporal being invites an even deeper reflection on how to define the self and what level of meaning authenticates that self. Another way that one might understand what is to follow is to consider the work as an exercise in philosophical anthropology. By this I mean the serious attempt to see how themes like time work across systems and how they are taken up anew by different thinkers in order to glean a better understanding of them.

If there is any source of inspiration behind this study, it lies in Ricoeur's achievement in *Time and Narrative* and his grand claim that the narrative function attains its full meaning only when it becomes a *condition* of temporal existence. So convincing is his analysis in light of this claim that I was tempted to ask the following: if narrated time is *the* time of our temporal being, would not an interest in the narrative mode of discourse be detectable in other authors who have similarly sought to describe that mode of being we call temporality? In other words, would not Bergson and Merleau-Ponty become test cases for Ricoeur's assertion? Would not some play or mention of the narrative function and language finds its way into the analyses of the former thinkers? The aim of the following work is to show just how strong the connection between time, narrative, self, and meaning is in both Bergson and Merleau-Ponty once viewed under the Ricoeurian optic to build a philosophical anthropology.[16]

The link between time and narrative, evident in varying degrees in each of these three thinkers, displaces the older metaphysical question concerning the "what" of time. The emphasis now becomes a question of "who" experiences, both personally and corporately, the passage of time and how. Ricoeur once remarked that "time is never lived directly, that it is never a mute, immediate lived experience, but one that is always structured by symbolic systems of varying complexity."[17] For example, no culture can refer back to its own conception of time without resorting to the vital "narrative" activity that is expressed linguistically in an immense variety of legends, epics, and stories. As narrators, human beings obtain a grip on their experience and find their way through the chaos of life's vagaries, which the wise of past cultures often contrasted with the immutable order of the stars.[18]

Ricoeur's interest in narrative is not his alone. The recent philosophical interest in narrative arises from a number of related disciplines such as literary criticism, psychology, linguistics, and historiography. The impetus behind this preoccupation with the narrative form has been the growing realisation that language is not a mere tool for mirroring reality but a formative part of that reality, in fact, it is constitutive of what we come to call the real.

Perhaps the most contentious development of this "linguistic turn" has been the idea that what we call "the self" is not something that exists as an extralinguistic existent or Cartesian agent. The self, rather, arises as a byproduct of our narrative practices. It is through narrative practices of all types that we eventually discern the character of our own "self," gain self-understanding, and forge meaning in our temporal lives.[19] What a growing body of literature points out is that the narrative function is the privileged medium for understanding human experience. The function doesn't merely describe the self and meaning but helps form them. Therefore, the sense of identity that will define this particular study is a nonessentialist view, one that is not dependent on an immutable substance or continuity theories. Rather, as Ricoeur proposes, narrative identity takes shape by the stories we tell and exchange with one another. These stories are rooted in national, religious, and familial traditions, offering master narratives that consciously and unconsciously serve as models for our own stories.

For those familiar with the literature, studies such as Brockelman's brief study, *Time and Self* and David Carr's *Time, Narrative, and History* have the greatest similarity with what is to follow.[20] While Brockelman states the connection between time, self, and "life values and attitudes," he does not develop the tripartite theme as a dynamic configuration. What he does emphasize and what will be important for our study is the realization that "'personal identity' is a kind of story." Brockelman clearly elaborates the temporal nature of human action and how the preconscious or prereflective life attitudes and values embedded in our actions must be recuperated through a process of secondary reflection. It is this reflective relation that intrudes a certain separation or transcendence within the self and permits the range of self-consciousness to develop through narratives in dialogical communion with others. His succinct thesis statement reads, "I shall develop the transcendental argument that the various realms of narrative discourse through which human beings find life construed with meaning (novels, stories, sacred history, drama, mythology, theology, history) find their existential roots in the temporal and narrative structure of personal identity. Without the narrative condition involved in being a 'self,' there could be no literature, history, poetry, or religion."[21]

Carr's study, meanwhile, is much more extensive and argues that narrative "is on the one hand the unity of the *lived* and the *told*, and on the other hand the unity of the *individual* and the *social* or *historical*." His strong thesis is that action, life, and historical existence are themselves structured narratively — independent of their presentation in literary form — and that "this structure is practical before it is aesthetic or cognitive."[22] However, Carr takes issue with many authors, including Ricoeur, who accord to narrative a universal aspect that makes it the only way we confront temporal chaos and stave off Father Time's attempts to devour us all.[23]

To close this section, I have left the most contentious point for last — the question of meaning, the third component of the dynamic configuration to be discussed. The problem of meaning is no less ambiguous and unresolved than the problems of time and self, both briefly unpacked above. As previously stated, what I hope to make clear is that the notions of self and meaning constellate around time. Too often previous studies plunge forward with discussions of meaning and authenticity while either overlooking the problem of time or acknowledging it but not giving it the foundational place it deserves. The works of Charles Taylor are emblematic on this point. In a recent work on meaning and authenticity, he quite readily asserts that "we are embodied agents, living dialogical conditions, inhabiting time in a specifically human way, that is, making sense of our lives as a story that connects the past from which we have come to our future projects. This means . . . that if we are properly to treat a human being, we have to respect this embodied, dialogical, temporal nature."[24] However, nowhere in his extensive corpus of works does Taylor give a full accounting of what he means by temporal nature. While he consistently defends the point that human identity can only be defined against what he calls "horizons of significance,"[25] he does not hierarchize these horizons. In failing to do so, Taylor does not permit us to see how a particular horizon of time in which each "self" is embedded takes on a preeminent significance with regard to what will be seen as good and valuable. True, many people see their identities defined partly by some moral or spiritual commitment to a religious or political affiliation, but such affiliations are often grounded with respect to a particular eschatology or worldview that engenders a particular conception of time. In constantly emphasizing, for example, the notion of becoming and the projection of future possibilities as a basic feature of human existence, Taylor rightly acknowledges his own allegiance to a particular Heideggerian formulation of how time is to be understood.[26]

As the following analysis hopes to reveal, formulations of human time, self, and meaning are codependent. Taylor's work is not an exception to the rule.[27] But my point here is not to take issue with Taylor, or to define meaning, but to let the analysis show how the *philosophical play with time,* within a system of thought, encourages a formulation of meaning to arise, whether it be based on a single category, as in the case of Bergson, or, in a more hermeneutic fashion, as in the case of Ricoeur.

HISTORICAL BACKGROUND

Historically, outside of the theme itself, there has been no continuity to the philosophical study of time. Each author, from Plato to Augustine, from Kant to Ricoeur, picks up the torch anew and attempts to throw fresh light on the basic conundrums of time. The only discernible shift that marks this history is the appearance of what is normally understood as "modern philosophy." Loosely defined, modern philosophy is a movement of thought originating with René Descartes (1595–1650) that has perpetuated itself up to, and into, the twentieth century. It sought to realize one of philosophy's traditional goals of achieving a basic, fundamental knowledge of what is (*ta onta*) by turning inwards, into the epistemic-knowing subject itself (conceived in either psychological terms or transcendentally). The subject becomes, henceforth, the ground for the certainty of our knowledge of what we will refer to as "the external world." The result is the transformation of the epistemic-knowing subject into something foundational, provided the knowing subject is understood as somehow self-transparent. In being transparent to itself, consciousness of self becomes a center of indubitable knowledge and treated as more fundamental than any form of positive knowledge.

A key byproduct of this historical movement is the temporalization of time.[28] By this I mean that after the Enlightenment period, the question of time becomes more and more a problem associated with the machinations of the epistemic-knowing subject. Philosophers and thinkers became more preoccupied with time as a basic constituent of human subjectivity rather than something independent of the subject. Modern philosophy marks a shift from the more traditional strategies of defining time external to the self to inquiring how time is integral to knowing oneself and the external world. It is in this sense that time is temporalized, and temporality becomes a constitutive force in the construction of someone's perception, someone's intention. In the following chapter much will be said on this matter, with direct references to key figures in the modern discussion of time: Kant, Husserl, and Heidegger.

The following study is a product of this temporalization of time. As ordinary time is temporalized and brought closer to the self, the sense of this new temporal time is fragmented into a number of possible variations and possible interpretations, as is the self. It was Kant, for example, who first argued against seeing space and time as either simply real or simply ideal. Space and time, rather, are subjective conditions of sensibility — the pure forms of intuition — and necessary conditions of the possibility of experience. In other words, there is no direct grasp of naked reality. Objective reality is that which we experience. Such experience is always the product of an imposed spatio-temporal framework that prevents us from ever knowing things as they are "in themselves," that is, the "noumenal" state that is assumed to underlie the phenomenal world as we experience it. Time as such is no longer the time of nature, but the time of experience. However, in this new guise, time does not lose its vestiges of Newtonian uniform time.

Under Kant, time becomes the infinite container in which all experience transpires.

A consequence of this split between the noumenal and the phenomenal is the theoretical doubling of the self or ego into an empirical and transcendental subject. The odd thing is that even with such doubling at hand, we cannot know about the self as it is in itself since all knowledge is only of appearances. Self-knowledge would have us make an object of ourselves, and employ time as a form of intuition. As such, knowledge of our inner states is as conditioned by time as all other empirical intuitions. The result is that all we can ever hope for is empirical self-consciousness — knowledge of the appearance of the self — but no knowledge of ourselves as we really are.

My point here is simply to hold up Kant as exemplary of modernity's long engagement with delineating the self in light of how time is characterized fundamentally in the modern period. While locating the beginning of modernity's preoccupation with time and self with one philosopher or another is a matter of taste, it is certainly in the course of modernity's history that the idea of a self stabilized in time becomes problematic. This problem finds its extreme formulation in such postmodern thinkers as Jacques Derrida where, under the auspices of his idiomatic neologism of *différance,* the traditional sense of "self-presence" as an origin and locus of meaning in time is challenged and seemingly dispersed.[29]

MASTERS OF DISRUPTION

Let me finish this section by enunciating more precisely why the French continental tradition, characterized by Bergson, Merleau-Ponty, and Ricoeur, is a valuable test case for the triple thematic of time, self and meaning.

If there is one term that succinctly captures the *Zeitgeist* of the twentieth century it is "crisis." Underlying any review of current events and literature, whether focused on humanitarian issues, human rights, political debacles, philosophical currents, or even a change in aesthetic taste, is a vision of the last century as a century of crisis.

The last century, more than any other, posed indomitable crises for the individual. The growing domination of technocracy, scientism, and the rise of totalitarian control over human intelligence made it obvious that classical systems of ideas inherited from the Enlightenment or before no longer assuaged our need to find meaning in our daily human experience. The explosion of technology alone, for example, reflected human domination over nature and forced human beings into conscious reflection not only on the end of history, but on the very historicity of our own consciousness.

French philosophy, at least since the time of Descartes, offers a valuable counterbalance to the pandemic rise and domination of scientism, with its reductionistic tendencies that cultivate crises. While the aim of this counterbalance has been obviously to critique science, the method makes it unique, in claiming that only philosophy is able to reveal something of lived experience that escapes the abstractness necessary for successful empirical science.

In his magisterial work on French philosophy in the twentieth century, Gutting summarizes this counterbalance by focusing on the problem of human freedom as *the* central issue over the last hundred years.[30] He refines this focus by conflating the question of human freedom with that of the immediacy and concreteness of human experience. In other words, "just what is given in immediate experience" that eludes the grasp of empirical science?

Broadly conceived, one can see the historical imprint of this theme in Descartes' desire to define his thinking self in an instance of reflexive thought; it is equally present in Pascal's epiphany and Marcel's secondary reflection. In this respect, I believe Gutting is correct. French thought in so many vocabularies, contexts, and categories has provided a plethora of formulations as to what constitutes the immediate and lived experience, yet none are comprehensive and, ultimately, exhaustively adequate.

What Gutting may have overlooked, however, is that our desire to understand and retrieve concrete lived experience from analytical reductions and instrumental categories is more aptly understood as the need for the self to understand and retrieve the richness of the present moment. In this sense, the last hundred years of French thought can be equally conceived as temporal-centric, seeing conceptualizing the present, or, more precisely, grasping the self in the flux of time, as its perennial task.

In his *Conversations with French Philosophers*, Rötzer sees the interpretation of self-understanding in the present, not individual freedom, as the guiding leitmotiv that underpins much of modern and postmodern French thinking.

> If the horizons of traditional self-understanding are concealed, or, like the story of perpetual progress unto perfectibility, no longer convincing, everyone's everyday self-understanding is already at the starting point of *philosophical reflection about the conditions for, and possibility of, inquiry into what now is.* If Hegel had already characterized philosophy programmatically as an undertaking that grasps its own time in thought, then this intention is undeniably appropriate for the experiences of contemporary consciousness, shaken as it is with crises, incomprehensible changes, and possible dead ends for the project of modernity. . . . In the hollow space of the present, each must put together and develop flexible, uncertain, fleeting identities inscribed in a more or less reflexive interpretation of the fundamental constellation of consciousness.[31]

Stated in these terms, consciousness of the present is as much a question as it is a task. Yet it is the very task that Bergson, Merleau-Ponty, and Ricoeur set for themselves, albeit in different ways. What exactly are the broad contours of this task? As will be aptly elaborated in the next chapter, the present has two faces, *the present given* and *the present as giving.*

The *present given* is that story we tell about time as being objective, self-existent and autonomous, something outside of ourselves, irreversible in its direction, towering over our lives and deaths. We use the objective present as a tool. It is the time we use to measure movement by counting successive instances or "now points." This sense of the present attempts to exclude the observer and his or her impressions of the present as much as possible. To achieve this we employ the position of the arms of a clock, various timepieces, and astronomical objects. When we ask what time it is, we inadvertently give the present a spatial quality by *assuming* that the "now" can be located between a preceding "now" and a successive "now" separated by a gradation of space. This is clearly seen on analogue timepieces, less so on digital timepieces where only the numerical instant appears, yet the assumption is the same. Further, the duration of the objective instant is inconsequential to this conception of time. A millisecond or nanosecond is still an arbitrary grid we employ to gauge events happening. The given present is the temporality we impart to Nature and employ to describe the causal connections we observe to be occurring and thereby to have some measuring stick to say "how fast" or "how slow."

The *present as giving* begins with the human experience of corporeal movement and perception, the impressions I have of being a body that observes and reacts intersubjectively with others and the natural world. My body does not need objective time to be able to experience and move about animate and inanimate objects outside myself. Rather, the movement of my body to undertake and perform an action is a consolidated effort between the memory of previously executed actions and an anticipated pattern. In brute terms, *every* action is the result of a temporal synthesis based on our body's ability to register impressions, process them, and act appropriately.

For this reason, regardless of habit and repetition, corporeal action is more than a mechanical reaction. Our perceptual ability wonderfully masters the need to pick out necessary and vital environmental cues (that constantly change) to ensure our action is not awkward but efficient. The sequences of actions by which we do the most mundane things from opening doors to drinking a glass of wine are a unique temporal synthesis every time we undertake them — supported by remembering (memory) and projecting forward my past experience as a foreseeable outcome (anticipation).

In the execution of a bodily action or nonaction (which would nonetheless still be an action unless we were dead), our impressions are heavily infused with memorial remnants, subjective colorings, and psychic data that flavor the present peculiar to the unique individuals that we are. Sometimes, for example, our passage on a commuter train passes quickly as our inner time consciousness becomes absorbed by our own inner machinations mulling over a broken love affair, a forthcoming holiday, or the desire to achieve something. Other times, we constantly look at our timepiece, impatient with the chronological duration of our commute. As such, the uniformity of measured time doesn't dictate our experience of it. Further, just having to go into certain environments may recall a childhood trauma or other unconscious memories that color the experience, making it either pleasant or unpleasant, and influencing its duration to seem like an eternity or a brief delight, regardless of the objective measurement of the duration.

More, even though I am framed by a world I call objective, the inner time of others dislodges me from my own spatio-temporal center of action. My inner sense of time cannot be a fixation on *my* world, challenged as I am by the fact that I do not have any special access to the memories and anticipations of another. His or her inner time never appears to me, yet it is the center out of which he or she acts. To this end, my own sense of self as being a center is always being decentered and recentered in the alterity of the other.

In this way, our inner sense of time, the present as giving, has features that cannot appear in the objective world. For this reason, quoting Merleau-Ponty, each of us is "the upsurge of time" unique to our lived experience. Each new birth of flesh breaks the anonymous continuity of an objective exterior time by the very real need to move, to perceive and to react to the natural world and others.[32] As one author notes, "In the common world, inner time gives itself as not being able to be given. It gives itself as something that, from the perspective of the common world, appears as a disruption of the given."[33] Such disruption delivers us from the tyranny of any perceived sense of casual determinism since the sequences of our actions are not governed strictly by necessity.

In this light, Bergson's *la durée réelle,* Merleau-Ponty's *le surgissement du temps* and Ricoeur's the historical present should be understood as so many different attempts to grasp this disruption, which cannot appear in the objective world. As we shall see, each attempts to master the hiddenness of the present, this disruption in chronological time, in order to reclaim some aspect of our irreducible humanity that science does not honor. This is why I refer to them as "masters of disruption." Perhaps only outdone by Augustine, no other set of philosophers in any particular school or epoch has offered us such a diverse and unique series of attempts to respond to the question: "what is the present?" While not working in tandem, or necessarily following each other's lead, yet sharing the same French cultural and philosophical climate, Bergson, Merleau-Ponty, and Ricoeur aptly reveal how interrogating the present constantly intercepts any neat and efficient closure to defining the self and human meaning. Each of their contributions is novel and unique, leading us to take Ricoeur's claim seriously, namely, that time cannot, ultimately, be thought; it can only be lived and our lives recounted.

STRUCTURE OF PRESENTATION

Chapter 1 summarizes Ricoeur's discussion of the aporetics of temporality in regard to several thinkers (Aristotle, Augustine, Kant, Husserl, Heidegger). Sufficient space is permitted to show how Ricoeur identifies the aporias within those thinkers (Augustine, Husserl, and Heidegger) who attempt to interiorize time — to seek a phenomenological "pure time" — in contradistinction to ordinary time or world time. An understanding of these aporetics and the ultimate inscrutability of time will be important in gauging the success of the works of Bergson and Merleau-Ponty. This introductory chapter does not attempt to introduce the larger hermeneutical project of Ricoeur but concentrates on his central thesis in *Time and Narrative,* providing a brief sketch of his "poetic solution" to the problem of time under the auspices of the narrative function.

Chapter 2 is an exposition of Bergson's famous notions of intuition and real duration (*la durée réelle*). This exposition is a critical one. It aims to reveal how the role of the "intuition of duration" is extended to encompass not only the category of time but consciousness and "life" itself. This tension reflects Ricoeur's warning of how any attempt to define "time" with a direct but silent intuition of time runs into insoluble contradictions by trying to account for what it leaves behind — ordinary time. Parallel to this is Bergson's ambiguous appreciation of

language. As a pre-postmodern philosopher, Bergson lacked a fundamental understanding of how language may be constitutive of such fundamental concepts as time and self. In many of his works he is critical
of language's ability to translate the quality of inner experience wherein
intuition melds with the *élan vitale*. On the other hand, Bergson gives
special priority to poetry and to the storymaking function as basic tools
of our social existence. In *Creative Evolution,* he goes so far as to attribute
to language our liberation from an oblivious attachment to matter. But
for the most part, Bergson, outside of his own magnificent uses of tropes,
refuses to use language to mediate intuition. Last, the central meaning that authenticates the deepest sense of self is freedom. Yet, it is difficult
to see how sheer intuition and consciousness, as Bergson describes them,
safeguard our freedom without a discourse about intentions and
motives.

Chapter 3 is devoted to the thought of Merleau-Ponty, with almost
exclusive regard to his *Phenomenology of Perception*. After giving an
overview of his philosophical project, the chapter is divided between
his diffuse remarks on temporality throughout the *Phenomenology of
Perception,* and then a more focused exposition of the second chapter
in the third part of the text entitled "Temporality." My concentration
on this text hopes to elucidate his attempt to situate temporality
between an empirical and idealist account of time. While his depiction
of temporality bases itself somewhat on Husserl's notion of internal
time-consciousness, Merleau-Ponty's analysis of phenomenal time
never gives in to the temptation of basing time solely in its phenomenological constitution. In the end, time is a dimension of subjectivity and not a feature of the objective world; however, subjectivity does
not constitute time, and time is not simply an attribute of the self. The
difficulty with this thinker is to connect his desire to detail our preobjective existence and the expression of the incarnate in language and
literature. What results is a continual deferment to ambiguity with regard
to the self and meaning. The self is always unfinished, able to reconstitute its identity in finding levels of authentic expression in the midst
of sedimented significance. Borrowing a term from Montaigne, I designate this sense of self the ambiguous self. The chapter ends on a critical

note, criticisms that will be taken up in the concluding chapter, "Creative Time."

Chapter 4 takes a more detailed look at Ricoeur's entire thesis with emphasis on the formal aspects of narrative composition as a prelude to discussing the "historical present" as the "third time" between what he calls "cosmic time" and "mortal time." It may only be at this juncture, in the light of the analyses offered by Bergson and Merleau-Ponty, that we will more fully appreciate his depiction of this "narrated time" as the really "human time" of our lives. I will focus on the final volume of *Time and Narrative,* which culminates in a sort of hermeneutics of historical consciousness that is developed through an understanding of how the narrative form — both historical and fictive — mediate each other and accomplish their individual aims by borrowing from each other. The correlative sense of self that erupts at the intersection of these two narrative chains is what Ricoeur will call narrative identity. It is an identity that mediates a fragile tension between *idem*-identity and *ipse*-identity. In the end, narrative identity does not master the meaning of time, but works with the aporias in search of meaning. Meaning arises as we, the reader, stand before a text that invites us into a world that may provoke us to act and think differently. Here we fully understand that in avowing the mystery of time, narrative allows us to work with a prefigured sense of time that is refigured in the act of reading. Nonetheless, in the end, time remains inscrutable. Time is not conquered as much as we are taught to give depth and richness to its ceaseless passage.

Chapter 5 summarizes Ricoeur's contributions one more time; subsequently, the thought of Bergson and Merleau-Ponty are more rigorously compared to it. The chapter aims to show clearly where the desire to proffer a "pure" intuition of time or a purely "lived time" falter in trying to say the "all" about time. The result of any one master idea attempting to say the "all" about time is to splinter or bifurcate the self, given the tension of holding the two streams of time (mortal and cosmic) in balance. While both Bergson and Merleau-Ponty commented amply on the role of language, narrative, and literature, their sense of narrative does not arrive at Ricoeur's assertion that time becomes human to the extent that it is articulated through the narrative mode. The very last section of this chapter notes in the course of this study how often the term "creative" arises in speaking of human time, whether it be Bergson's *durée réelle*, Merleau-Ponty's notion of temporality, or Ricoeur's narrated time. Perhaps human time is essentially the opportunity for human creations to take fruit. Part of such creations is the search for meaning in time. There is also the metaphilosophical question of the role narrative plays in dispersing the distinction between literary genres and levels of discourse. Have we really read three philosophically astute theses on time, or, can we see such texts as autobiographical attempts to enframe the author's narrative identity over time?

ONE

The Aporias of Temporality

The first word that you ever spoke was: light.
Thus time began.
For long you said no more.
— Rainer Maria Rilke, *Book of Hours*

THE ORDINARY SENSE OF TIME AND SELF

Thinkers of all sorts, from scientists to philosophers, have attempted to give a final account of time. Time has been portrayed in a multiplicity of forms, hypostatized in a thousand metaphors, and described through a plethora of symbols. However, when separated from theogonies, genealogies, and mythologies, the human desire to understand time in its totality, on its own account, in all of its modalities from the personal to the cosmic, has found little satisfaction over the centuries.

The central problem is that time has yet to be definitively thematized so as to make it clearly intelligible.[1] The internally consistent accounts of time found in science, psychology, philosophy, aesthetics, or practical action, when compared, are incompatible; there is no "right" time. Regardless of the account, time transcends its analogical representations; its essential characteristics are never completely captured by any one of them. Another way of stating the intractability of the time problem is that we are unable "to think it away."[2]

There is a common notion, however, that behind both the chronometry of daily life and the felt sensation of duration, as well as behind the biological time of physiological processes and the metrics of astronomy, there subsides a more fundamental or absolute time that is at once primordially continuous and infinite. It is this sense of a great, pervasive, but hidden time that has often persuaded metaphysical thinkers to define time on the basis of permanence over change. This tendency is no more clearly epitomized than in Plato's seminal and classical statement that "time [is] an eternal moving image of the eternity which remains forever at one."[3]

While Aristotle (384–322 B.C.E.) was later to identify time with movement,[4] our modern understanding of time has its more recent historical basis in Galileo Galilei (1564–1642). Galileo realized that all important features of local motion — the distance covered, the speed, and the change of speed — could be expressed in terms of displacements given the magnitudes of elapsed distance (space) and time.[5] It is here that time, understood as an independent variable in the description of motion, finds its conception. Most significantly, time was now conceived as something independent of the environment. Subsequently, this implied that motion was better described in terms of time, not time in terms of motion as the ancients had held. Also implicit in Galileo's approach was a certain refinement to the sense of uniformity that characterizes the flow of time. Without such refinement, time could not have become the independent variable that it has.

Some 80 years after the discoveries of Galileo, Isaac Newton (1642–1727) codified this understanding of time for physics in the famous definition: "Absolute, true, and mathematical time, of itself, and from its own nature, flows equally without relation to anything external, and by another name is called duration: relative, apparent, and common time, as some sensible and external measure of duration by the means of motion, which is commonly used instead of true time; such as an hour, a day, a month, a year."[6] Terms such as "absolute," "true," "mathematical," "itself," and "equally" all work to distinguish time from any particularity whatsoever and give it a metaphysical pre-eminence of perfect uniformity and unalterable presence. The most common analogy to this understanding of time is a line linking together mathematical points. Ricoeur states, "According to this representation, time is constituted merely by relations of simultaneity and of succession between abstract 'nows,' and by the distinction between extreme end points and the intervals between them. These two sets of relationships are sufficient for defining the *time when* something happens, for deciding what came *earlier* or *later*, and *how long* a certain state of affairs might last."[7]

Absent in this description is the need to introduce the distinction between past, present, and future particular to the agency of a human spectator. There is no need to single out a unique moment of time as the present, separating the past from the future. The "now" is always anonymous, a purely quantitative and seemingly independent datum. Until perhaps recently, classical science has never felt it necessary to distinguish this anonymous "now" with regard to a human observer. This single oversight lies at the heart of Ricoeur's argument concerning the aporetics of temporality, which we will discuss shortly. At the level of physical reality, as described by science, there is an admission that time does not flow as much as it is asymmetric. That is, there is an irreversibility to time that is better indicated by the analogy of an "arrow of time" to differentiate orientations of physical time — "before" and "after."

Asymmetry, however, does not allow the notion of "becoming" as one of the fundamental characteristics of physical reality.[8] What a scientific standpoint fails to recognize, nonetheless, is that even this admission of time's asymmetry presumes the presence of an intermediary who can initiate some form of temporal demarcation, even as basic as a "before" and "after." The anonymous "now," therefore, is never anonymous. Any distinction of the smallest duration must be attributable to a human spectator or observer. For Merleau-Ponty, the natural milieu is too much a plenum for there to be time. It is the self that is the "upsurge" of time. More precisely, Bergson remarks, "without an elementary memory that connects the two moments, there will be only one or the other, consequently a single instant, no before and after, no succession, no time."[9]

What allows time to be used as a common parameter of measurement is its quasi-spatialization. As we become accustomed to saying metaphorically that events "move" into the past, we become equally accustomed to conceiving an order in which events occupy different "places." Events thereby become hypostatized and the heterogeneity of *real change* is reduced to a homogeneous succession. This quasi-spatialization of time transforms succession into juxtaposition and presents uncompleted moments of time as a completed, simultaneous whole.[10]

While mimicking a primordial regularity built into nature, the common notion of the relentless uniform flow of time is deeply rooted in modern Western civilization. It serves as the commonsense attitude toward the nature of time despite Albert Einstein's theories of relativity and the notion of space-time. As such, the average person in the Eurocentric West is an unwitting Platonist of the first order, in as much as he or she believes time to exist apart from and prior to him or herself. Its existence is paradoxical in that it is something that we cannot produce or effect, but can employ as a tool of order.

This commonsense or ordinary understanding of the nature of time has been variously designated throughout history as "objective time," "scientific time," and "physical time." Most of these terms have their origin in the seventeenth century. It was the spirit of the Enlightenment, with its infatuation with the scientific method that invited the world to disregard the medieval understanding of nature as a multiplicity of forms and qualities at various stages of actualization and, instead, see the "real" world as inscribed in the laws of physics.

The key concept in this new science was "substance." Extended, observable, and calculable, the form and method of substance was mathematics. Pure mathematics became the ideal form of all valid knowledge and what could not be determined in this form became unreal, illusory, and imaginary. Unfortunately, the desire to universalize this form, and conceive of the world as a set of causal relations between substantial objects, becomes seriously flawed when applied to the entire field of knowledge, and, in particular, in any attempt to understand the self by analogy to the material world. Let us look at an example.

It was David Hume (1711–1776), in his *A Treatise of Human Nature* (1739–1740), who so innocently tried to extend the methods of Newtonian science to human nature itself.[11] Early in this famous work Hume states that time is to be understood in a particular manner. First, the idea of time is specifically derived from the succession of our distinct perceptions that have distinct existences and to which the mind can never perceive any real connection. Second, time is to be understood as individual moments that succeed each other, and that none of them, however contiguous, can ever be coexistent. And lastly, an unchangeable steady object that produces coexistent impressions could not affect the idea of time in our minds; rather, like a line where a succession of anonymous "nows" appear, time can only appear to the mind in light of some perceivable succession of changeable objects.[12] In short, the time of the mind is the time of number as measure, as used in physics.

Further on in the *Treatise* Hume claims that "when I enter most intimately into what I call myself, I always stumble upon some particular perception or other, of heat or cold, light or shade . . ." but that "I never can catch *myself*." This inability to "catch" himself as a self stems from the fact that there is no one perception that will account for the unity of the distinct existences of particular impressions. There is no one impression that can account for "the whole course of our lives." Consequently, for Hume, what we call the self is a fiction. It is only through the work of cause and effect and memory that "a bundle or collection of different perceptions" are linked together to give the illusion of a self.[13]

The problems Hume encounters arise because of change and would be unproblematic without the passage of time. What Hume seeks are the relations linking the various perceptions a person has at different times. He fails to "catch" the self because he cannot justify the thinking of various simultaneous perceptions as belonging to a single person. The self Hume describes lacks a principle of unity, or a unity of consciousness, that would order perceptions in a time conceived differently than serial succession. The mind for Hume was only "a kind of theatre where several perceptions successively made their appearance; pass, re-pass, glide away . . . There is properly no *simplicity* in it at one time, nor *identity* in different; whatever natural propension we have to imagine that simplicity and identity."[14] As such, the Humean mind could only entertain the metric "now" as the simple demarcation between a "before" and "after." In contrast to St. Augustine, the Humean mind could not distend itself into the living present wherein the past (memory) and the future (anticipation) have sway in the action (intention) of the lived present.

Hume often notes his skeptical frustration in the *Treatise*.[15] The occasion of this frustration was his inability to conceive the self outside the laws of cause and effect that determined his understanding of the self as a substantial entity in the world. Hume's starting point to describe the self was not a historicizing ego but the objective natural world as described by Newton. The self was a mere entity found in the world *in* time like other quantifiable substances. Hume could only grasp the identity of the self through the categories of resemblance and causality, just as he understood the identity of other natural objects. The spatio-temporal continuity of perceptions was par with the spatio-temporal continuity of a physical body as the criterion of self-identity.[16] Said in other terms, the fundamental meaning of the identity of the self for Hume was the identity of the causal laws that determined its behavior. These laws were the nature of the Humean self.

The meaning of time, therefore, did not issue from the experience of the self. Like Newton, Hume felt time was ready-made, absolute, instantaneous, and infinite. If the self could not exist within a time that was ready-made and under which other natural entities were substantiated and coordinated, then it did not exist. Because a self is never only a "now," Hume could never grasp more than a fragment of the self at a moment. Given his premises about the nature of time, his conclusion that the self is a mere fiction was correct.

Despite its utility, uniformity, and even omnipresence, this ordinary sense of time is deficient. As subsequent philosophers have shown, this representation of time cannot account for the particular manner in which a human subject *actually* reckons with experience through time. It does not account for the primacy of the future as the main orientation of human desire; it does not explain the fundamental capacity of recollecting the past in the present; it does not take into account the centrality of the present as the fulfillment of an intentional action. All of these expressions of being-in-time issue from a conscious subject and are not accounted for by the ordinary sense of time. As noted in the introduction, there are prephilosophical intuitions that we have of time's passage left unexplained by the conventional understanding of objective time.

One can quickly object here and argue that great strides have been made to overcome the Humean dilemma since the time of Kant and well into the twentieth century with the famous works of Husserl and Heidegger. Various phenomenological descriptions have attempted to show how the self is constituted through a time that it constitutes and how the self employs time in living by looking at its self-conscious acts.

At this point I turn to Ricoeur's analysis in *Time and Narrative*. One of his central claims is that there is no one time that can adequately account for both ordinary time and a purely phenomenological time that issues from the one "who" experiences time. Ricoeur argues, rather, for a "third time" between cosmic time (of which ordinary time is derivative) and phenomenological time. This third time finds its genesis at the intersection of human finitude and language, or, more precisely, where language as narration transmutes that finitude by ennobling it with various levels of signification. "As soon as the individual comes up against the finite limits of its own existence, it is obliged to recollect itself and to make time its *own*" (RR 465).

My present purpose in turning to Ricoeur's work is to follow his argument against ever delineating a purely phenomenological time that is peculiar to the self. He will accomplish this by tediously working his way through five major figures in the philosophy of time (Augustine, Aristotle, Kant, Husserl, and Heidegger) and showing how time without a present (natural time) and time with a present (phenomenological time) mutually contaminate one another yet remain impenetrably incommensurable. In short, no one philosopher can say all there is to say about time if they uncritically start from either pole. This will set the stage for a better appreciation of both Bergson and Merleau-Ponty, who attempted to delineate a particular sense of time oblivious to the difficulties Ricoeur will point out.

Discord and Concord in the Study of Time

Ricoeur's fundamental thesis in *Time and Narrative* is that "time becomes human to the extent that is articulated through a narrative mode, and narrative attains its full meaning when it becomes a condition of temporal existence" (TN1 52). Summarizing elsewhere, Ricoeur states,

> My basic hypothesis . . . is the following: the common feature of human experience, that which is marked, organized and clarified by the fact of storytelling in all its forms, is its *temporal character*. Everything that is recounted occurs in time, takes time, unfolds temporally; and what unfolds in time can be recounted. Perhaps, indeed, every temporal process is recognized as such only to the extent that it can be, in one way or another, recounted. This reciprocity which is assumed to exist between narrativity and temporality is the theme of my present research (FT 2).

The strategy to unpack this hypothesis is to concentrate on the tension between what Ricoeur calls the "concord" and "discord" in life that gives rise to the production of narratives.[17] From Augustine, Ricoeur more fully understood the instability of time—the suffering we endure from its ceaseless decomposition. Only by means of a *distentio animi* was Augustine able to see any possible, if fragile, concord over the discord that erupts between the instability of the human "now" and the stability of the eternal "now" of God. Jumping back several centuries, Ricoeur finds in Aristotle a thoroughly human product where concord constantly outstrips discord—namely in the construction of stories of all types, from epics to tragedies, through the dynamic operation of emplotment (*muthos*) and creative imitation (*mimesis*). The genius of Ricoeur's entire thesis is the *tertium quid* he finds between the two seemingly disconnected tensions of concordance and discordance in Aristotle and Augustine; this third tension will be more fully explored in the fourth chapter devoted to Ricoeur.

To make Ricoeur's confrontation with the aporias of time as coherent as possible, I have joined his remarks from the first volume of *Time and Narrative* concerning Augustine with those made at the beginning of the third volume where Augustine is incorporated into a larger discussion that includes Aristotle, Kant, Husserl, and Heidegger. My goal is to enumerate, in as orderly a fashion as possible, Ricoeur's critique of past attempts to grasp a typically human time as a prelude to contributions made by Bergson and Merleau-Ponty. To this end, the following discussion summarizes Ricoeur's detective work in uncovering the particular brands of aporia that plague the discussion of time in the works of Aristotle, Augustine, Kant, Husserl, and Heidegger. This journey through the dense intellectual history results in what Ricoeur calls the "ultimate aporia of time." This last aporia will guide our discussion of Bergson and Merleau-Ponty and why they too fail to offer a final solution to the enigma of time.

St. Augustine and the Hierarchization of Time

For Ricoeur, the time of the human subject, phenomenologically pursued, cannot be sought directly on its own terms free from theoretical difficulties or puzzlements, which Ricoeur formally calls "aporias." His attempt to delineate them is important because they stand over and against the power of temporal refiguration, which he valiantly tries to describe in his discussion between the epistemology of history and literary criticism.

Pure phenomenology for Ricoeur is the "intuitive apprehension of the structure of time" and "it is the attempt to make time itself appear" (TN1 83). However, Ricoeur denies that any such "pure" phenomenology can exist. To exist, it would have to free itself from the arguments by which it undertakes to resolve its own paradoxes inherited from earlier traditions and yet not engender any further contradictions (TN1 84). Unlike Edmund Husserl who was aware that "as soon as we even make the attempt to undertake an analysis of pure subjective time-consciousness — the phenomenological content of lived experiences of time (*Zeiterlebnisse*) — we are involved in the most extraordinary difficulties, contradictions, and entanglements,"[18] and yet incurred still more paradoxes by supposedly discovering "the absolute, temporally constitutive flux of consciousness,"[19] Ricoeur refuses such an analysis, denies the purity of such procedures, and is content to identify the continual appearance of aporias that prevent an absolute and pure analysis of time-consciousness that so many have sought. Ricoeur's most consistent reference throughout his discussion of the aporias of time is to the elegant portrayal of human time in St. Augustine.

The first chapter of *Time and Narrative* sketches the central aporetic nature of time in book 11 of St. Augustine's *Confessions*. Ricoeur understands that Augustine's study is psychological, and he concentrates on this mindful sense of time, excluding Augustine's wider meditation on eternity. I will summarize Ricoeur's treatment of Augustine by identifying the three aporias that Ricoeur finds important.[20]

First, there is the problem of the triple present. As soon as Augustine voices his famous exclamation, "What, then, is time? I know well enough what it is, provided that nobody asks me; but if I am asked what it is and try to explain, I am baffled" (14:17),[21] all the ancient difficulties regarding the being and nonbeing of time come to the fore. The skeptical argument is well known: time has no being since the future is not yet, the past is no longer, and the present is not always. Yet, we speak of time as having being in that things to come *will be,* that things past *were,* and that things present *are passing away.* What negates the triumph of skepticism however is the "experience" of time — the "sensory, intellectual, and pragmatic activities in relation to the measuring of time" (TN1 9). But regardless of the experience that time is passing, the stubborn skeptic wants to know how or where we measure the past and future. It was Augustine's genius to conclude that indeed the past and future do exist (17:22), and, unlike any intellectual predecessor, he insisted they could exist in the present. "It must be correct to say that there are three times, a present of past things, a present of present things, and a present of future things. Some such different times do exist in the mind, but nowhere else that I can see. . . . The present of things past is memory; the present of present things is direct perception; and the present of future things is expectation" (20:26).

While Augustine's triple present is an elegant solution to the past and future of time, Ricoeur is quick to point out the new puzzlements Augustine faces in proffering such a solution: first, all time is somehow in the present, and second, time is no longer "out there" but is intimately tied to the mind and is denied any type of cosmological reference point.

The second aporia surfaces in Augustine's attempt to explain "how" the triple present is present to the mind. The answer is the *distentio animi*. The inherence of time in the soul takes on its full meaning only when every thesis that would place time within the sphere of physical movement has been eliminated through argument. To this end Augustine has to deny the ancient insistence that the movement of celestial bodies constitutes time. Augustine refuses to accept the fact that astral movements are invariable and therefore the ultimate standard of how we measure the passage of time. In fact, Augustine argues that if all movement should stop, time would not (24:31); but the fact that we do measure the movement of a body by time implies to Augustine that such measurement takes place solely in the mind, as a type of extension (26:33). Furthering his examples by reference to recitations, Augustine purifies the present from being anything remotely instantaneous; it is extended rather, in relation to certain intentions (*intentio*). The mind distends (*distentio*) itself actively between present attention, past memory, and future anticipation in constant engagement given what it intends to accomplish (28:38). As Ricoeur summarizes, "the more the mind makes itself *intentio*, the more it suffers *distention*" (TN1 21). Augustine extrapolates this distention of the mind to stand not only in relation to the recitation of a psalm, but every action in life and the whole history of humankind (28:38).

But Ricoeur turns us away from the elegance of the answer provided by the *distentio animi* to the question of human time, and points toward the several enigmas that suddenly appear. How can it be, he asks, that expectation and memory can exist without any reference to physical change outside the mind? What independent mode of access do we have to the extension of the impression inasmuch as it is held to be purely "in" the mind? Last, and perhaps most enigmatically, Ricoeur asks to what degree anything has been solved by a soul that is constantly distending itself as it engages itself. Is this not, he asks, only a recognition that discordance always precedes the concordance of the intentions of expectation, attention, and memory? Is not the real revelation of *distentio animi* the fact that the time it engenders is never complete; is not the constant threat of potential decomposition presupposed in every act of extension, intention, and distention? (TN1 21).

The third aporia Ricoeur isolates in Augustine's thesis only deepens the above. It comes into focus when the notion of *distentio* is placed back into Augustine's larger meditation on eternity. The clash between eternity and the *distentio animi*, Ricoeur insists, forces us to inquire into "what is other than time" (TN1 22). It intensifies the existential experience of the *distentio animi* and invites us to recognize an internal hierarchy that relates our experience of change and that what does not change.

Wishing to understand how the *Verbum* created heaven and earth (7:9), Augustine has to refine his notion of eternity until finally he pinpoints an ultimate characteristic: "in eternity nothing moves into the past: all is present. Time, on the other hand, is never all present at once" (11:13). As such, a negativity is introduced. In order to push reflection on the *distentio animi* — that is, on the slippage of the threefold present — as far as possible, it must be compared to a present with neither past nor future. As Ricoeur states,

> It is the recoil (*le choc en retour*) effect of this 'comparison' on the living experience of the *distentio animi* that makes the thought of eternity the limiting idea against the horizon of which the experience of the *distentio animi* receives, on the ontological level, the negative mark of a lack or a defect in being. The reverberation . . . of this negation that is thought on the living experience of temporality will now convince us that the absence of eternity is not simply a limit that is thought, but a lack that is felt at the heart of temporal experience. The limiting idea then becomes the sorrow proper to the negative. (TN1 26)

In recognition of this negativity, Ricoeur points out that in the closing lines of book 11 of the *Confessions,* a final interpretation of the *distentio animi* is proposed. Encased in a lament, the *distentio animi* becomes not a "solution" to time but an expression of the way in which the soul, deprived of the stillness of the eternal present, is torn asunder: "but to win your favor," Augustine cries, "is dearer than life itself. I see now that my life has been wasted in distractions [*distentio est vita mea*]" (29:39). The themes of *distentio* and *intentio* now become acknowledgments of dispersal and discordance. All questions concerning the unity of time — our complete concordance with time and eternity, and the experience of the eternal as the absence of any lack — are transferred from the level of the existential but speculative play of the *distentio* and *intentio* to hope in the future. It is still in the midst of the experience of distension that the wish for permanence is uttered: "until I am purified and melted by the fire of your love and fused into one with You" (29:39).

Hence, the alienation, distance, and dissemblance between time and eternity calls for a return. In Augustinian terms, this alienation exists between the eternal *Verbum* and the human *vox* and is only assuaged by teaching and communication. The Word is the inner master sought and heard within: "It is true that I hear your voice, O Lord, telling me that only a master who really teaches us really speaks to us. . . . But who is our teacher except the Truth which never changes?" (8:10). In this way, our first relationship to language is not that we talk, but that we listen, and that, beyond the external *verba*, we hear the eternal *Verbum*. The essence of teaching, therefore, is to bridge the abyss that opens up between the eternal *Verbum* and the temporal *vox*, to elevate time, moving it in the direction of eternity (TN1 29).

During his analysis and the discovery of certain puzzlements, Ricoeur makes special note of when Augustine slips in and out of differing modes of discourse, from lamentation, to praise, to supplication, to interrogation, to discursive analysis and back to lament. In the circuitous monologue of the *Confessions*, what has the retreat to the soul — with the introduction of the threefold present, the *distentio animi*, and the role of *intentio* — wrought in regards to understanding time? Has Augustine really solved anything? Are not the same ancient paradoxes still in place — the permanence and transience of time, the need to associate and disassociate time with movement, the impossibility of grasping the temporal and eternal all at once? Yet, were not all these problems presupposed by Augustine prior to his initial query, "*quid est enim tempus?*"

In pointing out these three aporias, Ricoeur does not accord failure to Augustine's interrogation over and against the traditional paradoxes of time. Rather, what comes to light is that human temporal experience can be hierarchized and unfolded to reveal layers or levels of temporalization that, in Augustinian terms, run the gamut between the distended present and the unchanging present. In contrast to "what is other than time," human temporal experience is not abolished but deepened. In Augustine's analysis, while the older aporias are solved by deeper and deeper interiorization of human temporal experience, new aporias are produced or older ones are expressed in a new light. This multiplication of aporias is the price, Ricoeur insists, we must pay for every attempt to make time itself appear — which is the ambition that defines any phenomenology of time in the purest sense (TN1 30).

Despite this initial attempt in the first chapter of the first volume of *Time and Narrative* to seek out the various aporias found in Augustine's struggle with time, Ricoeur, in the opening pages of his third volume, reports that this initial investigation cannot stand as a complete study. Even though the first two volumes of *Time and Narrative* address the topics of history, narrative function, and "games" with time found in certain novels, Ricoeur feels that he has not sufficiently established the aporetic character of speculation on time with this initial excursion into St. Augustine. While Augustine's analysis allowed him to discover the paradox of the discordant-concordant structure of time, it did not take into account the further aporias that resulted from that discovery. In fact, Ricoeur wants to generalize the law that any progress in the theory of time, through the phenomenology of temporality, must ultimately pay the price of a higher and higher accumulation of aporicities. To prove his suspicions, the first section of the third volume of *Time and Narrative* rigorously investigates not only Augustine, but Aristotle, Husserl, Kant, and Heidegger. It is to these investigations that we now turn.

Aristotle and the Unity of Time

Ricoeur opens his third volume with a dynamic clash of perspectives between the time of the soul in Augustine's *Confessions* and the time of the world in Aristotle's *Physics*. He begins by doubting whether

Aristotle's sense of measurement and extension attributed to time can be derived from the *distentio* and *intentio* dialectic of Augustine. While Augustine sees measurement as a genuine property of time, he refutes a cosmological thesis that tied time to the movement of various material objects since the invariance or regularity of that movement could not be established. For Augustine the principle of measurement could only be found in expectation and memory; its duration dilates or deflates, so to speak, with regard to the intention at hand. However, outside of his famous example of recitation, he does not detail our access to the impressions of variable durations or how such durations could provide the fixed measure of comparison that he has refused to accord to the movement of stars and planets.

In recognizing this failure in Augustine, Ricoeur turns to Aristotle to see the problem of time from the other side, from that of nature, the universe, the world. Ricoeur understands Aristotle's assertion that time has roots in a cosmological tradition according to which time envelops us and dominates us without the soul having the power to produce it. Not only is the soul powerless to produce the imperious character of time but, paradoxically, it helps to conceal such a time (TN3 12). What is Aristotle's definition of time?

Ricoeur restricts his discussion of Aristotle to the significant set of passages found in the *Physics* (219a34–35).[22] He concentrates his attention on three particular points. First, Aristotle is careful not to elevate time to a principle that is reserved for change alone. Change (movement) is in every case in the thing that changes (moves), whereas time is everywhere in everything equally. The relation between time and movement is such that "time is neither movement nor independent of movement" (219a2). Second, Aristotle applies to time the relation of before and after when he states that, "since then before and after hold in magnitude, they must also hold in movement, these corresponding to those. But also in time the distinction before and after must hold, for time and movement always correspond with each other" (219a15–18). Last, the relation between before and after is completed by adding a numerical relation to it: "for time is just this — number of motion in respect of 'before' and 'after'" (219b).

Ricoeur observes that in this particular definition of time there is
an absence of any noetic activity of the soul despite its *necessary* implications in each of the emphasized points. Aristotle, he points out, consistently fails to stress the perception, discrimination, and comparison
of the active mind in relation to movement — that is, the need to distinguish two end points and an interval and the numerical identification
of an instant. What Aristotle specifies as important for the definition
of time "is not counted but countable numbers, and this is said about
movement before being said about time" (TN3 16).

Ricoeur believes Aristotle is blinded to ever according a role to the
soul in his definition of time, owing to the requirements of the tradition he represents. For Aristotle the initial definition of change (and
movement) is rooted in *physis*. *Physis* is the source and cause of change.[23]
It is *physis* that, by supporting the dynamism of movement, preserves
the dimension of time over and above any human attributes (TN3 17).
Despite the development of his philosophy since Plato and those prior
to him, Aristotle, Ricoeur surmises, is not free from the premonition
that time overpowers us with an awesome strength as heard in the pre-
Socratic voice of Anaximander when he supposedly stated that "The
source from which existing things derive their existence is also that to
which they return as their destruction, according to necessity; for they
give justice and make reparation to one another for their injustice, according to the arrangement of Time."[24] As such, Ricoeur argues, the
anchoring of time in *physis*, whose mode of being escapes the argumentative rigour common to Aristotle and resists his philosophical clarity, allows for two "inconceivable" elements to undermine the entire
Aristotelian analysis of time (TN3 18). The first element concerns the
unstable and ambiguous status of time itself, caught between movement, of which it is an aspect, and the soul that discerns it. The second refers to movement which, Ricoeur insists, Aristotle never clearly
defines as being anything more than "something indefinite"[25] or "the
fulfillment of what is potentially, as such."[26]

In concluding his critique of Aristotle, Ricoeur does not accord any
superiority to Augustine's emphasis on the necessity of the soul. What
prevents an easy assimilation of one system by the other is the

conceptually unbridgeable gap between the notion of the "instant" in Aristotle's sense and that of the "present" as understood by Augustine. For Aristotle, the instant is a discriminatory break in the continuity of movement that can be made anywhere. The Augustinian present, on the other hand, is an instant designated by a speaker as the "now" of his or her utterance. The spoken "now" implies an intention that lives within the slippage of a past, present, and future; it is not reducible to just a before and after. Again, for Aristotle, to distinguish the present from the instant and the past-future relation from the relation of before and after would be to threaten the dependence of time on movement — the single, ultimate principle of physics (TN3 21).

The actual dilemma between Augustine and Aristotle can be summarized as the inability of a psychology of time to replace a cosmology. Augustine, from the distension of the mind alone, cannot derive the principle of the extension and measurement of time. It is the dilemma of the assembled unity of time bursting apart as a function of memory, anticipation, and attention. Which is primary? The core aporia between these two authors concerning time is that a psychological theory (time of the soul) and a cosmological theory (time of the world) mutually occlude each other to the very extent they imply each other (TN3 14). Said otherwise, the physical definition of time cannot by itself account for the psychological conditions for the apprehensions of this same time (TN3 244).

Husserl and the Pure Hyletics of Consciousness

Ricoeur's recognition of the constant appearance of aporias in Augustine and Aristotle, between the dispersal of time in the soul and the unity of time in general, sets the stage for his last three investigations into Husserl, Kant, and Heidegger. In these latter three authors it is the oneness of time that is the continual problematic and source of ever more refined aporias.

Ricoeur's entire investigation of Husserl is restricted to the latter's obscurely edited text entitled the *The Phenomenology of Internal Time-Consciousness*.[27] The beginning of this text argues that only at the exclusion of objective time (world time) can we gain access to an internal (*inneres*) consciousness — a time-consciousness (*Zeitbewusstsein*). This compound German expression suggests two things that are one: one consciousness, one time. Husserl's aim is to work out a "hyletics"[28] of consciousness, "the apprehension [*Auffassungen*] of time, the lived experiences in which the temporal in the Objective sense appears" (24).[29] Ricoeur wishes to see if Husserl can indeed exclude all other times "in order to lay bare time and duration . . . appearing as such," thereby giving internal time-consciousness a proper phenomenological description (TN3 24).

Husserl proposed two major advances to arrive at his goal: the constitution of an extended present by the continuous addition of retentions and protentions to the source-point of the living present, and, the distinction between retention (primary remembrance) and recollection (secondary remembrance). Husserl, as is well known, starts his analysis of retention with the perception of as materially insignificant an object as possible, namely, a sound. By reason of its temporal nature, the sound is no more than its own occurrence, its own succession, its own continuation, and its own cessation (TN3 26). The sound is not a perceived object as much as it is a sensed object; it is a *Zeitobjekt* (40) that has a residual objective side that must be bracketed, not forgetting that this *Zeitobjekt* must be constituted in the sphere of pure immanence, that is, duration, in the sense of the continuation of the same throughout the succession of other phases.

Wherever one starts, "the 'now' is not contracted into a point-like instant but includes a longitudinal intentionality": it is at once itself and the retention of the tonal phrase that has "just" passed, as well as the protention of the imminent phase.[30] What we hear, therefore, is not just a "now," but "a continuity of phrases as 'before'" (44). In fact, the sound "begins and stops, and the whole unity of its duration, the unity of the whole process in which it begins and ends, 'proceeds' to the end in the ever more distant past" (44).

Ricoeur immediately picks up on something in Husserl's suggestive example, namely, that a jump must be made between the "fragments" of duration represented by the *Zeitobjekt* that is constituted by a sound that continues to resonate, and "temporal duration itself" (45).

Ricoeur feels Husserl has not supplied a sufficient explanation of duration in the sense of continuation, of "continuance considered as such" (43), and not simply succession. Can the iteration of the phenomenon of retention (protention) make up the single flux of temporal consciousness? (TN3 252). Despite the twists of language and the diagrammatic explanations, Ricoeur argues that it is impossible to bring together in one flow, as Husserl proposes, memories that are continually issuing from the living present, quasi-presents freely imagined along with their own sets of retentions and protentions, and recollections that do not stand in direct connection with the living present, yet which are endowed with a positional character not found in merely imagined quasi-presents. While Husserl feels he has advanced an adequate answer in the light of what he calls "coincidence" (*Deckung*) (67) which is supposed to transpose, on a wider scale, the phenomenon of the continuation of the present into the recent past, Ricoeur doubts that it accounts for what is called for, namely the "linking of time."

To make his point, Ricoeur points to the third section of *The Phenomenology of Internal Time-Consciousness* where Husserl attempts to explain how every kind of memory has a fixed place in the unitary flow of time, along with the increasing fading away of these contents as they fall back into an ever more distant and hazy past. To accomplish this Husserl splits up the intentionality that slides back and forth along the length of this flux, distinguishing from the primary (transverse) intentionality that is directed toward the modifications in how a particular object is presented, a second form of (longitudinal) intentionality that aims at the temporal position of this experienced object independent of its distance from the living present. "Consequently," Husserl states, "like two aspects of one and the same thing, there are in the unique flux of consciousness *two* inseparable, homogeneous *intentionalities* which require one another and are interwoven with one another" (109). In other words, despite the continual modification of temporal objects at the level of transverse intentionality, that modification subsists in a particular enduring form of time (the unitary flux) that must constitute itself.

In this sense, Ricoeur rightly points out the infinite regress inherent in Husserl's analysis; to have something that endures, there must be a flux that constitutes itself. To do this the flux, which must appear in person, requires yet another flux in which the first can appear. As such, the enterprise of pure phenomenology cannot be completed without positing this self-constitution (109). This self-constituting flux, however, as Ricoeur points out, refers to the totality of the flux of time considered as a form (TN3, 41). In other words, there is no flow to the originary time Husserl is trying to describe; "the absolute, temporally constitutive flux of consciousness" must occur "in" time regardless of belief to the contrary. There is a "fixity" to time that Husserlian analysis cannot dissolve by its own argumentation but must presuppose. In short, there seems to be an objective time that precedes the phenomenology of inner-time consciousness as proposed by Husserl.

The problem of a form or a fixity can be examined in regard to a major feature of the flux — its continuity. In section 41, Husserl considers what he now calls the "self-evident consciousness of duration" and its identity of continuity which "is an internal characteristic of consciousness." The strange attribute of this continuity, he argues, is its dependence on the discontinuous: "In any moment, no matter what, a greater or lesser fluctuation will always take place, and thus the continuous unity with respect to a given moment will be linked to a difference of another moment which provides an indirect separation from the first" (113). Ricoeur points out that the difference between two lapses of time is precisely a distinction, not a separation (*ver-schieden,* not *ge-schieden*). The difference between one moment and another (discontinuity) presupposes a background of changelessness (continuity) which is time itself; Husserl, immediately following the above, states that "discontinuity presupposes continuity, be it in the form of changeless duration or of continuous alteration" (113). But how are we to know it, outside of the mixture of transcendent intentionality (toward the object) and longitudinal intentionality (toward the flux)? For Ricoeur it is clear that Husserl can only attest to the discontinuity in change by appealing to some other experience that has no break. "At the very most we can say that continuity and discontinuity are interwoven in the consciousness of the unity of the flux, as if the split arose out of the continuity and vice versa" (TN3 43). The result of this is a sharpened aporia where the multiplication of intentionalities does not exhaust the source of objective time. The absolute, temporally constitutive flux of consciousness presupposes a time it does not constitute.

In short, Ricoeur argues, no matter what his strategies, Husserl cannot draw from a phenomenology applied in the first place to the continuous expansions of a point source, a phenomenology of the whole of time. Despite his attempts to keep his level of analysis at the level of a pure hyletics of consciousness, such a discussion can only occur if it borrows from the determinations of an objective and constituted time supposedly bracketed in the beginning. What falls under severe scrutiny, therefore, is Husserl's methodology and the efficacy of the *epoché* to totally remove oneself from the "natural standpoint." The "natural standpoint" is an inescapable reality that must be confronted and not bracketed or banished. As Ricoeur summarizes: "the situation is as follows. On the one hand, objective time is assumed to have undergone reduction . . . on the other hand, if the discourse on the hyletic is not to be reduced to silence, the support of something perceived is necessary" (TN3 26).

Constituting time, therefore, cannot be elevated to the rank of pure appearing without some shift in meaning from the constituting to the constituted (TN3 244). Unfortunately, Ricoeur observes, Husserl did not seriously consider the irreducibly metaphorical character of the most important terms upon which his description is based such as "flow" (*Fluss*), "phase," "expire" (*ablaufen*), "proceed" (*rücken*), "sink back" (*zurücksinken*), and "interval" (*Strecke*).[31] These terms indicate that the Husserlian analysis is marked by certain homonymies between the "flow of consciousness" and the "Objective flow of time," or the "one after the other" of immanent time and the succession of objective time, such that the analysis of immanent time could not be constituted without repeated borrowings from the objective time that has been excluded (TN3 24). It is this particular paradox to which Ricoeur points out as the most significant aporia of the Husserlian analysis of a "pure" phenomenology of time.

Kant and the Invisibility of Time

What directly opposes Husserl's phenomenology of time and Kant's critical philosophy is the latter's assertions about the indirect nature of all assertions about time; that is, that time does not appear but is a condition of appearing. Ricoeur, in juxtaposing these two authors, wants to show that Kant, in the *Critique of Pure Reason* (1781, 1787),[32] is unable to construct a presupposition concerning a time which itself never appears as such, without borrowing from an implicit phenomenology of time.

Ricoeur begins his incursion into the *Critique* by expressing suspicion about Kant's constant reference to the nonthematized identity of the mind (*Gemüt*). It is not without phenomenological overtones, Ricoeur suggests, that the *Gemüt* is defined as "the capacity (receptivity) for receiving representations [*Vorstellungen*], through the mode in which we are affected by objects, is called *sensibility* [*Sinnlichkeit*]" (A19),[33] and that both external sense and inner sense rest on "a property of our mind" (A22, B37). Only Kant's separation of matter (manifold) from form (which "must lie ready for the sensations *a priori* in the mind *[Gemüt]*" (A20, B34)) negates an appeal to self-evidence and veils the phenomenological implications in the early stages of the *Critique*.

Kant's arguments about time also borrow from phenomenology. In the "Transcendental Aesthetic," and reminiscent of the Newtonian definition of time quoted earlier, Kant puts forward several arguments for the "Metaphysical Exposition of the Concept of Time." First, he tells us that we would not perceive two events as simultaneous or successive if the representation of time were not presupposed as underlying them *a priori* (B46); second, that time would not vanish if it were emptied of all of its events (A31); and, third, that time is not a discursive concept but a pure form of sensible intuition and that different times are but parts of one and the same time (A31, B47). This third argument, Ricoeur is quick to point out, is an axiom not produced by experience but *presupposed* by it. "If indeed different times are only parts of the same time, time does not behave as a genus in relation to different species — it is a collective singular" (TN3 46). Last, "the infinitude of time signifies nothing more than that every determinate magnitude of time is possible only through limitations of one single time that underlies it" (A32, B48).

Common to all these arguments is that time is posited *a priori* as the intuition of one unique time; there is an ideal nature of time that assures its oneness (TN3 47; 251). Kant can only deny a direct vision of this time, Ricoeur suggests, by accenting this presuppositional character of time. As a presupposition, the character of time becomes inseparable from the relational and purely formal status of space and time. In assuring that the level of discourse of the "Aesthetic" remains at the level of the presuppositional, all other levels of discourse, especially of any lived experience, is silenced. This strategy, Ricoeur suggests, is regressive and simply assumes the privileged form of an argument from absurdity (TN3 47). What else could be meant when Kant states that time "is nothing but the form of our inner intuition. If we take away from our inner intuition the peculiar condition of our sensibility, the concept of time likewise vanishes; it does not inhere in the objects, but merely in the subject which intuits them" (A37)?[34]

In short, the paradox of the *Critique* resides in its particular argumentation, which veils the phenomenology implicit in the thought-experiment that governs the demonstration of the ideality of space and time (TN3 48).

In "Analytic of Principles" the main reason for the nonphenomenality of time becomes more apparent: for every new determination of time, a detour, by way of the constitution of an object, is confronted that ultimately thwarts any appearance of time as such. For example, schemata, which for Kant are a necessary and universal procedure of imagination in providing an image for a concept (A140, B179), are the *a priori* determinations of time. They are the representation of a particular category under the form of time. Consequently, we can speak of "the *time-series,* the *time-content,* the *time-order,* and lastly to the *scope of time* in respect of all possible objects" (A145, B184).

Are such determinations "time" *per se*? Further in the "Analytic" we are told that these determinations are meaningless without the support of *a priori* synthetic principles that make the schemata explicit. These principles have no other function than to posit the conditions for the objectivity of the object. As such, therefore, time cannot be perceived in-itself: we can only have an indirect representation of it through simultaneous intellectual and imaginative operations applied to objects in space. In remaining a condition for objective appearing, time itself does not appear. In this respect, giving a figure to time by means of a line, for example, far from exposing time, is only an accomplice in indirectly manifesting time in the application of a concept to the object through the auspices of the imagination (TN3 49). Further, any representation of time at the level of schemata and principles is always accompanied by a determination of time, that is, by a certain practice of time (lapse of time) that adds nothing to the original presupposition of an infinite time to which all the other times are but successive parts. "It is only in the determination of particular successions that this indirect character of the representation of time becomes clearer" (TN3 49).

This twofold nature of the representation of time, then, at once indirect yet determined, refuses time a level of phenomenality in the "Analytic." An intuitive phenomenology of time recedes further and further as experience presumes formality. Time once again does not appear but only remains a condition for objective appearing.

This implicit strategy of detour is equally well expressed in the "Analogies of Experience" under the general principle that "all appearances are, as regards their existence, subject *a priori* to rules determining their relation to one another in one time" (A177, B218). Here we find the richest observations concerning the transcendental determinations of time as order. Kant tells us that there are three modes of time, namely duration, succession, and coexistence that correspond to the three rules of all relations in appearance in time (A177, B219). In the first analogy, the "Principle of Permanence of Substance," one reads

> Our *apprehension* of the manifold of appearance is always successive, and is therefore always changing. Through it alone we can never determine whether this manifold, as object of experience, is coexistent or in sequence. For such determination we require an underlying ground which exists *at all times*, that is something *abiding* and *permanent*, of which

all change and coexistence are only so many ways (modes of time) in which the permanent exists. (A182, B225–26)

Further on the same text states that

the permanent is the *substratum* of the empirical representation of time itself; in it alone is any determination of time possible. Permanence, as the abiding correlate of all existence of appearances, of all change and of all concomitance, expresses time in general. For change does not affect time itself, but only appearances in time. (A183, B225–26)

The paradox is that permanence somehow includes succession and simultaneity. Since time itself cannot be perceived (A183, A226), it is only by way of the relation between what persists and what changes, in the existence of a phenomenon, that we can discover this time that does not pass away, yet in which everything passes. This is what is referred to as duration of a phenomenon, that is, a quantity of time during which changes occur in a substratum that nonetheless remains and persists (TN3 50). In the same section, Kant stresses the fact that in mere succession, without appeal to permanence, existence would only appear and disappear without ever possessing the slightest magnitude. If time is not to be reduced to a series of appearances and disappearances, it must itself remain. But this can only be detected by observing what remains in phenomena, which we determine as substance when we put into relation what remains and what changes.

The permanence of substance upon which this description is based takes nothing away from the invisibility essential to time. Permanence remains an unvoiced presupposition of our ordinary perception and the apprehension by science of the order of things. In stating that, "the schema of substance is permanence of the real in time, that is, the representation of the real as a substrate of empirical determination of time in general, and so abiding while all else changes," and "to time itself non-transitory and abiding, there corresponds in the [field of] appearance what is non-transitory in its existence, that is, substance" (A143, B183), the immutability of time is presupposed as it corresponds to what appears in accordance with the schema (the permanence of the real in time) and the principle of the permanence of substance. Again, nothing about time has been necessarily demonstrated. Everything up to this point concerning the question of time has been presuppositional (TN3 50–51).

In his remarks so far Ricoeur is convinced that Kant's determination of time contains the lineaments of an implied phenomenology especially if in the reciprocity between temporalization and schematization the former is to contribute something to the latter. But, Ricoeur is quick to add, this phenomenology cannot be disentangled without breaking the reciprocal connection between the constitution of time and the constitution of the object, a break that is consummated precisely by the phenomenology of internal-time consciousness (TN3 54).

In turning to one of his last two chosen themes in the *Critique,* Ricoeur wonders whether Kant's remarks in the "Analytic" on *Selbstaffektion* support a phenomenology freed from the tutelage of a formal critical philosophy. In section 24, Kant returns to a paradox left in abeyance since section 6 of the "Aesthetic." Here we are told that inner sense in no way constitutes an intuition of what we are as a soul, hence as a subject in itself, but "represents to consciousness even our own selves only as we appear to ourselves, and not as we are in ourselves" (B152–53). This is as much as to say that a human being requires something more than spontaneous thought to know itself — it needs matter given to the senses. We know ourselves only to the degree we are inwardly affected by our acts, just as external objects result from our being affected by things unknown in themselves.

What is left to explain, however, is the following paradox: while we can appear to ourselves as an empirical object, we cannot know the self in itself. How can we behave passively, therefore, in relation to ourselves? (B153).

Responding to the question, Kant offers the following solution. In contradistinction to the spontaneity of apperception, inner sense contains "no *determinate* intuition" (B154). To correct this, Kant enlists a transcendental act of imagination known as "figurative synthesis" to necessarily mediate between myself as affected (known) and myself as affecting (unknown). The core of the argument is that the synthetic activity of the imagination has to be applied to space — drawing a line, tracing circles and so on — so that, reflecting upon the operation itself, we discover that time is implied (B154). By constructing a determined space I am conscious of the successive character of the activity of understanding. But I only know it to the extent that I am affected by it. Therefore, we know ourselves as an object, and not as we are, insofar as we represent time as a line. Time and space mutually generate one another in the work of synthetic imagination: "we cannot obtain for ourselves a representation of time, which is not an object of outer intuition, except under the image of a line, which we draw and that by this mode of depicting it alone could we know the singleness of its dimension." Determination in space now becomes determination in time. These are determinations we produce together so that "the determinations of inner sense have therefore to be arranged as appearances in time in precisely the same manner in which we arrange those of outer sense in space" (B156). Important to note is that self-affection here is always from the outside in that "so far as inner intuition is concerned, we know our own subject only as appearance, not as it is by itself" (B156).

Instead of clarifying the determination of time, such an explanation only infuses it with more confusion since we are temporally affected only insofar as we act temporally. What does this mean? There is no intuition of space that has not first been determined in its unity by the schema of understanding which engenders a double reference to time. Time provides thought with the means for its unfolding and for transferring the order of time to phenomena and to their existence, under the auspices of the schematism, so that if empirical objects now help us to determine ourselves in time, they do so only because we have already lent them time. As Ricoeur concludes, Kant was not wrong in calling this self-affecting of the subject by its own acts a paradox (B152). More notably, where this section in the *Critique* alludes to the necessity of the self effecting time, the glimmer of a phenomenological appearance of time is avoided and veiled once again by the appearance of yet another formal presupposition — the figurative synthesis.

In terms of critical philosophy in general, Ricoeur concludes that even though the "Transcendental Aesthetic" proclaims that time and space inhere originally in the subject, we can only enter into the Kantian problematic on the condition of abstaining from all recourse to any inner sense that would reintroduce an ontology of the soul which the distinction between phenomenon and thing-in-itself has bracketed. Where the determinations by which time is distinguished from a mere magnitude can themselves be based on an implicit phenomenology, its expression is muted by the constant presence of the categorical apparatus of the mind which corresponds to the physics of nature alone. By tying the fate of time to a determined ontology of nature, Kant has prevented himself from exploring qualities and properties of temporality other than those required by his Newtonian axiomatic system — succession, simultaneity, and permanence (TN3 59).

In the end, Kant's characterization of time only reconfirms Ricoeur's initial suspicion: any singular definitions of time fail to cover the whole problematic of time. Where Augustine failed to derive the extension of physical time from the simple distension of the soul, so too Husserl's attempt to make time itself a pure experience by excluding physical time strikes the impassable problematic of Kant; that is, a) that time as such is invisible; b) that it could not appear in any living experience; c) that it is always presupposed as the condition of experience; and, d) from this last fact, that time could only appear indirectly in objects apprehended in space and according to the schemata and categories of objectivity. Consequently, neither the phenomenological approach in Husserlian terms above, nor Kant's transcendental one is sufficient unto itself. Each refers back to the other. But this referral presents the paradoxical character of a mutual borrowing, conditioned on a mutual exclusion (TN3 57).

Heidegger and Within-Time-Ness

The last philosopher Ricoeur investigates in his study of the aporias of temporality is Martin Heidegger. Ricoeur restricts himself almost solely to the latter's early and incomplete work, *Being and Time*.[35]

Ricoeur believes that Heidegger's brand of hermeneutic phenomenology "dissolves" the aporias of time in both Augustinian and Husserlian thought (TN3 61). This is achieved by leaving behind the ground upon which these aporias took shape in favor of a new kind of questioning. There are three points to be made here. First, Heidegger's existential analytic has as its referent not the soul but that of *Dasein*, being-there; that is, the being that we are. This is a substantially different point of departure than in any of the previous authors. As Heidegger himself states: "Dasein is an entity which does not just occur among other entities. Rather it is ontically distinguished by the fact that in its very Being, that Being is an *issue* for it" (32).[36]

Second, in an existential analysis, nature cannot constitute an opposite pole in regard to Dasein inasmuch as "the 'world' itself is something constitutive for Dasein" (77). Hence, in the thematic layout of *Being and Time,* Heidegger will go to great lengths in part one to express the determinations related to the concept of (my own) existence and to the possibility of authenticity and inauthenticity contained in the notion of mineness which "must be seen and understood *a priori* as grounded upon that state of Being which we have called '*Being-in-the-world.*' An interpretation of this constitutive state is needed if we are to set up our analytic of Dasein correctly" (78). In fact, it is Heidegger's strategy to thoroughly discuss the worldhood of the world, and to allow ourselves to be permeated by the sense of the surrounding world before discussing the structures of Dasein. It is only after such a thorough-going description that it becomes easier to see how the arguments of *Being and Time* separates itself from the older problem of a subject and object dichotomy, or, for that matter, a dichotomy between soul and nature (TN3 62).

Third, Heidegger's hermeneutic phenomenology goes beyond, for example, Husserl's attempt at making time appear as such, in that beyond the dilemma of the visibility or invisibility of time, the path of a hermeneutical phenomenology starts where seeing is depreciated in favor of understanding and interpretation. Ricoeur emphasizes that if Heidegger can claim to escape the alternative of a direct but silent intuition of time (Husserl) or an indirect but blind presupposition of it (Kant), this is thanks to the labor of language that makes the difference between interpreting and understanding (188). Interpreting in this sense develops understanding, explicating the structure of a phenomenon as this or that. In this way, the understanding that we already possess of the temporal structure of Dasein is brought to language (TN3 63).

In regard to time, Ricoeur focuses on what he considers to be Heidegger's three most important contributions. The first concerns Heidegger's insistence that the question of time as a whole is enveloped by the basic structure of "Care" (*Sorgen*). It is "Care" that reveals self-hood as fundamentally temporal in the sense that time is equiprimordial with Dasein's self-concern — our being-in-the-world is always already a "being-within-time-ness" (333). Second, with emphasis given to the future, the future (coming-towards), the past (having-been), and the present (making-present) form a fundamental unity, that is, an interpenetrating set of orientations. These orientations, or ecstases of time, ground the unity of the self by configuring experiences in a temporal way. "Temporality is not, prior to this, an entity which first emerges from *itself*; its essence is a process of temporalizing in the unity of the ecstasies" (377). The last, and by far the most important, concerns the unfolding of this ecstatic unity in such a way that it reveals a constitution of time that may be said to be layered. This hierarchy has three levels: a unification of resoluteness in the face of death (fundamental or primordial temporality); a datable and public historicality recapitulated only in repetition; and a within-time-ness that is splintered and consumed by our everyday preoccupation with things that nonetheless could orient us toward the unified structure of care in its originary and authentic intimacy.

While Ricoeur applauds this attempt to radicalize the various levels of phenomenological time, he sets out to uncover the hermetic nature inherent to the analysis in *Being and Time* and to substantiate the claim that Heidegger ultimately succumbs to the same impenetrable aporia endemic to any vision that tries to lessen the sharp contrast between mortal time and cosmic time (TN3 268). To explain this further, let me highlight the precise site of the aporia that Ricoeur feels Heidegger failed to overcome.

Ricoeur begins his most serious appraisal of Heidegger with the latter's third level of temporalization — within-time-ness (*Innerzeitigkeit*). Two questions are important with respect to this level: in what way is within-time-ness still connected to fundamental temporality, and in what way does its derivation from primordial temporality constitute the origin of ordinary time? (TN3 80). The importance of these questions rests with Ricoeur's suspicions as to whether the ordinary concept of time, the time of all the sciences and cosmic time as well, can be said to be derived from a level of pure temporality.

For Heidegger, temporality (*Zeitlichkeit*) is first, time (*Zeit*) is second. The most important phenomenon of temporality and its realization is the future because human existence "cares" for the future more than for anything else; the future means also death. Death is what challenges human existence. The resoluteness, therefore, with which we face our own being-towards-death, in the most intimate structure of Care, provides the criterion of authenticity for all of our temporal experience. We move in the direction of the inauthentic pole when we proceed from temporality (17, 328) toward historicality (*Geschichtlichkeit*) (19, 376, 385). The problem of historicality belongs to a set of concerns that deals with how we understand the stretching along (*Erstreckung*) of life between birth and death, movement and self-constancy. Historicality moves further away from temporality when this stretching along loses its authentic richness as an orientation toward death and assumes the characteristics of something measured between birth and death. It is easy, Heidegger suggests, to forget that the world is always already a historical world because its existence is coextensive with the existence of Dasein (388–89). Instead, we often take up historicizing within-the-world, history that aims to express more about Dasein's particular concerns in recovering the past. This stretching along, however, is saved from sheer arbitrariness and dispersion owing to Dasein's capacity to recapitulate — to repeat (*Wiederholung*), to retrieve — our inherited potentialities within the projective dimension of Care.

More specifically, we move toward a pole of inauthenticity when we enter the structures of everyday life that stand over and against those of temporality ruled by being-toward-death and of historicity ruled by repetition. This slippage is readily discernible — Heidegger suggests — in light of what he calls within-time-ness. It is the sense of time we have when time is designated as that "in which" events occur.

Within-time-ness is where we reckon with time (*Rechnen mit*) yet become forgetful of the nature of temporality. "Reckoning with" is first of all to highlight the world-time that we already find ourselves in with regard to historicality. Initially, being in time of within-time-ness is something quite different from measuring intervals between limiting instants; it is first of all to reckon with time and so to calculate. It is because we reckon with time and make calculations that we have the need to measure, not the other way around. It should be possible, therefore, to give an existential description of this reckoning before the measuring it calls for. It is here that expressions such as "having time to," "taking time to," "wasting time" and so on, are revelatory of its nature. The same is true of the grammatical network of verb tenses, and likewise of the far-ranging network of adverbs of time: then, after, later, earlier, since, till, while, until, whenever, now that, and so forth.

While within-time-ness is still a feature of Care, it is a level of Care that easily falls prey to our thrownness among things, where the description of temporality becomes dependent on the things in the world. Heidegger calls these things of our concern *das Vorhandene* ("subsisting things which our concern counts on") and *das Zuhandene* ("utensils offered to our manipulation") (98–101). Being alongside (*bei*) the things of our concern is to live Care as "preoccupation" (*besorgen*) (298). The time of preoccupation is "ordinary time," the time of everydayness. It is the time measured by clocks. The orientations of past and the future in such time has less to do with a futural self-orientation toward death than merely expressing some orientation to objects that exist alongside us.

At the level of within-time-ness, and preoccupation in general, what predominates is the ecstasis of the present, or rather enpresent, in the sense of making-present (*gegenwärtigen*). Just as primordial temporality places the accent on the future and historicality on the past, preoccupation puts the accent on the present. Of the three ecstases the present is where the description of concern, in the modality of preoccupation, can most easily slide back into the description of the things of our concern and remain tied to the sphere of *vorhanden* and *zuhanden*. And it is in looking at three particular characteristics of within-time-ness — datability, lapse of time, and publicness — where the ordinary representation of time does level off, that we more readily see how things with which we are occupied often come to determine the sense of time more than our general existential orientation governed by care.

Datability is connected to "reckoning with time," which precedes actual calculation. If within-time-ness is easily interpreted in terms of the ordinary representation of time, it is because the first measurements of the time of our preoccupation are borrowed from the natural environment—from the play of light and dark within a day and over a season. But a day is not an abstract measure; it is a magnitude which corresponds to our concern and to the world into which we are thrown. The time it measures is that in which it is *time to* do something (*Zeit zu*), where "now" means "now that . . .," to which are added the "when" and "before" in order to find the phenomenological meaning of this interplay of relations. We must remember that it is Being-alongside that connects preoccupation to the things of the world. If time is reduced to a system of dates organized in relation to a point of time taken as an origin, the work of interpretation is forgotten by which we moved from making-present, including all that waits and withholds, to the idea of an indifferent "now." An aspect of within-time-ness is leveled off, therefore, when datability no longer precedes the assigning of dates but rather follows it. When this happens, saying "now" becomes synonymous with reading the hour on the face of the clock, thereby disguising the making-present that awaits and retains, that is, the third ecstasis of temporality.

A second feature of within-time-ness is consideration of the lapse of time, of the interval between a "since then" and an "until," generated by the relations between "now," "then," and "before" (TN3 83). In the lapse of time there is a stretching-along, characteristic of historicality, but interpreted in the idiom of preoccupation. It is here we find the origin of our ability to assign a temporal extension to every "now," to every "then," to every "before," as when we say "during the meal" (now), "last spring" (before), "next fall" (then). This sense of "a lapse of time" underwrites what we mean when we "allow" an amount of time for this or for that or say we "employed" our day well or poorly, forgetting that it is not time consumed as much as it is an expression of our preoccupation which, by losing itself among things of its concern, loses time as well. This lapse of time, however, is leveled off into a mere abstraction of passing "nows" when the stretching out characteristic of historicality no longer precedes the measurable interval but rather is governed by it.

The final feature of within-time-ness is public time. The title of "public" time is something of a misnomer. It cannot be misconstrued as a neutral time, indifferent to the distinction between things and human beings. Rather, within-time-ness implies a public time because human action is common action. As Heidegger states: "in the 'most intimate' Being-with-one-another of several people, they can say '*now*' and say it 'together,' though each of them gives a different date to the 'now' which he is saying: 'now that this or that has come to pass . . .' The 'now' which anyone expresses is always said in the publicness of Being-in-the-world with one another" (463). However, Being-with (*Mitsein*) has always been and may always be reduced to anonymity. Therefore, the everyday condition only reaches making-present through the impersonal and abstract "now." The character of making-public, founded in the "Being-with" that relates mortals to one another, gives way to the allegedly irreducible characteristic of time, its universality. The net result is that time is held to be public because it is declared to be universal. In this sense, the temporality of within-time-ness is leveled off to the ordinary sense of time.

The problem of the "leveling off" in each of these three features of within-time-ness was of major concern to Heidegger. "Leveling off" was his thematic strategy to explain the diminution of authentic time to inauthentic time, and hence the genesis of the concept of time as it is employed in all the sciences starting from fundamental temporality. Heidegger chose, Ricoeur suggests, "within-time-ness" to situate this genesis because it makes the ordinary concept of time first appear in great proximity to the last decipherable figure of phenomenological time. It is only upon this pivotal point, where time flips back to the side of beings other than the one that we are, that we see the fading of the tie between temporality and Being-towards-death.

> The reversal that appears to give an anteriority to time in relation to Care itself is the final link in a chain of interpretations that are but so many

misinterpretations. First, the prevalence of preoccupation in the structure of Care; next, the interpretation of the temporal features of preoccupation in terms of the things alongside which Care stands; finally, forgetting this interpretation itself, which makes the measurement of time appear to belong to things present-at-hand and ready-to-hand themselves. The quantifying of time then appears to be independent of the temporality of Care. The time 'in' which we ourselves are is understood as the receptacle of things present-to-hand and ready-at-hand. What is particularly forgotten is the condition of thrownness, as a structure of Being-in-the-world. (TN3 84)

In the end, therefore, the history of the measurement of time is that of forgetting all the interpretations traversed by making-present. At the end of this forgetting, time itself is identified with a series of ordinary and anonymous "nows."

Having distinguished Heidegger's thesis in this particular fashion, Ricoeur formulates his doubts as to the efficacy of the entire project by asking that if, as Heidegger suggests, "human temporality cannot be constituted on the basis of a concept of time considered as a series of "nows," is not the opposite path, from temporality and Dasein to cosmic time, in accordance with the preceding discussion, just as impracticable?" (TN3 88). The crux of the matter is whether or not Heidegger has convincingly shown a plausible transition, either in one direction or the other, between indistinguishable anonymous instants and the lived-through present (*le présent vif*) (TN3 88). In Ricoeur's reading of Heidegger, no plausible transition exists. The temporalizing of Dasein does not engender the succession of anonymous instants; its making-present is a function of the absolute unity of the temporal ecstases. If ontological temporality does not itself articulate succession, how, then, can succession be derived from it? As was noted in Ricoeur's study of Aristotle, movement (change) belongs to the principles of physics that do not include in their definition a reference to a soul that discriminates and counts. Hence, that time should have something to do with movement, and something to do with Care, seems to Ricoeur to constitute two irreconcilable determinations in principle that Heidegger does not satisfactorily confront (TN3 89).

One factor Heidegger failed to contend with properly, Ricoeur argues, is science's contemporary debate over time. The very term, "ordinary time," that Heidegger consistently employs is diminutive in regard to the scope of problems posed to science by the orientation, continuity, and measurability of time. In noting the discoveries in geology, biology, and astronomy, Ricoeur points out the present incommensurability in the diverse meanings attached to the term "time" employed by the various disciplines. There is simply no single scientific concept that can be opposed to any phenomenological analysis. What modern studies indicate is that it is illegitimate to presume a homogeneity of time-spans projected along a single notion of natural "history." "The fact that this alignment along a single scale of time is ultimately misleading is attested to by the following paradox. The length of time of a human life, compared to the range of cosmic time-spans, appears insignificant, whereas it is the very place from which every question of significance arises" (TN3 90). The paradox finds its keenest lacuna in acknowledging how the notion of history was extrapolated from the human sphere to the natural sphere while, in return, the notion of change, specified on the zoological level by that of evolution, has been able to include human history within its perimeter of meaning. In short terms, no matter how much effort is exerted in expressing the profound temporal unity of ecstases to ground the mode of existence that is Dasein, there is still something past which is independent of human existence and its historicality.

For Ricoeur there is no solution to this paradox. One must simply draw a line, as suggested by Collingwood, between the notions of change and evolution, on the one hand, and history on the other.[37] Ricoeur himself summarizes,

> In this respect, the notion of the 'testimony' (*témoignage*) of human beings concerning events of the past and the 'testimony' of the vestiges of the geological past does not go beyond the mode of proof; that is, the use of inferences in the form of retrodiction (*rétrodiction*). Misuse begins as soon as the notion of 'testimony' is severed from the narrative context that supports it as documentary proof in service of the explanatory comprehension of a course of action. It is finally the concepts of action and narrative that cannot be transferred from the human sphere to the sphere of nature. (TN3 91)

The practical side of this epistemological break concerns the time of phenomena. It is impossible, Ricoeur insists, to generate the time of nature on the basis of phenomenological time and vice versa. Where the former is a time without a present, the latter is time erupting through the presence of the present. The fundamental distinction that decisively divides the two is that a time without a present is an anonymous instant while time with a present is a present defined by the instant of discourse such that the present is designated reflexively.[38] Consequently, Heidegger's attempt to further the internal diversifications of Care into historicality and within-time-ness must be understood only as a desperate attempt to approximate the equivalence of sequential time within the limits of his existential analysis. However, the burgeoning epistemological break noted above negates the possibility of such an equivalence.

THE ULTIMATE APORIA OF TIME

Ricoeur's laborious investigation into the various studies of time results in the observation of an ultimate aporia, an aporia that sums up the failure of all our thinking about time. In simple terms, the gap (*l'écart, la brèche*) between a phenomenology of time (mortal time) and the autonomy of time with respect to movement (cosmic time) is unbridgeable; the former cannot produce the latter (TN3 91–92).

Ricoeur concludes his discussion of the aporias of temporality with four extended comments (TN3 92ff.). First, to the degree that every existential analysis is beset with it, this aporia forces every existential analysis to distend, stretch, and unfold as many levels of temporality as possible in an attempt to reach, by an ever-increasing approximation, its other (cosmic time) that it cannot generate. This stretching to claim a source for the disparity among time perspectives provokes continual internal diversification at the existential level. Heidegger's distinction between temporality, historicality, and within-time-ness is a prime example.

Second, to less than perceptive minds, where such distinctions between the existential and empirical levels of time have become indiscernible to feeling, the result has been the overlapping of one mode of discourse about one time with another. The loss of this one distinction has bestowed upon philosophy the aporetical virus that guards the conundrum of time. Equally true, this aporia has encouraged humankind to create numerous elegies, ranging in their modulations from lamentation to resignation, never ceasing to sing of the contrast between the time that remains and we who are merely passing.

Third, in Heidegger's most expansive attempt to proceed from the authentic and primordial to astronomical and scientific time, each level is achieved by a new stage of interpretation, which, as Ricoeur points out, is at the same time a newer level of misinterpretation. The result of this multiplication of interpretative levels is really a production of meaning producing a surplus of meaning at the level of world-time. This production of meaning by way of a hermeneutic phenomenology bears three consequences. First, with the increase in meaning between Being-towards-death and world-time, two polar opposites are more clearly defined and come into sharper relief — mortal time and cosmic time. Second, the irreversible descending order of temporalization, from the primordial to the least authentic, as described in *Being and Time,* becomes questionable; it is not as irreversible as Heidegger would have us believe. As Ricoeur argues, if you study closely the three figures of temporalization — temporality, historicality and within-time-ness — the second presupposes the third and the first presupposes the second. Last, what we learn from hermeneutic phenomenology is that its contribution to seeking the source of time is not its designation of a primordial source, but the fact that it "pluralizes" the figures of temporality. Ricoeur indicates that Heidegger himself suggests that the three degrees of temporalization are equiprimordial, thereby demoting any priority given to the future. Consequently, the future, past, and present each play an important role when we pass from one level to another. The result is that the process of temporalization is further differentiated but not necessarily ordered (TN3 95).

Ricoeur's last comment on the ultimate aporia concerns history. For Ricoeur, the final redemption of our thinking on time finds its source in the problem of history which arises in Heidegger's distinction between fundamental temporality and its leveling off at the point of within-time-ness. History appears to Ricoeur as a sort of fracture zone between mortal time and cosmic time where the production and over-lapping of meaning compensates for the epistemological break between the two times. Ricoeur observes with interest that the greater the distance between the two poles of time, the more the position of histor-icality becomes problematic. Is it not history, Ricoeur asks, that can bridge the abyss between our memory of the dead (Being-towards-death) and the investigation of institutions, structures, and transfor-mations (world-time) that are stronger than death? (TN3 96).

Ricoeur suggests that the aporia he has uncovered outruns the accomplishments of phenomenology, resituating it within the great cur-rent of reflective and speculative thought as a whole in its search for a current answer to the question, what is time? (TN3 96). How, there-fore, does Ricoeur respond to the aporetics of temporality that he has so laboriously uncovered in the various phenomenologies of time?

While leaving to a later chapter a much more detailed account of Ricoeur's thesis, the short answer is that he elaborates on the mediat-ing role of the narrative function. Narrative activity in general does not provide a speculative resolution to the ambiguity and paradoxes of our experience of time. Ricoeur suggests, however, that narrative, while preserving the paradoxes of time, *is* the basis for at least a poetic res-olution to the problem of time's enigma. By telling stories and writ-ing history we provide "shape" to the chaotic, obscure, and mute in our experience of time's passage. Ricoeur argues that historical narra-tive and fictional narrative *jointly* provide not only "models of" but "models for" articulating, in a symbolic way, our experience of time.[39]

Ricoeur's markedly different approach to time in general, affects notions of both self and meaning since the narrative function casts such a wide net over our discursive practices. Ricoeur's "human time" or "narrative time" is not borrowed from the time of science nor is it a purely phenomenological time. It is really a "third time" reinscribed on cosmic time through the living of a human mortal being where nar-rative is the privileged means of self-understanding. In summarizing his thesis in *Time and Narrative*, Ricoeur once stated that his goal was "to discover how the act of *raconter,* of telling a story, can transmute *natural* time into a specifically *human* time, irreducible to mathematical, chronological 'clock time'" (RR 463).

In pursuing such a path, Ricoeur radically shifts the conventional strategy of asking about the "what" of time to inquiring about the "who." Such a strategy acknowledges the fact that each of our lives is unquestionably temporal and finite. A particular moment of birth and a particular moment of death bounds each lifetime. While such temporal existence is always lived against an impersonal background of cosmic phenomenon, the temporal events over a lifetime belong to someone. Anyone who has lost a cherished loved one would readily acknowledge that the mere succession of neutral "now" points does not justly account for the life of a deceased friend or family member. Someone's life is a history, a story of what has been endured — love, betrayal, defeat, triumph, tragedy, and success. We accord dignity to the life of someone by remembering, often inchoately, the long chain of interconnected stories that identify that person as the one whom I loved, who went to war, and who never came home. In the end, all that we are left with are memories and the stories that bring those memories to life in the (present) moment we recount them.

The temporal passage of a lifetime becomes unique to someone in the stories that accrue to him or her over a lifetime. The fate of human temporal passage, therefore, is not to remain anonymous and impersonal except by malicious or accidental intent. The ominous passage of time is humanized — won back from a faceless passage — by our ability to tell the story of "who" lived and endured the cacophony of experience that comprise the content of a life lived. This is Ricoeur's formal thesis. To repeat, "Time becomes human to the extent that it is articulated through a narrative mode, and narrative attains its full meaning when it becomes a condition of temporal existence" (TN1 52). For Ricoeur, the narrative function organizes language in a way to reflect the human experience of time. This correlation is not accidental but "presents a transcultural form of necessity (TN1 52).

As mentioned, two interlocking themes arise from this thesis concerning the problem of meaning and identity. Out of the reciprocity

he detects between time and narrative, Ricoeur embraces the conviction that the "language-game" of narration, to use Wittgenstein's
term, "ultimately reveals that the meaning of human existence is itself
narrative" (RR 463). None of us live on the pinpoint of a lived present devoid of history. Our existence is enmeshed in stories and histories of all sorts (international, national, religious and family).
Recognizing this enmeshment is what Ricoeur will call the historical
present. The sense of this "present" is not the "now" point of some
chronometer's measure. Rather, it is the rich but complicated time of
initiative wherein we acknowledge the past and anticipate the future.
It is a consciousness or awareness that we occupy a place and time that
is encased in traditions that are not set and unchangeable but open for
interpretation in the time yet to come. More, the historical present is
the humble recognition that we do not create our own present but
find ourselves present to a matrix of stories that impart to us a sense
of place and meaning that often demands debate, discussion, and
eventual consensus.

Meaning as such is stored in as many ways as it is told, read, and
memorialized in a culture. Meaning in time arises in our individual lives
because we tell stories about "good times" and "bad times" that eventually become part of the narrative density to which we already belong.
It is out of this narrative density in which we each participate that we
identify the particular style and character of the one who recounts. To
examine our lives, to ask "who am I?" is not to identify with some form
of substance or self-transparent *cogito;* rather, it is to identify with the
innumerable stories weaved into the fabric of our character that gives
each of us a type of self-constancy in the historical present. For Ricoeur
our own existence "cannot be separated from the account we can give
of ourselves. It is in telling our own stories that we give ourselves an
identity. We recognize ourselves in the stories we tell about ourselves.
It makes no difference whether these stories are true or false, fiction
as well as verifiable history provides us with an identity."[40]

The result of linking narrative with time, meaning, and identity is
what Ricoeur calls "narrative identity." Narrative identity is not
grounded in some permanently subsisting substance. It is thoroughly

hermeneutical in nature and arises out of our narrative practices. Narrative identity assumes our embeddedness in an ongoing history and that interpretation is a vital activity to discern identity over a lifetime. As Ricoeur will often remark, narrative identity is "fragile," "unstable," and as much a problem as it is a solution. Nonetheless, such a notion ingeniously links imagination, emplotment (configuration), and reading into a hermeneutical circle that deepens our experience of life and time. Central to our understanding of life and identity, Ricoeur adds, is that both are made up of actions that bring into actuality what is only potential. The meaning imparted to actions is rarely, if ever, unequivocal. Not knowing itself directly, narrative self must embark on the difficult journey of interpreting its actions as they are mediated by cultural signs, symbols, and texts. We will recross this path in chapter 4, detailing more closely the fusion between the world of the text and the world of the reader.

Let me conclude this chapter by emphasizing some central points and the path to be followed. In terms of the philosophical study of time in general, Ricoeur has bestowed upon future thinkers two important thematic tools. First, his deft detective work at uncovering the paradoxes of past discussions on time allows us a new diagnostic light with which to appraise these works and to highlight the infectious aporia that befuddles any attempt at a specifically phenomenological description of time. Second, Ricoeur's dedication to the narrative function renders any philosophical discussion of human time somewhat suspect if it avoids a similar dedication. Such suspicion marks this century's long philosophical shift from expecting a solely metaphysical speculation on time to the present demand for the hermeneutical interpretation of its various expressions.

In the following chapters I turn this new diagnostic light upon two thinkers that antedate Ricoeur. Both Bergson and Merleau-Ponty specifically attempted to detail time as lived, and neither of them is dealt with to any great degree by Ricoeur. Interrogating them verifies Ricoeur's discussion of the existence of this aporia (the occultation between cosmic time and mortal time) and shows how it baffled "pre-Ricoeur" attempts to give an unambiguous account of lived time. In the course of *Time and Narrative*, Ricoeur states that without approaching human time through narrative and the historical consciousness that it demands, a phenomenology cannot escape the dilemma of dealing with time either as a direct but silent intuition or an indirect, but blind, presupposition (TN3 63). This particular challenge will animate our three-way dialogue between Bergson's *durée* as an intuition of time, Merleau-Ponty's presupposition of a phenomenal time, and Ricoeur's narrated time. While time as duration and phenomenal time are both "solutions" to the time of the self, each time easily falls prey to the trap of ideality. In designating a particular but ideal site (psychological intuition and phenomenal existence) to instantiate time, both Bergson and Merleau-Ponty avoid giving their versions of human time the historical robustness it demands. In short, Bergson and Merleau-Ponty cannot avoid the accusation of having posited either a direct but silent intuition of time or an indirect but blind presupposition respectively.

Further, I would like to see if, in attempting to detail the time of the self, the element of narrativity in the analyses of either Bergson or Merleau-Ponty precedes Ricoeur's connection between the two different themes, or whether either of their solutions can be even remotely related to the strategy suggested by Ricoeur.

To close this chapter let me emphasize a distinction the reader must keep in mind. It deals with the contrast between the human experience of time and time's mystery, that is, the sense we have that time is beyond passage, change, motion, mutability and our own finiteness. In his discussion of St. Augustine, for example, Ricoeur never fails to contrast the saint's experience of time with that which is beyond human time, namely "eternity." For didactic reasons, Ricoeur prefers to understand this contrast to human time, in Kantian terms, as a limit concept and simply refer to it as "the other of time."[41]

> The eternal present does not appear to be a purely positive notion except by reason of its homonymy with the present that passes. To say that it is eternal, we must deny that it is the passive and active transit from the future toward the past. It is still insofar as it is not a present that is 'passed through.' Eternity is also conceived of negatively, as that

which does not include time, as that which is not temporal. In this sense, there is a double negation: I must be able to deny the features of my experience of time in order to perceive this experience as a lack with respect to that which denies it. It is this double and mutual negation whereby eternity is the other of time that, more than anything else, intensifies the experience of time. (TN1 236, n. 35)

In the course of this study, as I shall point out in our discussion of Bergson and Merleau-Ponty, "the other of time" takes on a different meaning. Both Bergson and Merleau-Ponty differentiate a time that is opposed decisively to the impersonal and autonomous instant of what we will variously call scientific time, objective time, world time, or just ordinary time. They both specifically distinguish a time peculiar to the self — a time that is really human in the sense that it could not exist outside the agency of a conscious self. However, once the distinction is drawn and the analysis deepens, neither Bergson nor Merleau-Ponty provides an adequate explanation for the time they exclude from their respective analyses. In the same way that the *distentio animi* of Augustine cannot effectuate eternity, the analyses of Bergson and Merleau-Ponty cannot explain how the time of the self is connected to or effectuates scientific or ordinary time. This latter objective time, a time that supposedly exists independent of the self, becomes "the other of time" for Bergson's durational sense of time and, to a less degree, the sense of temporality discussed by Merleau-Ponty.

Two

Bergson and Time as Duration

> If a man were to inquire of Nature the reason of her creative
> activity, and if she were willing to give ear and answer,
> she would say — "Ask me not, but understand in silence,
> even as I am silent and am not wont to speak."
> — Plotinus, *Enneads*

INTRODUCTION

A review of the history of Western philosophy finds the French philosopher Henri Bergson (1859–1941) a curious anomaly. Almost 60 years after his death, Bergson's works have yet to be definitively assimilated into one movement or school.[1] Their originality and style have prevented them from being eclipsed and forgotten. And while his thought was initially criticized by many thinkers as being anti-intellectual, anti-scientific, irrational, and essentially vitalist, today his ideas remain relevant and are debated both in the sciences and the arts.[2]

The scientific community's current appreciation of Bergson is typified by Ilya Prigogine when he remarks that Bergson was the first thinker to seriously challenge the scope of science and give an acceptable summation of what science cannot do, namely, deal properly with change and time. More specifically, Prigogine states that it was Bergson who very early on tried to convince us "that only an opening, a widening of science can end the dichotomy between science and philosophy. This widening of science is possible only if we revise our conception of time.

To deny time — that is, to reduce it to a mere deployment of a reversible law — is to abandon the possibility of defining a conception of nature coherent with the hypothesis that nature produced living beings, particularly man. It dooms us to choosing between an anti-scientific philosophy and an alienating science".[3] Despite his failed debate with Einstein early in the last century, there has been a gradual renaissance among science scholars evaluating Bergson's importance. Some see Bergson's ideas as the basis for contemporary complexity theory, which attempts to lessen science's dependency on mathematical logic by acknowledging the unpredictable and unquantifiable qualities of time.[4]

The current revival of philosophical interest in Bergson can be dated from the mid-1960s. Prior to World War II, French thought had been dominated by a preoccupation with Hegel, Husserl, and Heidegger. In the wake of the "linguistic turn" in philosophy and the rise of "anti-Hegelianism" in France during the sixties, interest in German philosophy began to wane, and Bergson's ideas found a new life in those thinkers who recalled his critique of negation in the Hegelian dialectic some 40 years previously in *Creative Evolution*. Moreover, there was the growing recognition among thinkers such as Levinas and Merleau-Ponty that Bergson's ideas had been unjustly scapegoated and dismissed prematurely, having become more of a negative rallying theme for the generation of French thinkers that reached philosophical maturity in the 1930s and later.[5] Yet, of all the names associated with a philosophical revitalization of Bergson, the most important may be Gilles Deleuze. In a work simply entitled *Bergsonism*, Deleuze uses Bergson's notion of "difference-as-multiplicity" to overcome traditional representational and dialectical modes of thought. In tweaking out the consequences of classical Bergsonian notions such as "duration," "difference," and "tension," Deleuze elaborates a revolutionary approach to film theory that goes beyond psychoanalytical and semiological interpretations, which tend to locate meaning below the surface level of signs.[6]

On the other hand, regardless of acknowledgments by such notables as Prigogine and Deleuze, Bergson's name is hardly mentioned in poststructuralist, hermeneutical, and postmodern conversations today. The most striking feature of Bergson's thought that would seem to exclude him from our present interest in these areas concerns his pronounced suspicion of language. On his own philosophical highway, Bergson never made the "linguistic turn" toward the "promised land" of hermeneutics. However, in the following discussion, I hope to uncover Bergson's engagement with language as ambiguous to say the least, and to show that his suspicion of language and symbols is not airtight. The summary of Ricoeur's aporetics of temporality has provided us with a sharp backdrop with which to investigate Bergson's notion of time. Not only does Bergson run into the aporias delineated by Ricoeur, but, given his specific interest in the time of the self, Bergson recognizes, even inadvertently, the necessity of language and narrative in establishing the self and meaning.

Historical Context

Henri Bergson entered the intellectual milieu of late nineteenth century France at the crossing of two divergent currents of thought. Suspect of the first, positivism, Bergson drew much inspiration from a diverse number of thinkers sometimes collectively known as spiritualists. These included such thinkers as François Pierre Maine-de-Biran (1766–1824), Jean Gaspard Félix Ravaisson-Mollien (1813–1900), Jules Lachelier (1832–1918), and Émile Boutroux (1845–1921).

All of these authors held to a form of thought that was a counterweight to the rationalistic ethos of the Enlightenment. In varying degrees, they believed in the spontaneity of the human will and saw some form of "Spirit" (*Pneuma, Nous, Raison, Logos*) as a key to the nature of reality that acted as its ground and rational explanation. The characteristic trait of this movement was its emphasis on inner experience in search of evidence to identify the self above and beyond the prevailing arguments of positivists concerning human determinism.

Bergson's entrance into the intellectual limelight of his era was effected by his novel discussion of time as duration although his real interest was never the subject of time itself. In fact, his major works neither dealt with the historical development of time as a philosophical problem nor did they attest to any desire to understand time anthropologically. For example, despite the extreme similarity, and often identical modes of analysis of time's mind-related nature, Bergson never once makes reference to St. Augustine's meditation in the *Confessions*.[7] This lack of interest might be accounted for by the fact that Bergson's interest in time was only accessory to his attempts to rescue the notion of the human subject from being regarded as nothing more than an atomic fact in a universe that current science was anthropocentrically redescribing as a machine.[8]

As stated in the "Avant-propos" of his doctoral thesis, *Essai sur les données immédiates de la conscience* (*Time and Free Will*, 1889), Bergson wanted to uncover the perennial problem of human free will as a pseudoquestion. Bergson felt he could best solve this timeless polemic on a psychological plane alone. He felt that both determinists and their adversaries treated mental states as being thing-like and separate. The error resulted from assuming mental events and states were reflections of physical events and objects that could be visualized in spatial terms. In this regard, Bergson was reacting strongly against the experimental psychology of Wilhelm Wundt (1832–1887) and especially the psychophysical laws of Gustav Fechner (1801–1887).[9] For example, Fechner, Bergson argued, was mistaken in believing that an interval between two successive sensations, S and S', was a real *difference* in the arithmetical sense as opposed to a simple *passing* from one to another.[10] Bergson's strategy was to deny intellect its desire to translate perceptions and sensations into magnitudes and thereby be treated as possible physical events governed by Newtonian mechanics.[11] Once the habits of spatialization and visualization were no longer regarded as legitimate ways to describe the activity of consciousness, Bergson argued that the real sustenance of consciousness could then be grasped — namely duration (*durée*).

Bergson began his intellectual journey starting with a suspicion harboured against his first philosophical hero, Herbert Spencer (1820–1907). Spencer tried to establish psychology as a branch of evolutionary biology. In his *Principles of Psychology* (1855) Spencer argued that mental processes, like physiological processes, are modes of adaptation of the organism to its environment. By establishing the general similarity of mental processes and life processes, Spencer enumerated, from the simplest organisms to the highest thought processes in human beings, the various modes of awareness and response to environmental stimuli. He revealed how the progressive extension of the correspondence of internal and external relations in time and space, in generality and specificity, indicated the necessary connection between the progressive correspondence and the progressive complication in organic structure, especially with regard to the nervous system. For Spencer, the more highly developed the nervous system the greater the chance the organism has to survive because the milieu wherein the organism reacts is widened in term of space and time. The evolutionary principle illustrated is that the place of a living being in the hierarchy of organisms is generally determined by the spatial extent of its sensory field as well as by the temporal span of its memory and anticipatory abilities.[12] Spencer became famous for his claim that of all organisms, the steady process of adjustment to the wider spatio-temporal surrounding culminates in the species *Homo sapiens.*

What is important to understand about Spencer's thinking is his unquestioned assumption that the natural world (outer world) is best described through Newtonian physics in terms of matter, motion, and force,[13] which creates the highest state of awareness of any living organism. Both mental and physiological modes of adaptation are therefore coopted into a mechanical picture of nature. When he states that "the harmony between the inner tendencies and outer relations arises from the fact that the outer relations produce the inner relation,"[14] he is concluding that the human mind somehow mirrors the structure of reality which was itself understood through a corpuscular-kinetic view of matter. The result of such a conclusion is that Newtonian time was assumed to be mental time; that human mental apprehension of time was only knowable through sequence and the succession of mental states.[15] In other words, mental relations constituting our ideas of time are the result of inner relations, by perpetual repetition, being organized into correspondence with outer relations.

> The abstract of all sequences is Time. The abstract of all coexistences is Space. From the fact that in thought, Time is inseparable from

sequence, and Space from coexistence, we do not here infer that Time and Space are original forms of consciousness under which sequences and coexistences are known; but we infer that our conceptions of Time and Space are generated, as other abstracts are generated from other concretes: the only difference being that the organization of experiences has, in these cases, been going on throughout the entire evolution of intelligence.[16]

Such notions as this gave the argument for human determinism seemingly reasonable theoretical foundations. Humankind was thought to be caught in a matrix of relations governed by the laws of mechanics in a type of Hobbesian universe of perpetual motions. Time was simply conceived as the absolute and static medium "in" which all events occurred.

Bergson's Basic Methodology

Bergson began his intellectual interrogation of time in the light of Spencer's convincing arguments. Bergson's genius was to wonder why all sense impressions and events were not brought to consciousness at once. What good was time, he queried, if all possible events could be unfurled before us at once:

> This, in days gone by, was the starting-point of my reflections. Some 50 years ago I was very much attached to the philosophy of Spencer. I perceived one fine day that, in it, time served no purpose, did nothing. Nevertheless, I said to myself, time is something. Therefore it acts. What can it be doing? Plain common sense answered: time is what hinders everything from being given at once. It retards, or rather it is retardation. It must, therefore, be elaboration. Would it not then be a vehicle of creation and of choice? Would not the existence of time prove that there is indetermination in things? Would time not be indetermination itself? (CM 93)

For this reason Bergson mounts an investigation into the immediate data of consciousness (*les données immédiates de la conscience*). He desires to know if human inner introspective data is stained by admixtures unconsciously borrowed from the outer world or if such data is somehow mentally "pure." If the latter case, then Bergson would have an avenue to a region where the genesis of human free acts would be possible outside of any interference from any assumed natural causality. The key, therefore, becomes the necessity to show that time exists, "purely," on its own, unsupported by the supposed structure of Newtonian physics.

Hence, where the French title of his first work, *Essai sur les données immédiates de la conscience,* indicates his method, its English translation, *Time and Free Will,* best indicates Bergson's intention. If we are aware of our inner states immediately, and if this immediacy is not patterned on successive or sequential states, then the free flow of time, as experienced interiorly, is the key to human freedom. In other words, Bergson must ascertain if there is in fact a human time — a time specific to the self — a time that will ultimately be more than the mere succession of "nows" as noted by science. He intends to proceed, therefore, with a psychology of time — the time of the "inner life."

How does Bergson work his way back to or find access to the immediate data of consciousness? Finding association psychology too artificial, he discerns that the time of inner life is too often ruled out by intelligence through a confusion in language (CM 14). Real time, he feels, is habitually assimilated into the idea of space. His real fight, therefore, is a fight against the illusion that space and time could be easily juxtaposed. Where things in space fall under the law of causality, Bergson hopes to show that consciousness has no resemblance to things in space but subsists through time wherein such a law does not apply. Bergson's strategy to recover the real difference between time and space is to employ a set of contrasts that would unquestionably show differences of kind and not just of degree between the two.[17] These contrasts in his works have since become famous: duration-space, instinct-intelligence, intensity-extensity, quality-quantity, heterogeneous-homogeneous, continuous-discontinuous, inner-outer multiplicities, recollection-perception, and matter-memory. This tactic breaks through the composites of human experience and untangles two component elements that differ in kind but whose differences, through ages of intellectualizations, have become almost indistinguishable.

Almost working as an alchemist, Bergson needed to work his way back to the "purity" of things and discern time in its distilled formulation which he calls pure duration (*durée pure*). In fact, throughout his entire literary corpus, there will be no more important theme, a point from which he constantly sets out and to which he constantly returns, than the recognition of the intuition of duration (*l'intuition de la durée*).[18] The key word here is intuition, which is defined in contrast to intelligence.

Bergson's concern with number, space, and succession in his early work was preparatory for a famous critique of the intellect that he makes much later in *Creative Evolution*. Intellect for Bergson is the main tool science uses to seek influence and mastery over matter. When the intellect addresses living processes, movement, and growth, it seeks to immobilize, fix, and arrest all change. Hence, in reducing its object to number, space, and succession, "the operations of our intellect tend to geometry, as to the goal where they find their perfect fulfilment" (CE 210). Consequently, Bergson sees science as the tendency to realize order against disorder. Intellectual action on materiality is the course that satisfies this tendency. To refer to material objects is to have the possibility of seeing and touching them; the intellect's desire to structure and order the material world ultimately means localizing matter in space, so much so that, in the end, matter becomes geometry itself. However, mental phenomena are built up without means of sight and touch. Here, the terms are no longer given in space so that we can only count them by some process of symbolical representation that ultimately would not be inner life.

For knowledge of the inner life, that is consciousness, Bergson reserves the term intuition. While describing it variously throughout his works, Bergson never defines "intuition" despite its importance. Essentially, intuition signifies immediate consciousness; it is an enlargement of knowledge by contact and coincidence with reality unimpeded by the habits of the intellect (CM 32). An act of intuition is an effort to reascend the slope natural to the intellect and go from reality to concepts instead of vice versa (CM 183). Through intuition, we are brought to a knowledge of the world of unorganized matter which, beneath the inert and static surface that science reveals to us, constantly moves, changes, and endures. Intuition, ultimately, is what attains "the spirit, duration, pure change" (CM 33). Moreover, where intellect turns to matter (science), intuition turns toward life (the self) in general. Intuition is an attention to life, the reversal of intellectual habits, wherein the human subject is able to recapture the vital impulse (*élan vital*) that is the underlying cause of the organization of all living matter (CE 105). Where the intellect deals with the already-made, intuition is contact with becoming.

Despite the poetic intensity of his description, Bergson's notion of intuition should not be misconstrued, as it has been historically, as being some sort of altered state of consciousness or a semi-dream state.[19] Further, it is not "instinct or feeling." Bergson was quite adamant in asserting that intuition is an effort, "a difficult way of thinking" (CM 88) and "a strenuous (*vigoureux*) effect of reflection" (TF 233). Unless we are willing to give up certain habits of intellectual thinking, Bergson warns, our knowledge will remain superficial and contingent on bodily experience alone and our lower needs. Intuition, rather, broadens experience, travelling from needs and the merely useful to the *immediate*. "By unmaking that which these needs have made, we may restore to intuition its original purity and so recover contact with the real" (MM 241).

Intuition's flavor of "other worldliness" derives from our own narrow perception of reality as defined by classical physics. Intuition resembles, perhaps in spirit, Husserl's *epoché* in being a disciplined attempt to cast off the prejudice of everyday thought and allow phenomena once again to speak for themselves. As Merleau-Ponty once remarked, intuition is "a sort of Bergsonian 'reduction' which considers all things *sub specie durationis* — what is called subject, what is called object, and even what is called space . . ." (S 184).[20]

In short, as Bergson attempts to separate what is truly human from the merely scientific, he wants to detail an expression of our human existence that in no way falls prey to quantification and rectilinear measurement as does the category of substance which is subject to geometry and spatialization. In doing so he hopes to find a region where freedom is not only possible but realizable.

THE REDISCOVERY OF INTENSITY

In *Time and Free Will,* the first major distinction Bergson makes is between what he calls extensity and intensity. This is an important distinction because it is the means by which Bergson will show a marked difference between physical causality as we know it in nature and the relationship of inner states where such a law has no currency (TF 200).

Bergson notes that in the description of psychic states it is often the practice to remark on the states of consciousness, sensations, feelings, and passions as being able to grow and diminish. We often say that we are more or less warm or cold, greatly or less disturbed and so on. These impressions are dealt with as subjective unextended objects.

The puzzle for Bergson is to solve why we have come to describe sensations in terms of quantities attributable to objects with well defined outlines. Bergson offers two examples to explain his point. In terms of representative sensations he asks us to concentrate on the action of holding a pin in the right hand and with it prick the left hand more and more deeply. At first there is only a tickling soon succeeded by a prick and finally a pain localized at a point that spreads over the whole zone. Upon further inspection we realize that our eyes are squinting and our heart rate increases; in fact, our entire body has become hypersensitive to the intrusion. And the more we reflect on it, the more clearly shall we see that we are here dealing with so many qualitatively distinct sensations, so many varieties of a single species. But, Bergson points out, in common parlance we spoke at first of one and the same sensation which spread further and further, of one prick which increased in extensity.

The reason for this confusion is that without being aware, we localize in the sensation of the left hand, which is pricked, the progressive effort of the right hand, which pricks. We thus introduce the cause into the effect and unconsciously interpret quality as quantity, intensity as a magnitude of extension (TF 42). For Bergson, this example encapsulates how all other impressions of our representative sensations are normally understood — namely, that the intensity of sensations varies with the external causes thereby leading us to assume the presence of quantity in an effect that is inextensive and in most cases indivisible.

Contrastingly, in terms of deep seated emotions or affective sensations, the same confusion is often incurred but with important differences. In regard to deep feelings of joy, sorrow, and aesthetic pleasure, who has not experienced, Bergson asks, an emotion that enters feebly and remains isolated and foreign to the remainder of the inner life; little by little it permeates a larger number of psychic elements, shading them with its own color until the point is reached where one's whole outlook seems to have changed radically. When we remark in the course of all this that our souls are filled or become occupied with the effects of the emotion, it must be taken to mean that its impression has altered the shade of a thousand perceptions or memories, and in this sense pervades them, although it does not itself come into view (TF 9). What actually has occurred is a qualitative transformation in the multiplicity of simple states that consciousness dimly discerns. The deeper we penetrate into the depths of consciousness, Bergson insists, the less right we have to treat psychic phenomena as things which are set side by side as causal links or, as one would imagine, for example, domino pieces. What has happened, rather, is an evolution of qualitative differentiations and not a change in magnitude. Bergson reminds us that "this wholly dynamic way of looking at things is repugnant to the reflective consciousness, because the latter delights in clean cut distinctions, which are easily expressed in words, and in things with well-defined outlines like those which are perceived in space" (TF 9). Hence, in the course of his observations, Bergson concludes that the idea of intensity is thus situated at the junction of two streams, one of which brings us the idea of extensive magnitude from without, while the other brings us from within, in fact from the very depths of consciousness, the image of inner multiplicity (TF 73).

Bergson's next goal is to recognize what form the multiplicity of our inner states takes if the exterior causes are not introduced as extensive magnitudes. Bergson illuminates this multiplicity through its distinction from the process of counting in successions. In other words, what is the difference between numerical multiplicity and psychic multiplicity? The former is nothing more than the multiplicity of homogeneous units juxtaposed in the homogeneous medium of ideal space. In counting sheep, for example, we deliberately disregard individual qualitative differences between them; in considering their number we disregard their distinguishing individual features and only pay attention to a categorizing commonality that allows us to treat them as homogeneous units (TF 76).

Similarly, the units with which we form the number "3" seem to be indivisible as we pass abruptly from one to another because we are compelled to fix our attention successively on each of the units of which it is compounded. The indivisibility of the act by which we conceive any one of these units is then represented in the form of a mathematical point, which is separated from the following point by an interval of space. What is of the mind is the indivisible process by which it concentrates attention successively on different parts of a given space; the parts which have thus been isolated remain in order to join with the others, and, once the addition is made, they may be broken up in any manner whatsoever. They are therefore parts of space, and space is, accordingly, the material with which the mind builds up number — the medium in which the mind places it (TF 84). This process of spatialization, however, is only accomplished because what has been isolated and separated, like numbers, implies the simple intuition of a multiplicity of parts or units, which are *absolutely alike* (TF 76).

To further his point, Bergson asks us to reflect on the sound of a bell from a tower. Upon hearing the tolls, two alternatives are possible. Either we retain each of the successive sensations in order to combine it with the others, and form a group which is reminiscent of a rhythm, in which case we do not count the sounds but limit ourselves to gathering the "qualitative" impressions produced by the whole series; or, we explicitly count the sounds which means separating them. This separation, however, calls for some homogeneous medium in which the sounds can be spread and tallied, stripped of their qualities, and in a way emptied, thereby only leaving traces of their presence which are absolutely alike (TF 86–87).

As in all counting, Bergson wants to point out the problem of the medium. If the sounds are separated, they leave empty intervals between them; if we count them, the intervals remain though the sounds disappear. Yet, how could these intervals remain if not in space since the series of sounds have finished their enduring and no longer exist? It is in space, therefore, that the operation occurs. The passing sounds are retained by a reduction to the homogeneity afforded to numbers which is quite unlike the qualitative expression found as we penetrate further into the depths of consciousness. For the deeper we fall into these depths, the less quality yields to number. The more we let consciousness speak for itself, Bergson states, the more "we find ourselves confronted by a confused multiplicity of sensations and feelings which analysis alone can distinguish" (TF 87).

In other words, on its own terms, consciousness beholds more than number; like Augustine's *animus*, consciousness has the potential to be distended and to engage in a synthetic activity allowing it a certain degree of freedom from the causal laws of nature and the reduction of its existence to number.

La Durée Réelle

Bergson radically differentiates our rapport with matter from our rapport with consciousness in terms of multiplicities. On the one hand there is the multiplicity of natural objects to which the conception of number is immediately applicable in both extension and magnitude. On the other hand, there is the multiplicity within the states of consciousness which cannot be regarded as numerical without the help of some symbolic representation — namely without the aid of space.

For this reason, our interior life cannot be strung out in a line as if psychic states could be set side by side; perceiving a line as a line necessitates taking a position outside of it and taking account of the void that surrounds it. Furthermore, projecting this dimension of multiplicities into spatial discreteness is to cast them in a new form not originally attributable to them, thereby making an addition. But if no such projection is made, Bergson insists, we would find that our "sensations will add themselves dynamically to one another and will organize themselves, like the successive notes of a tune by which we allow ourselves to be lulled and soothed" (TF 104).

As such, only once the habit of spatialization is arrested in regard to our immediate conscious life are we able to make a direct note of successions which melt into and permeate one another, without precise outlines, without any tendency to externalize themselves in relation to one another, and without any affiliation to number. This, Bergson remarks, is pure heterogeneity, succession without distinction; it is the mutual penetration, interconnexion, and presentation of elements in such a way that everything at once represents the whole and cannot be distinguished or isolated except by abstract thought. Once the ego refuses the intellect's habit of confounding external extensity with inner intensity, what remains is pure change.[21] Hence, mental states are really derived states which actually float on the surface of continual change — change being the seamless endurance of the inner life. This seamless endurance is what is most immediate to our consciousness without interval or fixity; it is real duration (*la durée réelle*) — otherwise known as the real time of our individual lives:

> *real duration* is what we have always called *time*, but time perceived as indivisible. That time implies succession I do not deny. But that succession is first presented to our consciousness, like the distinction of a 'before' and 'after' set side by side, is what I cannot admit. When we listen to a melody we have the purest impression of succession we could possibly have — an impression as far removed as possible from that of simultaneity — and yet it is the very continuity of the melody and the impossibility of breaking it up which make that impression upon us. If we cut it up into distinct notes, into so many 'befores' and 'afters', we are bringing spatial images into it and impregnating the succession with simultaneity: in space, and only in space, is there a clear-cut distinction of parts external to one another. I recognize moreover that it is in spatialized time that we ordinarily place ourselves. We have no interest in listening to the uninterrupted humming of life's depths. And yet, that is where real duration is. Thanks to it, the more or less lengthy changes we witness within us and in the external world, take place in a single identical time. (CM 149)[22]

For Bergson, real duration is the indivisible continuity of change. It is the felt experience of change once the communicating surface between the ego and external objects becomes relaxed (TF 126). It is an experience of quality — a richness and depth that becomes confused when mathematical time, or quantity, is projected onto that experience. Real duration is not a measure of life, it is life in its unmeasured movement of ceaseless qualitative change and constant invention. Since it is the *élan* of the inner life, any attempt at imagining it tends to spatialize its flow; any attempt to logically categorize it tends to hypostatize its fluid quality; any attempt to substantialize it renders it inert.

Bergson argues that at the level of inner life, psychic states, while being just as much a phenomenon of nature as falling stones, are not subject to the law of causality. This law states that every phenomenon is determined by its conditions such that the same causes produce the same effects (TF 199). In nature the same cause can appear twice or innumerable times because the intellect reduces heterogeneous contingency to quantifiable homogeneous elements which are anonymous and interchangeable. This is the basis of all predictability in science. For example, after initial experimentation and quantification, we begin to expect a given force to move a given mass; we begin to expect water to boil once we excite its molecules to a certain temperature; we begin to expect a certain volume of gas to exert a certain pressure given a certain rise in room temperature. In every case the conditions for a predictable set of results can be continuously reproduced because the human intellect has reduced change to number and made the elements of change identical and therefore determinable.

However, at the level of psychic phenomena, deep-seated psychic states are radically heterogeneous to one another. As Bergson says, "it is impossible that any two of them should be quite alike, since they are two different moments of a life-story" (TF 200). Further on he states that "even the simplest psychic elements possess a personality and life of their own," such that "they are in a constant state of becoming, and the same feeling, by the mere fact of being repeated, is a new feeling." In other words, on the stage of consciousness, the same inner causes will not reproduce the same effects because a deep-seated inner cause produces its effect once and for all and will never reproduce it again. In short, if the causal relation still holds good in the realm of inner states, it cannot resemble in any way causality in nature. The relation of "before" and "after" can no longer hold because complete novelty has no antecedent (TF 101, 190). This is duration — "the same moment does not occur twice." Said otherwise, homogeneous elements do "not bear the mark of time that has elapsed and thus, in spite of the difference in time, the physicist can encounter identical elementary conditions;" duration, on the other hand, "is something real for consciousness that preserves the trace of it" such that identical conditions do not exist (TF 200).

It is important to note Bergson's slow but consistent insistence that as he penetrates the structure of inner life, the passage of time for the human subject becomes less and less impersonal and anonymous because each moment possesses it own "life-story." In other words, each present moment is infused with a person's unique history. There can no longer just be a "before" and "after" because no longer does *any* cause determine *any* effect whatsoever. The passage of time as duration becomes the touchstone of human individuality. In duration the personal past influences the personal present, not as static state of affairs, but as dynamic processes (TF 198) such that the person can prefigure (*préformation*) the future to a degree that allows a choice unpredicted by preceding circumstances (TF 211). Without the "survival of the past in the present there would be no duration but only instantaneity" (CM 179). The mathematical present, therefore, is a pure abstraction for Bergson and has no real existence (CM 151); it is not the time which distinguishes human existence.

In making such an assertion, in preferring to exclude all reference to the time of science in regard to the self, Bergson is now forced to account for time solely at the phenomenological level. In this respect, Bergson's dissertation on duration becomes an expert document on expounding the nonlinear aspects of time since he asserts that the time of the human subject is structured differently than time employed in the sciences. Duration, hence, becomes described in the most nonstatic and most nonlineal fashion.[23] As already quoted above, and throughout all Bergson's works, duration is consistently described through musical metaphors (TF 100, 111, 127, 147: CE 11, 27, CM 87, 147–49).[24] The musical metaphor of duration is an apt one since it adequately points to the complete nonspatiality of duration and excludes it from ever being employed for any form of physical measurement. At this point, duration is something strictly of the mind.

Subsequently, like Augustine, Bergson will employ with force the *distentio* of the mind to the fullest. The present becomes "a field of attention" that can be made shorter or longer. An individual may restrict the present to the sentence now being spoken, may enlarge it to include an entire lecture, may further stretch it to gather up great portions of the past, and, in moments of personal crisis, may elongate it to envelop the beginning and near end of one's life. "The present occupies exactly as much space as this effort" of attention. Moreover, Bergson goes on to state that

> An attention to life, sufficiently powerful and sufficiently separated (*dégagée*) from all practical interest, would thus include in an undivided present the entire past history of the conscious person — not as instantaneity, not like a cluster of simultaneous parts, but as something continually present which would also be something continually moving: such, I repeat, is the melody which one perceives indivisible, and which constitutes, from one end to the other — if we wish to extend the meaning of the word — a perpetual present, although this perpetuity has nothing in common with immutability, or this indivisibility with instantaneity. What we have is a present that endures. (CM 152)

Following Ricoeur's example, we cannot proceed without taking stock here of the puzzlements or aporias that Bergson has so far engendered. First, the "indivisibility" of duration was arrived at by asserting the nonidentity of psychic "states." In other words, as in the case of Husserl's "absolute, temporally constitutive flux of consciousness," continuity was only obtained by analysis of the discontinuous which in turn eventually has to be excluded because it contaminates the purity of the indivisible. To what degree, we ask, can duration ever be separated from that which distinguishes it? Moreover, duration is the counterpoint of spatial phenomena; regardless how ingenious the arguments ensuring that duration is understood as something entirely of the mental realm, it is introduced as something to be distinguished from other natural phenomena in space. Inadvertently then, the struggle to differentiate duration begins with its identity with other natural phenomena. Second, the present somehow embraces one's "entire past history." Precisely in what way are we to understand the presence of the past in a present that is described as continual movement? Lastly, time is no longer tied to any natural reference point — to either the passage of stars, days, seasons, or to anything spatial whatsoever. Yet in what way is something supposedly so nonspatial as duration of any influence and importance to something as totally spatial as the human body?

Bergson will address some of these conflicts in his following works. Up to this point we have made little reference to Bergson's notion of "self" and its manifestation given its authentic time as duration. He does address notions of the self initially in *Time and Free Will* but we will forego any expanded discussion on the topic until we allow Bergson to fully expand his reflections on duration in the important work, *Matière et mémoire* (1896), that followed *Time and Free Will*.

THE RHYTHMS OF DURATION

Unlike *Time and Free Will*, Bergson's second major work, *Matter and Memory*, poses a direct critique of the mind-body distinction and the nineteenth century school of psychological associationism. Bergson proceeds with his critique by way of a radical reflection on the meaning of matter and the human body as a center of action. He takes the question of freedom beyond a solely psychological solution and hopes to show how consciousness can interact with matter in the production of free acts, without having to be determined by "things" as defined by realists or depend on the production of "representations" as defined by idealists.

For Bergson, the body is an object capable of exercising a genuine and therefore *new* action upon surrounding objects (MM 4). Human perception of the universe is an aggregate of images which may be entirely altered by a very privileged image — the body. This particular image occupies a center in which all others are conditioned; at each of its movements everything changes as though by a turn of a kaleidoscope (MM 12).

Bergson distinguishes his notion of "image" from that of either an idealist or realist. For the former, in the world of consciousness all images depend solely on the body, whereas for the latter, through science, an image is only related to itself and possesses an absolute value. Both positions, Bergson argues, are wrong since they regard perception as an operation of pure knowledge (MM 12–13). Bergson, rather, employs the term with respect to *une image privilégiée* which actively takes from matter what the body needs for its next action (MM 46).

Unlike David Hume, who stated that "the mind is a kind of theatre, where several perceptions successively make their appearances; pass, re-pass, glide away, and mingle in an infinite variety of postures and situations,"[25] the brain and the nervous system, for Bergson, in no way passively review representations (MM 20).[26] Both are instruments, analyzing perceived movement and selecting the executed movement (MM 7). In this way, perception is a part of things and does not come from consciousness but is the part of consciousness that is modified while in the midst of things. Perception, Bergson argues,

> expresses and measures the power of action in the living being, the indetermination of the movement or of action which will follow the receipt of the stimulus. This indetermination . . . will express itself in a reflection upon themselves or, better, in a division, of the images which surround our body; and, as the chain of nervous elements which receives, arrests and transmits movements is the seat of this indetermination and gives its measure, our perception will follow all the detail and will appear to express all the variations of the nervous elements themselves. Perception, in its pure state, is, then, in very truth, a part of things. (MM 68)

Bergson not only talks about pure perception (*la perception pure*) but further distinguishes it from conscious perception (*la perception consciente*). The latter is "a *variable* relation between the living being and the more or less distant influence of the objects which interest it" (MM 24). Conscious perception is our everyday perception impregnated with our past. It is full of memories that practically supplant our actual perceptions using the latter merely as "signs" to recall former images. In contrast, pure perception abides by no memory whatsoever. This is the very primordial and fundamental act of perception whereby we place ourselves into the very heart of things. This type of perception resembles a mere type of contact; almost a fragment of reality (MM 22, 237). In pure perception we recognize

> a system of nascent acts which plunges roots deep into the real; and at once perception is seen to be radically distinct from recollection (*souvenir*); the reality of things is no more constructed or reconstructed but touched, penetrated, lived; . . . Pure perception, in fact, however rapid we suppose it to be, occupies a certain depth of duration, so that our successive perceptions are never the real moments of things, as we have hitherto supposed, but our moments of our consciousness. (MM 74–75)

Given these two qualities of perception, which are differences in degree not of kind, our consciousness illuminates at each moment of time the part of the past that is in immediate need for a potential action. As such we see that the body is the center of perceptions and not their source. To perceive, in Bergsonian terms, is not to know or to acquire knowledge; perception is not a representation or a photographic image of what is about to happen. The image of an extended object can become a representation but not before being an image virtually. This virtuality is the result of a constant tension between the body and matter. The diverse perceptions of the same object given by different senses will not, when put together, reconstruct the complete image of the object; they will remain separated from each other by intervals which measure, so to speak, the gaps in my needs. Simply said, perception adds nothing to the reality which was not there before. On the contrary, it excludes something from the full reality. "To perceive means to immobilize" (MM 275). It consists in detaching from the totality of images, the possible action of the body upon them. It creates nothing. The principle of this selection is that those influences that do not reflect the eventual actions of the body pass on, while those that concern its activity are reflected and come to consciousness. In short terms, conscious perception is a transition from an image as being in itself to it being for me in the aid of movement.

What is key to perception for Bergson, however, is the necessity of memory.[27] He distinguishes between two kinds. Both forms of memory operate, for example, in learning by heart a passage of poetry. Each time the passage is read, each reading, in all of its details, as an unrepeatable event, is stored in pure memory (*souvenir pur*) (MM 179). Yet, once the passage is read over several times and the body is capable of reciting it, this recitation becomes more of a habit — like other motor dispositions, one of many skills I acquire and deposit in my nervous system. This latter kind of memory is more of a bodily memory (*la mémoire du corps*).[28] As such, pure memory is inextensive, powerless, and does not share in any degree the nature of sensation, yet preserves all past experiences; its very nature is to be unconscious and to precede images. On the other hand, the bodily memory is made up of the sum of the sensori-motor systems organized by habit; it is a quasi-instantaneous memory to which pure memory, unextended and unconscious, serves as a base (MM 197). Bodily memory operates at the point of action such that the memory of the past offers to the sensori-motor mechanism all the recollections capable of guiding it in its task and of giving to the motor reaction the direction suggested by the lessons of experience.

Understood in this way, Bergson sees the body as a conductor interposed between objects and events. The body is an advancing boundary between the future and the past — a point where the past drives into the future. The present becomes, therefore, an attentive recognition, a kind of circuit between matter, perception, and memory that ceaselessly summons the conscious being to action (MM 130). The present is the pivot where perception and recollection are always interpenetrating each other. From the present come the appeals to which memory responds. From the sensori-motor interactions of the present, memory is warmed into life.

The temporal present is therefore not a mathematical point that can be merely registered as having passed. It is rather, in terms of the psychical state, a perception of the immediate past and a determination of the immediate future. The past, in so far as it is perceived, is sensation that translated a very long succession of vibrations. The immediate future, in so far as it is being determined, is action or movement. Bergson explains that, "My present, then, is both sensation and movement; since my present forms an undivided whole, then the movement must be linked with the sensation, must prolong it in action. Whence I conclude that my present consists in a joint system of sensations and movements. My present is, in its essence, sensori-motor. This is to say that my present consists in the consciousness that I have of my body" (MM 177). The consciousness that Bergson speaks of here is in fact a type of tension that dissolves the hardened categories that the intellect establishes between the unextended and extended and quality and quantity.[29] This suggests that we must interpret the traditional distinction between perception and the material world in such a way as to take movement seriously. This means understanding the body as enduring; enduring here means seeing the body as action, movement and change within a scale of various rhythms of participation with matter. The action and movement spoken of here is not "motion" as studied in mechanics as the function of axes and points (MM 268). It is not the relative movement of interest to either the geometer or physicist. The movement that Bergson points out expresses itself at the narrowest threshold where the heterogeneous, qualitative, and indivisible character of sensation unites with the homogeneous and divisible character of motion. It is nothing other than duration.

> In reality there is no one rhythm of duration; it is possible to imagine many different rhythms which, slower or faster, measure the degree of tension or relaxation of different kinds of consciousness and thereby fix their respective places in the scale of being. To conceive of durations of different tensions is perhaps both difficult and strange to our mind, because we have acquired the useful habit of substituting for true duration, lived by consciousness, an homogeneous and independent time. (MM 275)

It is here, above all other references, that Bergson clearly delineates the path to human freedom. Throughout *Matter and Memory*, mind and matter were defined by positive characters and not negations. Where pure perception places each of us within matter, perception is penetrated by means of memory. The body is therefore not a determined movement but a center of indetermination, a privileged movement in the world given its repertoire of memories. Necessity would only rule a living being who adopted the rhythm of duration of matter. By condensing that duration into our own, we conquer necessity for, as stated above, there is no one rhythm of duration. Independent actions upon surrounding matter become more and more assured to the degree we force ourselves from (*se dégagent*) the particular rhythm which governs the flow of matter (MM 279). Given the aid of memory, every moment is a *new* presentness of activity where the possibility of a free action arises. This is why Bergson insists that "consciousness" is "before everything else, memory. . . . all consciousness . . . is memory, — conservation and accumulation of the past in the present" (ME 7–8).

This Bergsonian theme may be roughly sketched given a cone SAB (MM 211). SAB is the totality of the recollections accumulated in memory; the base AB, situated in the past, remains motionless yet with ever

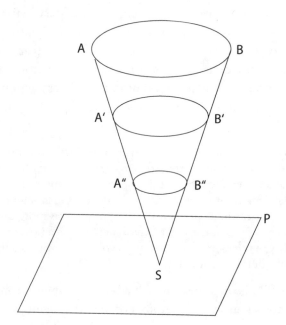

increasing shades of participation as the treasures of the past become more important for the present S. S is the bodily present moving forward on P, which is the plane of consciousness that has become the actuality of concrete perceptions.

As such, memory here does not consist in a regression from the present to the past but, on the contrary, in a progression from the past to the present. For a recollection to appear in consciousness, it is necessary for it to surface through the different planes of consciousness (AB, A'B', A"B") to where action is taking place. The living being scatters itself over AB to the measure that it detaches itself from its sensory and motor states in sleep and dreams; on the other hand, a being tends to concentrate itself in S to the measure that it attaches itself more firmly to the present reality, responding by motor reactions to sensory stimulation. Between S and AB, therefore, there is a constant oscillation of recollections that would "take the clearly defined form of a bodily attitude or of an uttered word" upon reception at S (MM 210).

Seen in this way, perception and memory are not the operations aiming to a type of pure knowledge. Holistically, they are facets of a dynamic circuit within a circuit advancing the boundary between the future and the past given the present action of the body. Unfortunately, the diagram is two dimensions and static. In reality, the reader should conceive of the entire cone image moving in two directions at once. There is no immobilization at any point in time. Every action therefore resides in a tension of consciousness with regard to duration. According to Bergson,

> Not only, by its memory of former experience, does this consciousness retain the past better and better, so as to organize it with the present in a newer and richer decision; but, living with an intenser life, contracting, by its memory of the immediate experience, a growing number of external moments in its present duration, it becomes more capable of creating acts of which the inner determination, spread over as large a multiplicity of the moments of matter as you please, will pass the more easily through the meshes of necessity. (MM 332)

The logic of Bergson's thesis is reducible to stating that matter is necessity and consciousness is freedom. For the living being, life is freedom inserting itself within necessity and turning it to its profit. In the most succinct terms, consciousness is coextensive with life (ME 17). Placed at the confluence of consciousness and matter, sensation condenses, in the duration which belongs to the person and characterizes his or her consciousness, immense periods of what can be called by analogy the duration of things. The tension of duration of a conscious being becomes, therefore, the measure of its power of acting — the quantity of free creative activity it can introduce into the world. Bergson writes that

> if you abolish my consciousness, the material universe subsists exactly as it was; only, since you have removed that particular rhythm of duration which was the condition of my action upon things, these things draw back into themselves, mark as many moments in their own existence as science distinguishes in it; and sensible qualities, without vanishing, are spread and diluted in an incomparably more divided duration. Matter thus resolves itself into numberless vibrations, all linked together in uninterrupted continuity, all bound up with each other, and traveling in every direction like shivers through an immense body (MM 276)[30]

What Bergson envisages, therefore, is a type of vibratory universe where everything is in movement and existing in differing tensions (rhythms) of duration.[31] More explicitly in *Creative Evolution*, Bergson will write "the universe endures" (*l'univers dure*) (CE 11). Where *Time and Free Will* dealt with the problem of psychological duration, *Matter and Memory* transcends the limits of psychology and tries to determine the reality of duration at an almost cosmic level. Where time was traditionally associated with space, Bergson correlates duration with "life" (consciousness) in an all-encompassing manner. "Besides consciousness and science, there is life" (MM 261); "[t]he evolution of life, from its early origins up to man, presents to us the image of a current of consciousness flowing against matter, determined to force for itself a subterranean passage, making tentative attempts to the right and to the left, pushing more or less ahead, for the most part encountering rock and breaking itself against it, and yet, in one direction at least, succeeding in piercing its way through and emerging into the light" (ME 27).

Regardless of this universalization in his philosophical vision, Bergson's point reveals a genuine temporality, or real duration, inherent in a conscious being. Key to this sense of duration is the indetermination of the future that, for him, explicitly points to the possibility of contingency in our actions. We are not automatons in a mechanical world of cause and effect. The flow of life is not irrevocably patterned and ready-made, devoid of any creative potential on our part. If our very essence as living beings is to "durationalize" matter, then there exists some assurance that we can forge our own freedom despite the seemingly endless web of determinate or causal factors in which we each seem enchained. The intuition of duration, therefore, is genuinely disruptive of our physical enmeshment in the objective world as the intellect conceives it.

Key to understanding what Bergson is driving at is to remember his chief methodology, intuition. Intuition is always contrasted with intellect. Intellect is the aspect of consciousness that helps us comprehend the environment and use the material world efficiently. While the intellect is essential to life, it does not have privileged access to reality. Its *modus operandi,* rather, is to represent reality by immobilizing it. Matter exists, for Bergson, as images. Images come about in the act of movement, defining a range of possible actions, either real or virtual, in relation to other images. The body, as a perceptive center, organizes itself in relation to other images. Only part of this organization, however, involves the role of the intellect and its need to immobilize and spatialize. Intuition, for its part, reaches in two directions, inward toward the depths of the self and outward, grasping the ambient duration. As Deleuze summarizes: "Duration is always the location and the environment of differences in kind; it is even their totality and multiplicity. . . . Intuition is not duration itself. Intuition is rather the movement by which we emerge from our own duration, by which we make use of our own duration to affirm and immediately recognize the existence of other durations, above and below us."[32] Having stated this, we must be careful not to attribute duration either a "location" or a particular "environment" *per se.* As one commentator aptly remarks, "nothing, in duration, gets to be a presence or a substance. Duration is not the collection of actualities, for it leaves room for a range of possibilities that may or may not become real. Insofar as duration is pure progressive differentiation, it is 'virtual movement.'"[33]

To summarize the equation succinctly, the movement of memory, for Bergson, always results in human action, and such action is human duration inserted into matter. Duration itself becomes differentiated depending on the matter it encounters, the materiality through which it passes. The result of this encounter is always virtual or continuous multiplicity. Intuition of this vital movement becomes obscured when we concentrate on the discrete multiplicities or actualities (matter) and deceptively believe the intellect has understood the whole in terms of what it can enumerate and analyze because it erroneously believes everything is ready-made and not still becoming. If this were so, creative acts would be impossible, and time would indeed be a useless category of existence.

It is Bergson's contention that life as movement — and duration as continuity of this movement — alienates itself by the very act of differentiation, thereby losing contact with the impetus or the whole that is never given. In this light, every species, every being attributed with *substantia,* is an arrested movement or a closure of continuous differentiation. Yet, as already stated above, Bergson argues that it is only in human beings, in the act of philosophical intuition, that this closure is circumvented; that the *élan vital* becomes self-conscious in our humanity, permitting a triumph over mechanism. Again to quote Deleuze,

> Duration, Life is *in principle* (*en droit*) memory, in principle consciousness, in principle freedom. 'In principle' means virtually. The whole question (*quid facti?*) is knowing under what conditions duration becomes *in fact* consciousness of self, how life *actually* accedes to a memory and freedom of fact. Bergson's answer is that it is only on the line of Man that the *élan vital* successfully 'gets through'; man in this sense *is* 'the purpose of the entire process of evolution.' . . . Man therefore creates a differentiation that is valid for the Whole, and he alone traces out an open direction that is able to express a whole that is itself open.[34]

At this juncture we must ask whether or not Bergson has succeeded in doing what Ricoeur has claimed impossible — to effect world time, or the time of nature, from a purely nonphysical or nonexternal source. As we have seen with Husserl, Bergson brackets the material world in favor of consciousness (but not intentional consciousness). Where Husserl proceeded with his *epoché* in hopes of having time appear as such, Bergson's purpose was to prove indetermination existed in the material world. Yet, for Bergson, in each receding step away from 'the natural standpoint' (the spatio-temporal world), duration becomes more and more encompassing. Where duration was the time of the individual in *Time and Free Will*, it becomes the time of life in general, and hence the world by the end of *Matter and Memory*. Ultimately, duration takes on an existence more exigent than ordinary time. In *Time and Free Will*, for example, Bergson attributes no reality to physical time, that variable which enters into the equations of physics; at least, he does not put it on the same level as extended space and inner duration.[35] As such, the argument for duration dims the distinction between the different categories of time. We must no longer conceive of there being a time of the world and time of the individual but rather, an infinite scale of times to accommodate the tension of duration in every existent possible.

But is the leap from the psychological to the cosmic credible? Problems arise on three counts. First, Bergson does not detail how reflection or attention sustains itself "in" duration. It is hard to imagine how concentrated intellectual effort and attention, as he calls it, can have the cosmic dimensions he purports it to have. Intuition, it seems, plays a double role in Bergson's thought. In some aspects it is understood as coincidence with an object and in other aspects it acts as a type of comprehension drafted in the course of an actual movement. Second, there seems to be a lapse of logic in Bergson's description. If pure change is more exigent than matter, then what is the purpose of ordinary or scientific time? In arguing that "consciousness is essentially free; it is freedom itself," (CE 270), Bergson fails to explain, positively, the purpose of the immobile, the static, and inert elements in the material world. Why must consciousness pass through matter? Is this a weakness or a strength? In giving priority to duration over clock time, he overlooks the fact that the former exists only relative to the latter. Bergson does not recognize that his elucidation of a "durational" consciousness is completely dependent on his understanding of the world as material and geometric. He fails to remember that succession and seriality had to be overcome to discover duration. This oversight leads to a contradiction. If attention to duration is the reestablishment of our grounding in pure change, what is the purpose of remembering, recollecting, preserving artifacts, or pursuing memorial efforts? Does not the possible attainment of pure change negate the necessity of history and time-marking in general? One can see now why Ricoeur adamantly recommends, in discussions of time, drawing a line between the notions of change and evolution on the one hand, and history on the other (TN3 91). Failure to do so only allows a phenomenological understanding of time to multiply its aporias and transcend the necessity of taking the historical past seriously.

Lastly, what is "the other of time (duration)" for Bergson? As Bergson's description of duration takes on cosmic proportions in his last writings, "the other of time" is not the eternity sought after by Augustine. In fact, the limit concept is reversed in Bergson's case; the "other of duration" becomes what duration, by its very definition, can never attain, namely the time of inert matter and identification with a magnitude. But here ordinary time is not a limit concept. Duration seems to violate the sharp distinction between the temporal and eternal order. Unlike the case of Augustine, in Bergson there can neither be laments and elegies for the loss of objective time nor a human desire to return to it; its loss is our gain. The "other of duration" becomes a time that duration refuses to acknowledge and must initially take flight from.

Up to this point we have not sufficiently detailed a self on the level of concordance-discordance such that it would be able to distinguish the anguish of the discrepancy. Where *Matter and Memory* dims the sharp distinction between the enduring inner life and timeless matter at the level of physical action, there has been little or no elaboration of what one might call a social self (*un moi social*), that is, a less abstract and theoretical depiction of self — one defined more by its relation to other selves. We will work toward this later theme by elaborating Bergson's remarks on the self in general and Bergson's critique of language.

THE PROFOUND SELF

Bergson opens *Creative Evolution* by reiterating the importance of intuition as the effort to recapture introspective data in its undistorted immediacy. As he had stated previously in *Time and Free Will*, mere intellect reduces heterogeneity to homogeneity, intensity to extensity, and duration to clock-time leading us to believe that fixed mental states are more real than the flow of our inner life. Contrarily, the intuition of duration finds within us neither separate mental states nor states which are strung upon the ego like beads upon a thread. In fact, the ego, the substratum that is often thought to support a psychic life, is only a static symbol conceived as a support for the artificial division of our consciousness into separate states; it has no real existence. The truth is, Bergson insists, that we change without ceasing and that such artificial states are themselves nothing but change; rather, they penetrate each other in a single endless flow (CE 3). The uninterrupted humming in the depths of our own consciousness is the indivisible continuity of change or *la durée réelle*.

> If our existence were composed of separate states with an impassive ego to unite them, for us there would be no duration. For an ego which does not *endure*, and a psychic state which remains the same so long as it is not replaced by the following state does not *endure* either. Vain, therefore, is the attempt to range such states beside each other on the ego supposed to sustain them: never can these solids strung upon a solid make up that duration which flows. What we actually obtain in this way is an artificial imitation of the internal life, a static equivalent which will lend itself better to the requirements of logic and language, just because we have eliminated from it the element of real time. But, as regards the psychical life unfolding beneath the symbols which conceal it, we readily perceive that time is just the stuff it is made of. (CE 4)

Duration as real time is therefore the very "stuff" which characterizes our inner life. Such a time is not fragmented, instantaneous, or divided; rather it is "the continuous progress of the past which gnaws into the future and which swells as it advances" (CE 4). Our character is the condensation of the history we have lived since birth. We challenge the future with the force of all our past preserved in memory

(CE 2). Our personalities, therefore, shoot, grow and ripen without ceasing. The irreversibility of duration prevents us from ever living a single moment over again. We are therefore creating ourselves continually; for a conscious being "to exist is to change, to change is to mature, to mature is to go creating oneself endlessly" (CE 7).

In this light, the time through which the self evolves is never the chronometry of successive and identical instants. The time through which the self feels itself experience the vicissitudes of enduring the physical elements of cold and warmth, the emotions of love and hate, the loss of loved ones, and unexpected joy is more a sensational wash of inner multiplicities. Time here is not a homogeneous container in which events simply unfold. Each moment is absolutely new. "Time is invention or it is nothing at all" (CE 341).

In short, the human subject for Bergson is dynamism. His is not a philosophy about things or substances (*une philosophie de la chose*).[36] He rejects any notion of the self as a *moi chose* or *moi immobile* in favor of the living self (*un moi vivant*) (TF 236); we are not the products of some artificial unification through an immutable ego. What in fact is most real to our own self is the least material and the least static. It is also something not foreign to the individual. For Bergson "there is at least one reality which we all seize from within, by intuition and not by simple analysis. It is our own person in its flowing through time, the self which endures" (CM 162).

But what is the result of so radically identifying the human subject with its immediate inner life, change, and duration? Bergson's answer, begun in *Time and Free Will*, states that "The self, infallible when it affirms its immediate experiences, feels itself free and says so; but as soon as it tries to explain its freedom to itself, it no longer perceives itself except by a kind of refraction through space" (TF 183). One cannot help but notice the striking similarity of this passage to St. Augustine famous query about time already quoted: "What then is time? I know well enough what it is, provided nobody asks me; but if I am asked what it is and try to explain, I am baffled." Elsewhere, Bergson points out that as long as we make no effort to perceive this continuity of change, we feel it is there, but, as soon as our consciousness thinks that it beholds

it, it is confronted with only an infinity of separate psychical states —
a multiplicity. Bergson concludes, hence, that it would seem to be the case
that "the unity of the person exists only so long as it is not perceived."[37]

What in fact has transpired in Bergson's case is that in identifying
the self so closely with time, the former problem simply supplants the
first. The self now becomes just as much a problem as the time of the
self. In fact, the solutions will follow a similar path. Where Bergson
sought to distinguish the immobile (space) from what constantly
changes in nature (psychic states) to define duration, he will now distinguish some immobile element at the level of personal identity by
which to contrast the self that defines itself by ceaseless change.

Just as space, therefore, was contrasted with time to distil duration,
Bergson contrasts the self defined by language (spatial) to a self understood beyond language (nonspatial) to distill the real self that is constantly in a state of becoming. As mentioned in the first quote of this
section, our deception about the static state of our inner life stems from
the requirements of language. It is language (*dupe du langage*), Bergson
charges, that deludes us about the multiplicity of heterogeneity and
intensity of experience, cogent with the duration of our existence
(TF 130–32; 165–66).

In *Time and Free Will*, Bergson argues that the consequence of trying to fit the self-as-becoming into the ready-made confines of ordinary public language is to confuse a "superficial self" (*le moi superficiel*)
for the fundamental or profound self (*le moi fondamental*) (TF 125;
129ff; 165–72; 231ff). The superficial self is the external projection of
the profound self. It is the self refracted through conceptual analysis
(intelligence) with its spatial and social representations (language). The
superficial self is only a surface confusion of crystallized images, divided
conscious states, and petrified sentiments that are ultimately parasitic
on a more deep-seated self.

Contrarily, the profound self is what is most intimately identified
with pure duration (TF 106). The profound self is our dynamic self —
our true personality.[38] At this level, Bergson remarks, "an absolute internal knowledge of the duration of the self by the self is possible" (CM
169; 176). The more we immerse ourselves into pure duration the more

false distinctions will fall away allowing us to grasp our freedom as an undisputed reality. The freedom inherent to human life resides beyond the social representation of stereotypes, power relations, and rationalistic theories of free choice. The self that is free for Bergson is the self that endures. "But the moments at which we thus grasp ourselves are rare, and that is just why we are rarely free. The greater part of the time we live outside ourselves, hardly perceiving anything of ourselves but our own ghost, a colourless shadow which pure duration projects into homogeneous space. Hence our life unfolds in space rather than time; we live for the external world rather than for ourselves; we speak rather than think; we 'are acted' rather than act ourselves. To act freely is to recover possession of oneself, and to get back into pure duration (*se replacer dans la pure durée*)" (TF 231).

Hence, the more the profound self, or "living self," (*un moi vivant*), is conscious of its identity with pure duration, the more disparate parts will enter into each other until the "whole personality concentrate itself in a point, or rather a sharp edge, pressing against the future and cutting into it unceasingly" (CE 201). As such, the fundamental self is future oriented; the deep-seated self finds its recognition in its becoming and not in what it attains.

In a shorter lecture given in 1914, Bergson recapitulates this dichotomous notion of the self in terms of his favorite ancient philosopher Plotinus (205–270 C.E.). We might consider ourselves, Bergson suggests, as having two different existences, one *de jure* and the other *de facto*. *De jure*, we are outside time and we feel ourselves to be of a purely contemplative essence. *De facto* we evolve in time and our life is in the sensible world, and we act.

> The *de facto* is . . . a diminution or a degradation of the *de jure*. To act is to wish or to desire a thing, to have need of it; to act is consequently to be incomplete, to set out in quest of self. To evolve in Time is to add unceasingly to what is; it is consequently to be unfinished and to lack the possession of existence in its fullness. More generally, the second mode of existence [*de facto*] is, as it were, a distension or a dilution of the first, since unity had thus been broken up into multiplicity, or, rather, has let fall from itself a dispersed multiplicity which is indefinitely striving to produce an imitation of unity in Time.[39]

In the course of his works, Bergson remarked sparingly about the superficial self in favor of the profound self but, in *Creative Evolution,* one sees the slow interpenetration of two themes — "life" and the profound self. "Life," for Bergson, is more than the mere arithmetical sum of individual organisms with various levels of consciousness. "Life" is a dynamic synthesis of unity and multiplicity which only duration can realize; "life" transcends finality as it transcends other categories. It is a current sent through matter, drawing from it what living beings it can (CE 265). "Life" in this sense is an effort to remount the incline that matter descends (CE 245). Where life is movement, materiality is the inverse movement. More succinctly Bergson says: "Life (*la vie*), that is to say consciousness launched into matter, fixed its attention either on its own movement or on the matter it was passing through; it has thus been turned either in the direction of intuition or in that of intellect" (CE 181).

> I am then . . . a unity that is multiple and a multiplicity that is one; but unity and multiplicity are only views of my personality taken by an understanding that directs its categories at me; I enter neither into one nor into the other nor into both at once, although both, united, may give fair imitation of the mutual interpenetration and continuity that I find at the base of my own self. Such is my inner life, and such is life in general. While, in its contact with matter, life is comparable to an impulsion or an impetus (*un élan*), regarded in itself it is an immensity of potentiality, a mutual encroachment of thousands and thousands of tendencies which nevertheless are 'thousands and thousands' only when once regarded as outside of each other, that is, when spatialized. (CE 258)

As Bergson proceeds to unfurl his thesis in *Creative Evolution,* the more the term "life" becomes differentiated. For example, we read that "in reality, life is of the psychological order," (CE 257) while in another place it is stated that "life in general is mobility itself," (CE 128) and later yet we read "life . . . will appear as a wave which rises [and] this rising wave is consciousness," (CE 269) until finally Bergson states that "consciousness is distinct from the organism it animates, although it must undergo its vicissitudes. . . . Consciousness is essentially free; it is freedom itself" (CE 270). Hence, where at one point duration for the profound self was consciousness, consciousness is now "life." This interconnection, however, is totally explicit for Bergson. Human existence, as it evolves, is the axial point between matter/life, movement/inertness, mere time/duration, necessity/freedom. It is only in the life of men and women that there exists "a subterranean passage" for consciousness to escape complete materialization (ME 27).[40]

Consequently, as in *Matter and Memory*, where duration becomes a type of cosmic time, in *Creative Evolution* Bergson eclipses the self with a universal dimension entitled "life." In yet a later work he will make such a transition explicit by stating "for we live a social and even cosmic life."[41] These are not really transitions perhaps, but what Ricoeur has referred to earlier as the "hierarchization" or layering of the experience of time at the level of the self. For example, if we follow the progressive distinctions from clock-time to duration to cosmic time, from the superficial self to the profound self to "life," from ordinary memory to bodily memory to pure memory, and from ordinary perception to conscious perception to pure perception, we can note the lines of differentiation Bergson produces in an attempt to have the self exact its absolute freedom and distinctiveness from the natural world. At each stage, when the already-constituted and natural are excluded or supplanted in hope of highlighting what is ever-growing, maturing, and becoming, the essence of what is reached for can never be an undivided unity in the way Bergson thought it could; whether it will be time or the self, the result will always be "a unity that is a multiple" (CE 258).[42]

In light of this, there is little hope of seeing how duration, "life," or consciousness could ever be responsible for constituting the time of nature or ordinary time. To reverse the direction of his analysis, that is, to show how "life" posits clock-time, Bergson would have to express a completely contradictory *telos* to what he has described as "life." Up to this point he has failed to express any reason why the *élan* of consciousness should posit clock-time; indeed it is such time that thwarts freedom and the work of consciousness itself. Said in other terms, why would the concordance of duration posit the discordance of the material world? Why would "indivisibility" and "pure change" posit their other? Why would a channel of freedom create its own world of bondage? In his particular strategy to extract the universal from the particular, the immaterial from the material, the pure from the impure, Bergson sets up a logic that is irreversible. Once the time of the material world is left behind, it can never be regained.

THE PROBLEM OF LANGUAGE

If the self is this "subterranean passage" of "life" and consciousness, why is it so rarely manifested in the common person and why is our feeling of condemnation toward a monotonous temporality at times so overwhelming?

For Bergson, our personality is alienated from the *élan* of becoming because language fails to translate inner experience; "there is no common measure between mind and language" (TF 164–65). It is language, Bergson argues, that makes us believe in the unchangeableness of our sensations and even the very nature of the sensation felt. Words impose a false stability on the fugitive impressions of consciousness. It is the public, stable, and impersonal word that intervenes between us and our private fluctuating sensations, thereby ascribing to them the sharp separateness of concepts that we employ to speak about them. Bergson states: "The most living thought becomes frigid in the formula that expresses it. The word turns against the idea. The letter kills the spirit" (CE 127).

This antipathy toward language is fueled by language's association with the intellect. The intellect operates in the material sphere using division, spatialization, and geometry for the achievement of practical results. Unlike intuition, the intellect was not designed to plumb the depths of our inner life. The most the intellect can do is to *theoretically apprehend* and analyze the experience of reality as duration using the terms of ordinary language — terms that are incapable of expressing the realm of pure change, novelty, and creativity. The intellect employs common stock words and everyday denotations that fail to reference "the very stuff" of which we are made — duration. In short, one cannot manufacture reality (real duration) by manipulating symbols

(CM 182). The whole is always greater than its parts. One can pass from the intuition of duration to analysis but not from analysis to duration (CM 180).

Given his negative regard for language, it is little wonder that many regard Bergson's thinking as mere metaphysical fancy.[43] To some degree this suspicion is well-founded. In a famous paper entitled, "An Introduction to Metaphysics" (1903), Bergson clearly states: "*metaphysics, then, is the science which claims to dispense with symbols*" (CM 162). By symbols here Bergson means all forms of notations from words to musical notes, including numbers and concepts. Yet there is surely a contradiction that shrouds such a claim. After all, how can someone claim the nonsymbolic status of duration, something that "cannot be expressed in the fixed terms of language," (TF 237) while using several hundred pages to beautifully describe it? How could someone so masterful in the use of metaphor be so suspicious of language? As one commentator notes, "according to everything Bergson seems to write about language, thought, and philosophy itself, it is far from evident how he . . . could ever have been able to write genuinely about time at all."[44]

There may be two possible explanations for the paradoxical relationship to language found in Bergson. First, Bergson is not well disposed toward the use of technical terms, not only in science, but in philosophy.[45] Metaphysics works best, he suggests, not in dispensing totally with concepts but freeing itself from "the inflexible and ready-made concepts" (CM 68) that fail to capture the flexible and mobile nature of its subject matter. The multiplication of technical terms by thinkers breeds a type of laziness. Technical terms become associated with ready-made ideas, and theories lose their creative employment in the activity of thinking. Bergson believes that there is no philosophical idea so profound and subtle that it cannot be expressed in everyday language.[46]

Second, Bergson has an ambiguous relationship to the role of metaphor. While he agrees that metaphors can suggest something of the inexpressibility of duration, he warns almost in the same breath that metaphors are not the answer (CM 42–43). In fact, he suggests the need "to get away from metaphor" (CM, 150). In the closing pages of *Creative Evolution* Bergson exhorts the philosopher to sweep away everything that is only an "imaginative symbol" in order to "melt back into" the flux and continuity of becoming that define duration. Yet, elsewhere, Bergson will argue that intuition gives birth to one of language's most metaphorical modes — poetry (CM 80). Even more so, in his work on comedy and laughter (*Le Rire*, 1900), he is more open to understanding poetic language as operating at another level. There, he concedes that it is the poet who can use words to "suggest — things that speech was not calculated to express."[47] He even goes on to say that it is through poetry that the "rhythms of life" can be translated, and — in a spirit somewhat akin to Martin Heidegger's exegesis of the quote, "poetically man dwells"[48] — Bergson concludes that "poetic imagination is but a fuller view of reality."[49]

   This strong distinction between poetic language versus scientific or even everyday language stems from Bergson's tendency to see language as employed by the scientist and by the poet as two distinct kinds (CE 201; 258; 326). In the *Creative Mind* he draws the distinction clearly: "If one were constantly to speak in abstract, so-called 'scientific' language, one would be giving of mind only its imitation by matter, for abstract ideas have been drawn from the external world and always imply a spatial representation: . . . The moment we reach the spiritual world, the image, if it merely seeks to suggest, may give us the direct vision, while the abstract term, which is spatial in origin and which claims to express, most frequently leaves us in metaphor" (CM 42–43). Yet, are there really two symbolic chains that exist without any points of convergence? As Ricoeur was later to make clear, there is no such thing as scientific or poetic language *per se;* there is only the poetic or scientific *use* of language owing to the polysemic nature of the sign. Where Bergson separated the two chains, Ricoeur notes their mutual necessity.

> Now we understand why we need two languages. We need a language that speaks by measurement and number, an exact coherent and verifiable language. This is the language of science. With it we fashion a model

of reality transparent to our logic, homogeneous with our reason and, in this sense, with ourselves. But were this language not limited and balanced by that of poetry, it would lead to one single kind of relationship with things — a relationship of domination, exploitation and domination by man with regard to things, and by man with respect to man. In this sense poetry preserves science by impeding the production of this fanaticism of the manipulable. Poetics preserves, for science itself, an idea of truth according to which what is manifested is not at our disposal, is not manipulable, but remains a surprise gift.[50]

As mentioned in the previous chapter, the creative intention of language for Ricoeur is to designate symbolically a possible horizon of existence that aims to transgress the already figured level of signification. But because language is symbolic, it remains open to a variety of interpretations, condemning us to various polemics of understanding. Bergson, however, at the level of durational existence, wants to rise above all conflicts of interpretation. As Ricoeur remarks in reference to Heidegger, the latter's vision teaches us that perhaps phenomenology is possible only as hermeneutics (TN3 62). Heidegger was not interested in direct seeing, appearing as such, or immediacy. For Heidegger, Being had been forgotten — covered up — and could only be sought through understanding or, to use another expression, by way of interpretation, where the anticipation of the meaning of Being frees it from forgetfulness and hiddenness.[51] For Ricoeur, Heidegger's hermeneutic methodology is really a labor of language; it is a labor of interpretation, of explicating the structures of phenomenon as this or that, whereby the understanding that we already possess of the temporal structure of Dasein is brought to language.

To say the least, Bergson's struggle to place language in his reflections on duration is obvious. Given his erroneous supposition of two different language chains, he will formulate many of the problems he attempts to solve as problems of language. For example, the struggle between realism and idealism, in relation to psychic-cerebral parallelism, is argued on the plane of notation alone. In Bergson's eyes, "we are . . . born conjurors" who unwittingly substitute one notation system for another and end eventually in self-contradictions (ME 237).

Yet, for all his antagonism toward language, Bergson goes on to assert that "a language is required which makes it possible to be always passing from what is known to what is yet known. There must be a language whose signs — which cannot be infinite in number — are extensible to an infinity of things. This tendency of the sign to transfer itself from one object to another is characteristic of human language. . . . Without language, intelligence would probably have remained riveted to the material objects which it was interested in considering. It would have lived in a state of somnambulism, outside itself, hypnotized on its own work. Language had greatly contributed to its liberation" (CE 158). In the course of his works, therefore, Bergson expresses almost diametrically opposed opinions about the status of language. It is seen as both a detriment and a necessity to his understanding of duration. Bergson could never conclude, like Merleau-Ponty, for example, that perception needs language. It is in fact language that destroys the mute silence of blunt sensations and imparts meaning to them. As Merleau-Ponty once stated: "I do not perceive more than I speak — Perception has me as has language" (VI 190). Bergson failed to see that the human subject is only able to orient and understand itself in the confused world of lived experience through the medium of language. He further failed to grasp that the formation of human awareness about anything, from the physical to the metaphysical, depends on a certain metaphorical economy in language. In Bergson we read of ideas that are simply posited and therefore above the hermeneutic grip of linguistic labor: "The intuition we refer to then bears above all upon internal duration. . . . It is the direct vision of the mind by the mind — nothing intervening, no refraction through the prism, one of whose facets is space and another language. Instead of states contiguous to states, which become words in juxtaposition to words, we have here the indivisible and therefore substantial continuity of the flow of inner life" (CM 32). In such a statement, who cannot hear Husserl's own pronouncement, concerning his own search for the absolute temporal flux of consciousness, that "for all this, names are lacking?"[52] Bergson goes as far to attest to the ineffectiveness of language when he states that "my initiation into the true philosophical method began the moment I threw overboard verbal solutions, having found in the inner life an important field of experiment" (CM 89–90). His suspicion that scientific language would never express the *élan* of duration's continual flow and novelty, is, therefore, more a rejection of language in general. Little wonder then that we are consistently reminded that duration is akin to something more universally communicative than words and language, namely music.

Bergson's failure to engage in this labor of language leads to what Ricoeur calls the "direct, but silent, intuition of time or an indirect, but blind, presupposition of it" (TN3 63). This is precisely what Bergson has presented. Not unlike Descartes's demand for absolute certainty, Bergson's location of duration in an inaccessible but immutable place such as "life's depths" (*la vie profonde*) (CM 150) or with "the inner regard of my consciousness" (CM 163) makes *l'intuition de durée* an impenetrable datum safely protected from any interpretation but his own.

The Social Self and the Necessity of Storytelling

Some 25 years after *Creative Evolution* (1907) we are confronted with a final work that still adamantly attests to the reality of duration but expresses it in a markedly different manner. In this final major work, *The Two Sources of Morality and Religion* (1932), Bergson tells us that these latter reflections "complete naturally, though not necessarily," the conclusions set out in *Creative Evolution* (TS 219).[53] In contrast to his earlier works, the most startling assertion concerns the necessity of a material world that completes a need inherent in that which is continually creating (TS 220).

The Two Sources of Morality and Religion starts from a sociological standpoint. While his early works elaborated the idea that human freedom issues from *"la vie profonde,"* in this last work Bergson wants to speak to our surface life where we are in continuous contact with other human beings whom we resemble, and with whom we are commonly united by a discipline which creates between all human beings a relation of interdependence. He therefore wants to speak about the self that is inserted "into the close-woven tissue of other exteriorized personalities." What binds each of us to each other, Bergson suggests, is the "necessary" state of obligation we each feel toward one another. This necessity of obligation, however, does not issue from the profound self but the social self, a social ego that is superadded to the individual self. "To cultivate this social ego is the essence of our obligation to society" (TS 6).[54]

The source of obligation for Bergson is something almost instinctual but not entirely; there is rather an interpenetration of instinct and intelligence at work in human beings. Both aid in the cohesion of a social milieu. Both have as their essential object the utilisation of implements; in the one case, invented tools, and therefore varied and unforeseen; in the other, organs supplied by nature and hence immutable (TS 17). Intelligence, however, has the possibility of going beyond a simple tool-making function. Expanding through its own efforts, intelligence developed unexpectedly and freed human beings from restrictions to which they were condemned by the limitations their nature had set. Human intelligence encourages a certain liberty that constantly tries to free the individual from "the totality of obligations" within a group (TS 15–17). To counterbalance this tendency of intelligence, nature provided its members with a virtual instinct (*l'instinct virtuel*) like that which lies behind the habit of speech (TS 18; 91). Virtual instinct is the force which causes the intellect to form certain representations and devise certain beliefs which thwart any attempt to neglect and free oneself from this "totality of obligation" in a society.

Bergson calls the forming of such representations and beliefs the story-making function of intelligence (*la fonction fabulatrice*) (TS 89).[55] It is perhaps one of the most underrated notions in Bergsonian scholarship.[56] The story-making faculty gives support to the natural cohesion of humankind and its obligatory rules by inventing divine and imaginary beings (gods) who add their authority to the commands and prohibitions of society, thereby ensuring that some protective deity will always be there to forbid, threaten, and punish. This led Bergson to conclude that religion in essence is a defensive reaction of nature against the dissolvent power of intelligence (TS 101).

Bergson sees the storytelling function as a continuous character of collective life. From ancient myths to modern novels, human beings are storytellers; the tendency is found "in everyone." Storytelling is understood here as "a fundamental demand of life" (*une exigence fondamentale de la vie*); it is indispensable to the existence of individuals as well as societies. "The storytelling function," Bergson states, "is thus to be deduced from the conditions of existence of the human species" (TS 166–67). Where some stories will be for pleasure, others will be for our compliance to the actual need for cohesion and are therefore "ideo-motory" (TS 179–80).

However, as if previewing this need for a narrative self that disparages conformity for uniqueness and demands a personal identity over a social one, we find another level of narrative function operational in Bergson's sociological reflections. Bergson's other mode of storytelling is cogent with an open and dynamic morality/religion. Here he concentrates on the characteristics of the "open soul" (*l'âme ouverte*) (mystics, saints, reformers, and moral leaders) who, through certain attunements to an emotive force in life, challenges society beyond its necessity for mere survival and protection and implores its members to engender everything meant by the word "love" (TS 27). These exceptional personalities, Bergson claims, borrow the images and symbols from the common storytelling function inherent in everyone to express their message — their story (TS 231). The vitality of this message is so great, so urgent, that the privileged personality is driven to do violence to speech to express it (TS 218). He or she is forced to refigure language using the language of passion and the art of dramatic literature in the hope of molding words to our deeper intuition (TS 31–34). In short, the "writer will attempt to realize the unrealizable" (TS 218). In pursuing this impulse, the word (*la vertu magique du langage*) bestows a power on a newly created idea, extending its previous relations and thereby influencing the past and opening a novel vision of the possible (TS 57).

In this latter mode of storytelling there is the potential for real human growth and the refiguration of identity. In listening to the story of an exceptional personality, our own confinement to social stereotypes can be broken and the path toward a more authentic identity opened up. "Let us hearken to their language; it merely expresses in representations the emotions peculiar to a soul opening out, breaking with nature, which enclosed it both within itself and within the city" (TS 39).

In a very clear passage Bergson indicates that our identities change to the degree that the life-story (narrative) of another finds a resonance within us, to draw us on to another chapter of our own narrative still to be lived and told.

> Why is it, then, that saints have their imitators, and why do the great moral leaders draw the masses after them? . . . Only those who have come into contact with a great moral personality have fully realized the nature of this appeal. But we all, at those momentous hours when our usual maxims of conduct strike us as inadequate, have wondered what such or such a one would have expected of us under the circumstances. It might have been a relation or a friend whom we thus evoked in thought. *But it might quite as well have been a man we had never met, whose life-story had merely been told us, and to whose judgement we in imagination submitted our conduct, fearful of his censure, proud of his approval.* It might even be a personality brought up from the depths of the soul into the light of consciousness, stirring into life within us, which we felt might completely pervade us later, and to which we wished to attach ourselves for the time being, as a disciple to his teacher. *As a matter of fact this personality takes shape as soon as we adopt a model; the longing to resemble, which ideally generates the form, is an incipient resemblance; the word which we shall make our own is the word whose echo we have heard within ourselves.* (TS 23; my emphasis)

The above passage is remarkable on two counts. First, Bergson rarely accords the spoken word such efficacy in reaching into "the depths of the soul" where duration becomes conscious and therefore becomes formative of the personality as the profound self. Pages later, in the same text, for example, he returns to his castigation of language and talks about "the dupe of language" and the need to "get away from metaphor."

However, the passage belies a second message that Bergson himself found hard to elaborate. The passage gives the impression that a personal narrative as an act of creation organizes a particular energy or duration that moves us from vague thoughts and chaotic pulsions to tangible, discrete words that have materiality and meaning. Such words carry vestiges of the originating creative force that inspired them to move us to a more profound consciousness of our identity. "Thought is a continuity, and in all continuity there is confusion. For a thought to become distinct, there must be a dispersion in words. Our only way of taking count of what we have in mind is to set down on a sheet of paper, side by side, terms which in our thinking interpenetrate. Just in this way does matter distinguish, separate, resolve into individualities, and finally into personalities, tendencies before confused in the original impulse of life" (ME 28). The last two passages taken together leave no reason to believe that the movement from "the original impulse of life" to personality cannot be achieved by either the written or spoken word. Hence, regardless of his prejudice against language in general, Bergson is hard-bent to deny that there is something in stories that can stir us to a certain consciousness, allowing us permission to possess the "echo we heard within ourselves" and thereby act out of our profound selves.

Yet, in what ways can life-stories be evocative? What is the mechanism that moves us to this state of consciousness which up until now has been described solely in terms of duration, intuition, memory, perception, and bodily action in hopes of skirting determinism?

In his essay "Intellectual Effort," Bergson explicitly addresses this evocation in terms of schemes and images. The effort exerted by an artist or novelist to express the deepest impressions, Bergson suggests, is an effort that begins abstractly and moves to the concrete, from scheme to images (ME 213). Schemes move vertically in our experience of invention, amassing from heterogeneous states into images that are homogeneous among themselves and upon which we act, write, speak, or create. Schemes descend progressively toward the images we want to evoke; schemes are intimated by depth and intensity while images move on a single plane carried out in extension (ME 201–02). It seems any created image that confronts us, whether it is written, spoken, musical, artistic, or mechanical, is only a cipher of the creative act from whence it came. All such acts of human creation have a dynamic source that can be accessed given effort and attention. According to Bergson,

> The scheme is tentatively what the image is decisively. It presents in terms of *becoming*, dynamically what the images give us statically as *already made*. Present and acting in the work of calling up images, it draws back and disappears behind the images once evoked, its work being then accomplished. The image, with its fixed outline, pictures what has been. . . . But for the flexible mind, capable of utilizing its past experience by bending it back along the lines of the present, there must, besides the image, be an idea of a different kind, always capable of being realized into images, but always distinct from them. The scheme is nothing else. (ME 227–28)

In this sense, language-as-narrative, as all creative expressions, can be, given our effort and openness, a conduit to the profound self, our truer identity. As much as he wishes to denigrate language, Bergson nonetheless seems to offer us a linguistic bridge between the two selves. By his own admission, storytelling is "a fundamental demand of life." Bergson, however, never fills out the larger implications of his suggestions. If so, it would have moved him to a hermeneutical position that sees self-understanding achieved through an encounter with representations, actions, texts, institutions, and monuments that objectify the self and mediate it. Instead, Bergson holds steadfastly to the vision that self-knowledge originates in consciousness, or, more specifically, philosophical intuition. Nonetheless, in *The Two Sources of Morality and Religion*, the implication is clear. Narratives of all types (political, moral, religious, and personal) can affect the self deeply, moving us from one level of consciousness (superficial) to another (profound). The difference seems to be a function of desire, effort, and attention.

In an implicit manner, therefore, one can vaguely see how the "the self" in Bergson's last work lives in a world configured by narratives. At one level, the self belongs to a web of narratives, both impersonal and individual, that encourage a social identity relative to communal forces, while another level of narrative challenges this very identity in the light of personal maturity and change. Consequently, this mixture, like so much in Bergson, is a living tension. Neither side of the self is authentic in itself nor should either side be taken as a *fait accompli*. If language-as-narrative can evoke us to a different level of consciousness, then it is not so difficult to see the conflict between our superficial selves and profound selves as a conflict of narrative modes. Where the superficial self remains with the level of narrative reflective of conformity and stereotypes for the sake of social cohesion, the profound self, in contrast, is in touch with the deeper pulses of life and learns to hear and tell a better story — its own *unique* story. In this latter case, an identity cannot be, as was first indicated, a totally self-presencing one, but rather, one dependent on models, biographies, and examples that aid in the telling of the uniqueness behind a name.

If Bergson had stopped his analysis here, then the correspondence between Ricoeur's narrative self and Bergson's profound self would be striking. The profound self, however, is open to a wider expansion, a wider horizon. There is, as in all levels of Bergson's analysis, just as personal duration became universal, the sudden addendum that the profound self is capable of cosmic feats. If the profound self is dedicated to its effort not to lose its intuition of duration then that intuition drives the self to deeper levels of recognition — to mystical intuition. At this level there are no aporias of temporality; here, "we shall cease to say, even of our body, that it is lost in the immensity of the universe." Our consciousness, in short, "reaches to the stars" (TS 221–22). For Bergson, immortality is not a fantasy in regard to intuition but the promise of life's vital impetus not to succumb to matter (CE 270–71). His thesis of immortality comes in the last several pages of *The Two Sources of Morality and Religion*, which rests on previous works that rejected the reduction of memory to physiological explanations and provided a novel view of memory that engendered the whole past (MM 220). Reminiscent of the diagram reproduced above, from a work he had written some 36 years previously, Bergson, in *The Two Sources of Morality and Religion*, states:

> We said metaphorically that we were proceeding thus from the summit to the base of the cone. It is only at its topmost point that the cone fits into matter; as soon as we leave the apex, we enter into a new realm. What is it? Let us call it the spirit, or again, if you will, let us refer to the soul, but in that case bear in mind that we are remoulding language

and getting the word to encompass a series of experiences instead of an arbitrary definition. This experimental searching will suggest the possibility and even probability of the survival of the soul, since even here below we shall have observed something of its independence of the body, indeed we shall have almost felt it. . . . Can the after-life, which is apparently assured to our soul by the simple fact that . . . a great part of this activity [is] independent of the body, be identical with that of the life into which, even here below, certain privileged souls insert themselves? (TS 226–27)

In opening his discussion up to immortality and the afterlife, Bergson takes the self beyond the temporality of all history and mortal time. Here, the profound self finds its furthermost limit from Ricoeur's narrative identity. The profound self must really be more properly designated as the durational self — the self that "is not limited to *playing* his past life again" (CE 180). Bergson's durational self is beyond the interest of refiguring time — it has gone beyond the matters of experience that are temporalized in the course of an individual's life time. Human meaning for the durational self is left behind in favor of what is least material and more creative, if not its very Creator (*à retrouver Dieu*) "who is . . . energy itself" (TS 221). As was done between *Time and Free Will* and *Matter and Memory,* as well as in *Creative Evolution,* Bergson, in *The Two Sources of Morality and Religion,* unwittingly passed over from one category of a problem to another. In this latter work the question of the self is eclipsed in favor of a metaphysical identity in general.

Despite some similarities, Bergson's appreciation of narrative is quite different from Ricoeur's thesis. Bergson sees narrative in light of a sociological necessity; on the one hand, *la fonction fabulatrice* provides communal cohesion while, on the other, it is a means to overcome the negative effects of that cohesion. In the latter case, the narrative function is brought close to the problematics of time and the self with respect to the "open soul" and its attention to duration, but there is no concrete reference to narrative as being either a condition of duration or its embodiment in a larger historical tradition that it challenges. Meanwhile, as we will see in a later chapter, Ricoeur's starting point is human action in history and the creation of meaning. Narrative is not argued for as a sociological necessity but as the very condition of imparting any meaning to our temporal existence at all.

MEANING

Has Bergson bestowed upon us anything more than an elongated poetic description of the "time-eternity" dualism?

Where Heidegger's hermeneutic phenomenology dispersed the figures of temporality, and generated a surplus of meaning by way of interpretation for each level beyond its previous source, Bergson offers no more than a single interpretation of the human experience of temporal passage. All Bergson really has told us is: a) that time employed metrically uses spatial metaphors to speak of the instantaneous "now;" b) that consciousness is durational and that neither our bodies nor minds experience temporal passage as instantaneous and punctual "nows;" c) and that there exists a luscious vocabulary for expressing human inner experience beyond the terminology of analysis. But the persuasive use of this poetic vocabulary does not necessarily refute the validity of the analytical research Bergson attacked in *Time and Free Will*. In placing a higher value on his ability to acutely express human inner experience, Bergson seems to have brashly concluded that he has surpassed any contributions that could be made by, for example, the psychology of associationism and psychophysics. Bergson's judgement that his notion of duration is more "real" than the result of experimental research was based on a serious prejudice that we will return to in our concluding chapter.

Of current interest, however, is what Bergson's description of the inner life meant for him. In finding what he felt to be a more fitting description of sensation and feeling, Bergson believes he has discovered the very source of human freedom. Ultimately, in relation to the world, the one meaning that authenticates the self for Bergson is freedom. At every level of differentiation of the self, from the intellect of the superficial self, to the intuition of duration of the profound self, to consciousness, to "life," and finally immortality, the degrees of freedom steadily increase as more and more the effects of matter are left behind.

The freedom posited is always presuppositional based on intuition alone. As Bergson himself states: "consciousness is . . . freedom itself" (CE 270). In fact, the importance of such a presupposition becomes more real with respect to Bergson's discussions of memory. For it is only in regard to his last work, in the light of the narrative functions, that memory seems to have any purpose outside of some physiological sense necessary for physical action. What use is memory if freedom is a function of something "pure," like intuition, which itself is free from any need of the rational discernment of alternatives and motives, as well as history and the interpretation of previous action?

The theme of freedom always operates between two poles — the material and the immaterial. Further, what self would choose only partial freedom since the guarantee of freedom seems to be nothing more than some sort of intellectual assent? Bergson never reckons with the discordance of life revealed through the language in laments and other elegies of the human condition. There is no need for testaments of struggle and the recognition of suffering. Apart from his last work, the misery of time is only rejected and never confronted. In fact, outside of the need to refer always to duration at the expense of discontinuity, there is little overlapping between the modes of discourse that describe mortal time and duration. At the level of duration there is no passivity before time since all is movement, which in turn may be no freedom at all. In an early work, Ricoeur criticized Bergson's notion of freedom:

> But what have we gained in thus returning to indistinct motives and vital coloration? We have to admit at once that such 'irresistible thrusts' do not make us free. It is no help if enthusiasm is imbued with our entire mentality, it is no help that somewhat spatial juxtaposition of ideas stamped by language and by society is replaced by a living interpenetration of continuous flux, it is no help even that I am present as a whole in an act — what is essential is that I should be the master of that flux rather than being subjected to it, in a word, that I should sustain it by attention, appropriate the very level on which I find myself.[57]

The impossibility of reversing this movement, of bringing duration back into clock time, indicates the illusion of freedom. Freedom is the negation of clock time — it cannot ameliorate or soften the awareness of life's shortness or its seeming insignificance. Again, who would choose struggle with mere interpretations of freedom when assent to duration guarantees the very reality of freedom? But what is the guarantee that such assent is possible? Has Bergson's thesis convinced us that intuition, in terms of "attention" and "reflection," renders the freedom he speaks about realizable? In this sense, the existence of what is "other than ordinary time" simply reduces itself to a function of belief. One final question therefore becomes crucial: outside of reading Bergson and perhaps listening to music, what sustains our belief in duration?

In the end, it is fair to conclude that the presupposition of meaning Bergson has the self engender only leads to hermeticism and even mystification. On this note, however, we shall leave the last word to Bergson: "I shall confine myself therefore to saying, in reply to those for whom this "real duration" is something inexpressible and mysterious, that it is the clearest thing in the world; *real duration* is what we have always called *time,* but perceived as indivisible" (CM 149).

But is such a corpus of thought as that of Bergson not redeemable at another level of interpretation than hermeticism? What are we to assume of his great assertions of time as becoming, continual creation, endless maturing, and the appearance of novelty? Is not the assertion, said in so many ways, that "consciousness is synonymous with invention and with freedom," (CE 264) beyond reduction to presupposition? Has not every novelist, artist, and poet given us centuries of proof that, against the range of cosmic time spans, it is only within a temporal life span — wherein consciousness matures and is perhaps now understood hermeneutically — that the question of significance and meaning arises and is continually addressed in so many novel ways? Should we not recognize, in the light of Augustine's original laments, Husserl's assertion of intentions as meaning, and Heidegger's "source" of time as care, that Bergson boldly adds his testament to the fact that mortal time is essentially creative; it being the only time wherein the question of meaning could arise?

On the basis of those whose quest is the time of the self against the immensity of nature's time, we can precociously conclude that any self-interrogation as to the time of the self is synonymous with a creation of meaning for that self. Whether we call it "fusion," as in the case of Augustine, "freedom" for Bergson, "the absolute temporal flux of consciousness" for Husserl, or "Care" for Heidegger, the interrogation of mortal time, the time of the self, is a confrontation with meaning. We approach here the origin of Ricoeur's own thesis when he asks: "How is narrativity, . . . a perpetual search for new ways of expressing human time, a production or creation of meaning?"

Three

Merleau-Ponty and Temporality

The greatest thing in the world is to know how to belong to ourselves.
— Michel de Montaigne

MERLEAU-PONTY AND BERGSON

In 1952, Maurice Merleau-Ponty (1908–1961) was appointed to the Collège de France, to a chair recently left vacant by the death of Louis Lavelle (1883–1951). It was the same chair previously held by Henri Bergson years before.

Upon close reading, one sees that Bergson's ideas cast a long shadow over much of Merleau-Ponty's thinking, even though the latter is understood to have been typically influenced by Husserl.[1] Like Bergson, Merleau-Ponty's thought begins with a critique of science and rationalism. In fact, there is some truth to the argument that Merleau-Ponty's early critical attitude toward philosophy as intellectualism was inherited directly from his reading of Bergson.[2] Furthermore, both Merleau-Ponty and Bergson, each in their own way, must be understood as having participated in the longer philosophical but diffuse tradition of French thought generally called Spiritualism. As mentioned previously, this was the tradition that forcibly rejected its epoch's fascination with a mechanical worldview and attached greater significance to the idea of life itself. Hence, in the two philosophies, we see several common elements: both appeal to the data of psychology; both desire to dissolve classical dualisms; both limit the relevance of science; both value direct contact with things rather than appearances; and both authors write in an unsystematic fashion, taking any system to be deceptive.

Perhaps the most striking similarity in the philosophies of Bergson and Merleau-Ponty, however, is the vital importance both place in the human body. The common terminology alone is amazing. In different ways, both speak of the body as a schema or a perceptive center and describe the body as a sensory-motor "apparatus" or "circuit." In both of their philosophies, the body is an instrument through which a subject acts upon the world but in itself is not reduced to a mere object; it is also an expression of a degree (or different degrees) of human freedom.[3] In this light, the theme of time each builds upon is never the ordinary or scientific time of the world. Whether it is time of the inner life (Bergson), or the primordial present of the phenomenal body (Merleau-Ponty), it is always time of the subject that is stressed and elaborated over and above what is inherited from the world.

Merleau-Ponty's interest in Bergson was not small. Not only did Merleau-Ponty write insightful essays on Bergson, but also Bergson's name figures prominently in Merleau-Ponty's lectures on "nature" and working notes on the incarnate subject.[4] Indeed, the third chapter in Merleau-Ponty's last work, *The Visible and the Invisible,* can be read as meditation on the Bergsonian problem of coincidence and intuition.

Much of what Merleau-Ponty says about Bergson's thinking generally could be applied to his own philosophical vision. Like Bergson, who did philosophy not by fleeing from the human situation but by "plunging into it," both thinkers will anchor their projects in perception. One cannot but believe Merleau-Ponty was describing his own philosophical agenda when he states of Bergson: "The absolute knowledge of the philosopher is perception. . . . Perception grounds everything because it shows us, so to speak, an obsessional relation with being; it is there before us, and yet it touches us from within" (IPP 16).[5]

Such similarities, however, should not veil essential differences. Bergson used the body as a channel to reveal the *theoretical necessity* of human freedom against the various arguments for human determinism. For Bergson, in a universe described as an aggregate of images, the body was the center of action that acted upon other images (albeit with a limited degree of freedom), bestowing movement upon and ordering matter in regard to human action. Merleau-Ponty, on the other hand, not only posits freedom in light of the action of the body, but tries to elucidate the body's *meaning* descriptively. He will not assume the human body is an object amongst other objects that can be discursively understood by science and objective mechanisms of empirical physiology alone. Rather, his signature idea is that the body is a privileged and mysterious mode of belonging to "a world" through gestures, speaking, perceptions, and sexuality. In this sense, Merleau-Ponty will refuse all oppositions between "consciousness" and "the world." Before any form of objectification, each of us is already in-the-world in a preobjective manner where the distinction between the subjective perceiver and the objects perceived is completely ambiguous. In short, Merleau-Ponty will refuse to annihilate our embodied relationship with the world in search of a purer, interior plane of consciousness. Where Bergson's analysis took us into higher and higher planes away from spatialized matter, and ultimately beyond an existentialist analysis, Merleau-Ponty will center his analysis on our embodied consciousness and our ability to become aware of our prereflective incarnation in the world without losing touch with that incarnate reality. He will enframe his description of the body within the world of matter as we experience it, filled with conflict, creativity, ambiguity, and struggle.

As an existentialist and phenomenologist, Merleau-Ponty's philosophy will almost entirely concern itself with a finite human consciousness caught up in world rather than observing its world from a distance. His whole endeavor, therefore, will tend toward an elaboration of an "engaged consciousness" (*la conscience engagée*) and not of mere "spectating consciousness" (*une conscience-témoin*).[6] Where Bergson fixes a dualism between matter and consciousness, Merleau-Ponty will turn consciousness back on matter to situate itself.[7] This dedication to human experience in the world explains the marked eclecticism of Merleau-Ponty's particular brand of phenomenology, which is a mix of classical phenomenology (Husserl), classical existentialism, Hegel, Heidegger, Marxism, Gestalt psychology, psychoanalysis, and structural linguistics.

There has been much discussion recently as to the proper place of Merleau-Ponty in the dialogues of postmodern thought. Some scholars argue that he should be part of this dialogue because of his attempts to overcome modern dualism and subjectivism; others have engaged Merleau-Ponty in dialogues with Jacques Derrida.[8] There is even an argument that much of Merleau-Ponty's last works cannot be read independently of Derrida's logic of supplementarity.[9] Alternatively, there is the counterclaim that Merleau-Ponty's thought does not neatly fall into either a modernist or postmodernist camp and that we should simply assent to the ambiguity inherent to his unique philosophical perspective.[10] In this chapter I am not interested in contributing to this repartee. What is of interest is to pursue the central theme of this work, namely, to understand how a particular notion of self — in Merleau-Ponty's case, the ambiguous self — arises from the enigma of his particular notion of time (the phenomenal present) and how meaning becomes inscribed on the basis of these two parameters.

MERLEAU-PONTY AND HUSSERLIAN PHILOSOPHY

Like Bergson's early preoccupation with Spencer, the young Merleau-Ponty was particularly inspired by Edmund Husserl. But unlike Bergson, Merleau-Ponty never ceased to acknowledge his indebtedness to his early philosophical mentor throughout his career. Merleau-Ponty's employment of the German philosopher is more interpretative than exegetical. In an essay devoted to Husserl, "The Philosopher and His Shadow," Merleau-Ponty claims that to remain faithful to such an author as Husserl automatically necessitates a "thinking again" of the original articulations (S 160).

Merleau-Ponty's interpretation of Husserl would eventually "existentialize" some of the latter's original themes and leave behind many of its idealistic notions. Originally, it was by way of the phenomenological reduction, the *epoché* (the suspension of judgements concerning the existential status of the objects of consciousness), that Husserl hoped to return to intentional consciousness as the source of all knowledge. As mentioned, Husserl was dissatisfied with "the natural standpoint." The sciences, he believed, never properly considered what it means "to perceive." Husserl's phenomenological task, therefore, was to penetrate the fundamental structures of consciousness reduced to essences and to understand how universal, absolutely necessary meanings were constituted by the transcendental ego; in fact, he wanted to understand how the entire world was wholly constituted by the transcendental ego.[11]

Merleau-Ponty's real engagement with Husserl begins with Husserl's later works, especially *The Crisis in European Sciences and Transcendental Philosophy*.[12] For Merleau-Ponty, as well as many of Husserl's future disciples such as Jean-Paul Sartre (1905–1985) and Heidegger, the meaning behind the experiential moment of being-in-the-world, of engaging with existence, became much more important than how the experience was actually constituted. Merleau-Ponty criticizes Husserl's project by stating that, "to return to the things themselves . . . is absolutely distinct from the idealistic return to consciousness . . . The world is there before any possible analysis of mine . . . The real must be described, not constructed or formed" (PP ix–x).[13] What fascinated Merleau-Ponty about Husserl's later work were the new possibilities it offered for grasping the relation between the human subject and his or her experiences in such a way that "the thing and the world exist only insofar as they are experienced by me or subjects like me" (PP 333).

Where Merleau-Ponty will laud Husserl for dissolving the age-old dichotomy between appearances and reality through intentional consciousness, he will on all counts reject the Husserlian attempt to find how such a consciousness is rationally constituted. Early in *Phenomenology of Perception*, Merleau-Ponty will redefine the extent to which the phenomenological reduction is applicable. In returning to the life-world (*Lebenswelt*), Merleau-Ponty will recognize the "impossibility of a complete reduction" (PP xiv) because immersion in the world will mean that we can never be totally removed from it as if it were possible to be some sort of transcendental spectator. Any attempt to do so only results in the world being immanent in consciousness where the aseity of things is thereby done away with. The eidetic reduction, Merleau-Ponty posits, is "the determination to bring the world to light as it is before any falling back on ourselves has occurred, it is the ambition to make reflection emulate the unreflective life (*la vie irréfléchie*) of consciousness" (PP xvi). Merleau-Ponty is not interested in understanding intentionality and the constituting power of the ego. For him, the intentional world is the world already there. For this reason Merleau-Ponty will put more weight in a more operative intentionality than redefining a pure intentionality in-itself.

Likewise, Merleau-Ponty will approach the question of meaning from his own unique perspective. Husserl's phenomenological project was an attempt to provide a foundation for the meaning of the world, and he refused to be satisfied with other than a genuinely rational explanation. While his faith in reason was unquestionable, he never explained the reasonableness behind such a faith. Merleau-Ponty, on the other hand, will not start out with such a faith. For him the ideal of rationality will mean progressively clarifying the meaning of the world. Meaning, therefore, will not be absolute or pregiven; rather it will be construed as something that evolves in the context of the world, which is the locus of all meaning. In taking up the call that "we are *condemned to meaning (sens)*" (PP xix), Merleau-Ponty wants to grasp rational consciousness itself, as it possesses itself on the basis of an unreflected existence from which it emerges and which it eventually transcends. The unreflected being is the world "already there" before reflection begins (PP vii). Since there is no pure and absolutely unexpressed life in human beings, the unreflected will only come into view through reflection. This reflection is not a return to an innocent identity but a deeper understanding of a fundamental experience, namely the experience of being-in-the-world (*être au monde*). To understand something, however, is to take distance; it is to "say" what we experience. Pursuing the fundamental until it becomes expressible is not a pure contact. Language as expression is creative or constitutive of what is brought to meaning and understanding for us. Language surrounds us in meaning (S 45) and ultimately becomes "the surplus of our existence over natural being" (PP 197). And, of all persons, it is the philosopher who remains awake (*s'éveille*) in the night of the unreflected and speaks for it (IPP 63). In Merleau-Ponty's view, life without the philosophical gaze and the penetration of reflection would dissipate into ignorance and chaos (PrP 19).

While Husserl's work on internal time-consciousness will be the groundwork by which Merleau-Ponty will forge his own remarks on temporality, the latter will reject the formers bric-à-brac of transcendental reflection such as eidetic reduction, states and acts of consciousness, noeses, noemas, images, hyletic data, and the transcendental ego. For Merleau-Ponty, the subject is not a transcendental observer looking at time from a dimension lying outside time. As we shall see, time, true time, exists for a subject as vital presence; it should not be metaphorically misconstrued as something that flows, moves or resembles a lineal progression of sorts. Merleau-Ponty admonishes us to neglect the vagaries of external time and to discover the temporality and historicity that we are. In doing so, however, it is our duty to see what aporias he entails and whether they express themselves in a manner predicted by Ricoeur.

Our discussion of temporality in Merleau-Ponty will deal almost exclusively with his remarks in *Phenomenology of Perception*. While the topic of temporality is specifically dealt with in a chapter in a latter part of that book, disparate remarks throughout the work cannot be overlooked and neglected. This methodological restriction will be extended in the latter part of the chapter in order to include much of what Merleau-Ponty had to say about language and literature outside of the *Phenomenology of Perception*. Meanwhile, some preliminary remarks about Merleau-Ponty's first major work on psychological behaviorism set the stage for introducing this early phenomenological work.

THE STRUCTURE OF BEHAVIOR

Perhaps derivative of Husserl's seminal call that "Wir wollen auf die 'Sachen selbst' zurückgehen," [We must go back to the "things themselves"][14] there is a typical style peculiar to Merleau-Ponty's authorship. Problems, polemics, and questions are set up with a particular pattern; the key to this pattern is the notion of a "return." We find references to a "return" throughout all of his works, especially his early texts.[15] There is the return to existence, the return to phenomena, to the unreflected, to the speaking subject, to the social and to silence. Merleau-Ponty's argumentative strategy is deployed in such a way that the reader is always invited to "return" and "rediscover." Such a style provides a context for the overcoming of various traditions while having the context itself avoid the risk of becoming either an abstraction or a dogma.

The context out of which the "return" emerges is already present in the opening sentences of Merleau-Ponty's first major work, *The Structure of Behavior* (1942). There he describes the metaphysics of modern science. Modern science is strapped with an ontological bias inaugurated by a distinction between the "real" and the "apparent" (or phenomenal). In modern psychology, for example, "the scientific analysis of behavior was defined first in opposition to the givens of naive consciousness" (SB 7). Science, as such, demands that we reject these characteristics as appearances under which a reality of another kind must be discovered. What Merleau-Ponty finds curious is the devaluation or even suppression of the phenomenal or appearing world in favor of the "real" world of "physical facts" that lies under or behind it and that allegedly gives rise to it as cause to effect.

In opposing the real to the phenomenal, Merleau-Ponty argues that the experience of the naive consciousness is negated; that is, *what is real for us, as given in experience, is neglected.* The gist of Merleau-Ponty's vision will always be to seek a reevaluation of this devaluation of the phenomenal, to return to the state of affairs that antedates this primary distinction. This return neither signifies a refusal to enter into any scientific analysis nor to scientifically determine what would be pre-scientific. Such a return to the prescientific on its own terms becomes a question mark for him, and his project is to find a way to approach pre-science so that it can itself teach us what it is.

In its simplest topology, *The Structure of Behavior* is a critical study of experimental psychology, behaviorism, and Gestalt psychology. *The Structure of Behavior* does not deal directly with natural and lived experience but rather with the interpretation or account of this experience by science. It is therefore a polemic against the reductionistic tendencies of empiricism. Empiricism, in the broadest of terms, defines behavior as the simple response to stimuli emanating from the environment. Hence, so-called psychological processes are reduced to their physiological simples and all behavior is to be understood in terms of external and casual relations between these simples. Merleau-Ponty will argue, rather, that behavior exhibits a form of general coordination or functioning which controls and orders the individual reflexes. Environments are not just envelopes of chaotic stimuli. Behavior is better understood as a dialogue or dialectic between an organism and its environment where each patterns the other, instead of simple environmental conditioning.

Using various arguments from Gestalt theorists, Merleau-Ponty argues that an organism functions in a globally structured way, exhibiting an overall coordination of its parts oriented toward the achievement of certain goals or intentions. *Gestalten,* in Merleau-Ponty's view, are neither empirical things (relations between parts) nor forms of consciousness (since they are not produced by thought and exist in non-self-conscious organisms) (SB 46ff.). Ultimately, he will argue that human experience does not consist in a series of isolated sensations haphazardly joined together, but is organized in terms of a field-structure where there is an internal relation between specific milieu and the corresponding behavioral style (SB 218ff.). Neither behavior nor experience is reducible to the mere sum of disparate parts but manifests a primitive structure.

For Merleau-Ponty, structure becomes a fundamental reality: a fundamental reality not in the sense of a first principle but as the decisive condition for the appearance of something — where this something stands out against something else (SB 168). This means that given a particular time and place, an organism's ability to structure behavior is "an instrument of knowledge and [that] structure is an object of consciousness" (SB 145). Furthermore, Merleau-Ponty contends this behavioral structure has it own meaning. Not to say that an animal is meaningful for itself or that it is the reflective consciousness of itself, but it is "to say that it is a whole which is meaningful for a consciousness which knows it, not a thing which rests in-itself (*en-soi*)"

(SB 159). Ultimately, in terms of the human order, "What defines man is not the capacity to create a second nature — economic, social or cultural — beyond biological nature; it is rather the capacity of going beyond created structures in order to create others" (SB 175).

In short, Merleau-Ponty refutes an empirical approach by insisting that the description of vital forms and physical systems is not merely of things that exist in themselves, but of nature that is present to consciousness. Structure, as Merleau-Ponty has been able to discern it, is "the joining of an idea and an existence which are indiscernible" (SB 206). But there is something peculiar about this. What exactly is present to consciousness? Structure, form, the whole, or *Gestalt* do not insinuate things but nonetheless engage perception. Structure exists only in being perceived; it is what a consciousness discerns as soon as it is engaged with its milieu. Consciousness in this sense does not constitute what it perceives but finds itself face-to-face with a world. "The gestures of behavior, the intentions which it traces in the space around the animal, are not directed to the true world or pure being, but to being-for-the-animal, that is, to a certain milieu characteristic of the species; they do not allow the showing through of a consciousness, that is, a being whose whole essence is to know, but rather a certain manner of treating the world, of 'being-in-the-world,' or of 'existing'" (SB 125).

When Merleau-Ponty, therefore, speaks of consciousness it is with "perceptual consciousness" that he is most concerned. "Correlatively the consciousness *for* which the Gestalt exists was not intellectual consciousness, but perceptual experience. Thus, it is perceptual consciousness which must be interrogated in order to find in it a definitive clarification" (SB 210). In opposition to Husserl, it is consciousness that lives in the world which must be interrogated and not the consciousness that has arrived at the complete possession of itself (SB 223). The aim of Merleau-Ponty is to confront us with the agent who participates in the scene he or she perceives where the world is meaningful for a consciousness which perceives it. The operative word here is perception; perception as the heart of the life-world. "If one understands by perception the act which makes us know existences, all the problems which we have just touched on are reducible to the problem of perception" (SB 224).

Merleau-Ponty is quite clear as to what he doesn't mean by perception. It is not a representation or intellection. His preoccupation with perception derives from his attempt to completely relativize the classical duality of a mind posed against a body. Neither mind nor body have a reality in and of themselves. Rather, they are two variable terms of a single structure which is nothing other than existence itself. Any relation that exists is entirely dialectical: "It is not a question of two *de facto* orders external to each other, but of two types of relations, the second of which integrates the first" (SB 180–81).[16]

Hence, by the end of his first work, Merleau-Ponty has posed more questions than he has provided solutions for. What, for example, is the relation between the perceiver and what is perceived? Who is the perceiving subject? What is the relation between thought and perception? Is time important? Wherein resides the possibility of existential meaning? We now turn to Merleau-Ponty's second work, *Phenomenology of Perception*.

PHENOMENOLOGY OF PERCEPTION

The *Phenomenology of Perception* is a difficult text in that it is not a systematic and orderly analysis with a clear genesis of thought. The preface stands more as a separate manifesto on phenomenology then an explanatory note to what follows.[17] Unfortunately, critical commentaries of this text are still rare and a final exegesis has still to be written. While the text is divided up into three distinct topic areas, with temporality being a subdivision of the last section, my own synopsis of the work will stress certain relations between the body, self, and time in an attempt to grasp all the disparate and prethematic remarks Merleau-Ponty spreads throughout the text prior to his main discussion of time.

The thesis in *The Structure of Behavior* made it quite clear that the world as it reveals itself in perception is not a chaos wherein everything acts aimlessly on everything else, but that perceptual consciousness offers a configuration of experience that manifests meaning. This meaning, however, is neither real nor a natural given in the world. The world is meaningful only for a consciousness that perceives it.

Where *The Structure of Behavior* criticized empiricism as a point of departure, this second work will interrogate intellectualism or idealism as well. In a very different voice than in his first work, Merleau-Ponty begins *Phenomenology of Perception* by asking who exactly it is that perceives. For the empiricist, perception is merely one event among many occurring in the world, its locus being the perceiver. The human body and its perceptions are studied analytically thereby becoming objectified; for the scientist, the perceiver becomes a physical system undergoing physico-chemical stimuli and responding in determinable ways. In studying the sensations which make up this occurrence, the empiricist adopts an impersonal approach whereby he totally neglects the fact that he *lives* perception and *is* the perceiving subject even in his very study of perception itself and that perception is the very condition of there being any facts at all for us.

For the intellectualist, on the other hand, the constituting activity of consciousness creates the structure of that which we perceive, and it is this structure as posited that is there whether or not we believe we see it. In positing such a structure to perception, the intellectualist can claim a level of certainty and clarity not unlike the empiricist. In short, the empiricist leaves no room for consciousness while the intellectualist subordinates everything to one universal constituting ego. The second position merely reverses the first in replacing being-in-itself (*en-soi*) by being-for-itself (*pour-soi*). Both approaches simply construct experience to fit their posited presuppositions (PP 39).

Meanwhile, the immediacy of perception is lost; the "figure" of "attention" is abducted from the "background" of perceptual experience that actively constitutes a new object and "makes explicit and articulates (*thématise*) what was until then presented as no more than an indeterminate horizon" (PP 30). As he states in his preface, Merleau-Ponty wants to "re-achieve a direct and primitive contact with the world," that is, the world that was there before any analysis of his own (PP vii; x).[18]

Like Bergson, Merleau-Ponty tries to uncover the erroneous attempt by science to interpret the unextended by the extended where for example, sounds and colors are treated as elements with magnitudes. Given a point-by-point correspondence between stimuli and perception, science diminishes the value of the immediate for the sake of identifying "'elementary' psychic functions" which are "objects purged of all ambiguity, pure and absolute — the ideal rather than the real themes of knowledge" (PP 11). Merleau-Ponty argues, to the contrary, that that which is perceived is ripe with ambiguity and must be understood as belonging to a context or "field" which shapes it (PP 4). Access to this field starts by a unanimous rejection of decomposing perception into sensations, of trying to reconstruct experience out of determinate qualities. He calls for a return to the preobjective realm that we have to explore ourselves if we wish to understand sense experience; we must overcome "the prejudice in favor of an objective world" (PP 6).

To overcome this *"préjugé du monde objectif"* Merleau-Ponty will not, as in the case of Bergson, return to the world of introspective psychology or intuitionism and the psychic datum. He equally rejects turning either to the "inner man" of St. Augustine or the presuppositions of Kant (PP ix–x). Rather, Merleau-Ponty suggests, we must understand, phenomenologically, the world as a "phenomenal field (*un champ phénoménol*)" (PP 54). The world is not a spectacle spread out before a disembodied mind; it is not something reducible to a set of determinate features. Our reflection on things is always perspectival; as incarnate subjects, phenomenological reflection becomes a recognition of our unreflected font of experience. Reflection in this manner is not for reflection's sake; it is not so that reflection can become self-transparent. We must neglect to understand our being as determined and go back to our actual experience of the world and rediscover the dialectical process of living experience whereby we ourselves, others, and things come into being. "The first philosophical act would appear to be to return to the world of actual experience which is prior to the objective, since it is in it that we shall be able to grasp the theoretical basis no less than the limits of that objective world, restore to things their concrete physiognomy, to organisms their individual ways of dealing with the world, and to subjectivity its inherence in history" (PP 57). To restore an understanding of "the perceiving subject as the perceived world," Merleau-Ponty begins *Phenomenology of Perception* proper with a critical examination of "the body as object and mechanistic physiology" (PP 73). What he hopes to show is that by understanding the body as our "point of view upon the world" it is no longer an anonymous idealized object but, rather, a project of sorts where the spatio-temporal structure of perceptual experience will be revived and shown as vital.

The Prethematic Discussion of Time in Phenomenology of Perception

To illustrate the shortcomings of traditional views about the status of the body, Merleau-Ponty discusses the phantom limb and anognosia. While neither phenomena can be fully accounted for by either physiology or psychology, both of the symptoms can be related to physiological and psychological conditions. This approach, however, overlooks the fact that subjects attempt to relate in the world as they did before their handicap. Merleau-Ponty wants to elucidate the fact that below the objective body there are preobjective ways of relating to the world.

The phenomenon of the phantom limb deals with the illusion that an amputated limb still exists and anognosia is the refusal of a paralyzed patient to acknowledge the paralysis (PP 76ff.). If a person conceives of the world in terms of the possible interactions his or her body can have with it, or as a series of actions he or she can perform upon it, the person with phantom limb or anognosia experiences the world through his or her former body. The paralyzed person still perceives and attempts to use the floor as something he or she can walk on; the amputee feels the cold night air as something that causes muscular cramps. "To have a phantom arm is to remain open to all those actions of which the arm alone is capable; it is to keep the practical field that one had before being mutilated" (PP 81).

The contrast between the whole body and the mutilated one helps us to see the body as bound up with the world by a whole number of intentional threads which are nothing other than its body. The body is not only a way of viewing the world but our general medium for having a world (PP 146). It is the way a subjective attitude both comes to know itself and express itself, a seat of intentionality where, in projecting itself onto the world, it makes the world the arena of potential intentions. There is in fact an operative intentionality "which produces the natural and antepredicative unity of the world and of our life, being apparent in our desires, our evaluations and in the landscape we see, more clearly than in objective knowledge, and furnishing the text which our knowledge tries to translate into precise language" (PP xviii). Operative intentionality is that particular intentionality by which consciousness projects a human setting around itself, and a patterning in which it lives. It is a relation of being rather than an act of knowing: "it is the unity of the world, before being posited by knowledge in a specific act of identification, [and] is 'lived' as ready-made or already-there" (PP xvii).

In this sense, operative intentionality is prethematic; it evaluates the potentialities of the whole environment and is the ground of any explicit and voluntary acts of intentionality while its own character remains "concealed behind the objective world which it helps to build up" (PP 138, n. 2). In saying that an operative intentionality is already at work before any positing or judgement occurs is to say that, in a way, before any intellectual operation of signification, existence is already fully significant. Our being-in-the-world, then, is really an intentional-being-in-the-world. Our intentional presence, in conjunction with the body, is a way of being-in-the-world; a way of having a "hold" (*la prise*) on things (PP 320; 374; 386). This bodily "hold" on the world is the basis of our more explicitly conscious and personal activity.

The preobjective naturalness of these intentions only becomes visible in light of a dramatic change to habituated body movements, as for example, with an amputation. Perceptual consciousness, as such, is not an absolute interiority, as pure presence of the self to itself, but as a bodily presence in the world — a bodily awareness of the world.

Yet, this bodily presence is never a simply defined fact. In the case of an itchy phantom limb that can't be scratched, something which was formerly one side of an interaction takes on a character of its own.

The subjectively experienced becomes an object, standing alone, independent of a person's perception or interaction with it. In other words, there arises an experience of the body that seems to make it no longer a personal body, the body of a particular person, but, rather, an impersonal or a generalized body.[19] We are made aware of this enigma in such cases as a phantom limb and anognosia by the fact the body gets stuck at a certain stage of experience, at a certain point in time. But how is this possible?

> This paradox is that of all being in the world: when I move towards a world I bury my perceptual and practical intentions in objects which ultimately appear prior to and external to those intentions, and which nevertheless exist for me only in so far as they arouse in me thoughts or volitions. In the case under consideration, the ambiguity of knowledge amounts to this; our body comprises as it were two distinct layers, that of the habit-body (*corps habituel*) and that of the body at this moment (*corps actuel*). (PP 82)

The habitual body signifies the body as it has been lived in the past wherein it acquired certain habitual ways of relating to the world. The habitual body already projects a "customary world" around itself thereby giving structure to its present situation (PP 82).[20] Since it outlines, prior to all reflection, objects which it "expects" to encounter at the other pole of its projects, this body must be considered an "anonymous," or "prepersonal" global intentionality.

It is because there is this prepersonal, preobjective and anonymous habit-body that subjects remain indefinitely open to a future which has been ruled out by their injury. In fact, this layered notion of the body is the coincidence of the past, present, and future. But the stubbornness of the past to manifest itself in a missing limb or paralysis brings to light the temporal structure which characterizes our existence as incarnate beings. In the cases of the phantom limb and paralysis, the real content of personal bodily experience becomes too painful to acknowledge and bodily experience refuses to proceed beyond an earlier stage. The habit-body (in the form of past experience) takes over and provides the content of present experience. "Impersonal time continues its course, but personal time is arrested" (PP 83).

The haunting of the present by a particular past experience is possible because we all carry our past with us insofar as its structures have become "sedimented" in our habitual life (PP 130). This haunting of the past is caused by a type of "organic repression" (PP 77). To the degree that our personal existence is biologically rooted, it is precarious and tends to repress the organism without "being able either to reduce the organism to its existential self, or itself to the organism" (PP 84). What the amputee in fact experiences, therefore, is "a former present" rather than merely recollecting or having a memory of it.[21] A phenomenon such as the phantom limb enlightens us as to the actual character of the past and thus to an appreciation of the role which our body plays in our being-in-the-world. The phantom limb is analogous to a repression of a traumatic experience where the subject remains emotionally involved in a particular past experience to such a degree that it imposes itself on the actual present.

> The traumatic experience does not survive as a representation in the mode of objective consciousness and as a 'dated' moment; it is of its essence to survive only as a manner of being and with a certain degree of generality. I forego my constant power of providing myself with 'worlds' in the interest of one of them, and for that very reason this privileged world loses its substance and eventually becomes no more than 'a certain dread.' All repression is, then, the transition from first person existence to a sort of abstraction of that existence, which lives on a former experience, or rather on the memory of having had the memory, and so on, until finally only the essential form remains. Now as an advent of the impersonal, *repression is a universal phenomenon,* revealing our condition as incarnate beings by relating it to the temporal structure of being in the world. (PP 83; my emphasis)

One might say that the phantom limb reopens time through memories evoking a certain past, inviting us to relive it as opposed to simply imagining it or rethinking it. In responding to this implicit summons, the amputee can cause his or her missing limb to reappear as a "quasi-present" without having either psychic or physiological parameters. Bodily existence is not reducible to the laws of mechanics but is intimately tied with being-in-the-world identified by intentions, projects, and movement; it is "a prepersonal cleaving to the general form of the world as an anonymous and general existence, [which] plays, beneath my personal life, the part of an *inborn complex*" (PP 84).

Each of us, healthy or unhealthy, experience, from time to time, an impersonal body as well as our personal body, and this impersonal body appears as a necessary condition for us to have any personal subjective experience. Merleau-Ponty accepts this paradox as a real and irreducible tension. The experience of the body teaches us a new mode of existence which is a strange mixture of being-in-itself (*en soi*) and being-for-itself (*pour soi*). In fact, Merleau-Ponty concludes that "the experience of our own body . . . reveals to us an ambiguous mode of existing" (PP 87). As one primary commentator suggests, "the constitutive paradoxes of perception are in no way subjective appearances which would dissipate as obscurities and confusion in the view of the objective world of science. On the contrary, they define the very condition of consciousness, the initial and constant status from which it cannot extricate itself."[22] It is ambiguous because the conflict calls into question the traditional distinctions of object and subject. The body not being just an object is also not a mere object of my subjective awareness as yet another discrete object in the world.

At the center of this ambiguity is temporality. "The ambiguity of being in the world is translated by that of the body, and this understood through that of time" (PP 84–85). Where Bergson initiated his discussion of duration with the immediacy of introspective data, Merleau-Ponty introduces his notion of temporality with the lived experience of the body. In both cases there is the retreat, one might say, to something that can be claimed as "authentic," "pure," or "original" to *human experience*. For Merleau-Ponty the body and its phenomenal field become the datum where time authentic to our existence will arise. Oddly enough, Merleau-Ponty does not truly bracket the scientific worldview (empiricism) or intellectualism from his analysis. He is willing to proceed under the shadow of ambiguity that will follow him at every stage of his analysis. As such, and ambiguously so, we are not "in" time but merely "inhabit" or "belong" to time (PP 139–40).

But is not this ambiguity really the early warning sign of a dispersion — the pluralization — of temporal levels that becomes possible once we posit the existence of a truer or more authentic time than the time of the world itself? Does not the distinction between the habit-body, and its prepersonal time, and the present body, with its personal time, indicate the dispersion of meaning possible once we aim to grasp a source of time outside ordinary time? How else are we to understand the pronouncement that "my body takes possession of time; it brings into existence a past and a future for a present; it is not a thing, but creates time instead of submitting to it." (PP 240)? Does not the founding of the habit-body on the "globally" intentional, as a "customary world," and as "universally" repressed, indicate a type of natural fundament, an original time, that comes into relief, as forewarned by Ricoeur, when a phenomenological analysis tries to distinguish between what is concordant and discordant, between what is continuous and discontinuous, between what is eternal and temporal?

At this point, it is hard to see a clear distinction between ordinary time and a phenomenological one. As gleaned from Ricoeur in the first chapter, the fundamental distinction between the anonymous instant of ordinary time and the present — understood phenomenologically — is that the latter must be defined by the discourse that designates this present reflexively (TN3, 91). This is why Merleau-Ponty's claim that the body "creates time," while positing a past, present and future, must be understood somewhat suspiciously. Such a time would be no more than an indirect presupposition. We've not been told precisely by what means we have access to understanding such a time other than the fact that it is. All we know is that Merleau-Ponty presumes there to be an autochthonous significance to our existence (PP 441) which is an historical unfolding of phenomena tending toward a unity to which we contribute as both actors and observers but not as a sole cause. As we shall see, this notion of autochthonous organization locates the ground of any meaning, and ultimately any knowledge itself, in the phenomenal world instead of the classical activity inherent to a mind (*Nous* or *Geist*).

In approaching the body in this preobjective sense, Merleau-Ponty claims that we are brought to acknowledge the existence of a "body schema" that operates below or prior to any scientific thematization:

> If my arm is resting on the table I should never think of saying that it is *beside* the ash-tray in the way in which the ash-tray is beside the telephone. The outline of my body is a frontier which ordinary spatial relations do not cross. This is because its parts are interrelated in a peculiar way: they are not spread out side by side, but enveloped in each other . . . my whole body for me is not an assemblage of organs juxtaposed in space. I am in undivided possession of it and I know where each of my limbs is through a *body image* (*un schéma corporel*) in which all are included (*enveloppés*). (PP 98)[23]

The body schema is the tacit knowledge that we each have of our body's position at any given time. The body and its parts should not be regarded as suspended in objective space. The body schema is a location with reference to the way in which my limbs enter into my projects; it is not a "*spatiality of position* but a *spatiality of situation*" (PP 100). The body schema reminds us of our prereflective orientation and motility insofar as we are aware of where our limbs are as the body projects itself toward the world of its tasks.

I can scratch, for example, the bite of a mosquito without having to search for the spot in objective space; it is not a question of locating it in relation to axes of coordinates but reaching with a phenomenal hand to a spot on a phenomenal body. I do not move my body like I move other objects external to me. "But my body itself I move directly, I do not find it at one point of objective space and transfer it to another, I have no need to look for it, it is already with me — I do not need to lead it toward the movement's completion, it is in contact with it from the start and propels itself towards the end" (PP 94). The whole operation takes place in the domain of the phenomenal rather than the objective. Prior to its conceptualization or thematized account as a biological entity, that is, an organism, the human body is before all a dimension of my own existence.[24] In this sense, the body is foremost a lived body (*le corps propre*). "The body image (*le schéma corporel*) is finally a way of stating that my body is in-the-world. As far as spatiality is concerned, and this alone interests us at the moment, one's own body (*le corps propre*) is the third term, always tacitly understood, in the figure-background structure, and every figure stands out against the double horizon of external and bodily space" (PP 101). The function of the lived or phenomenal body (*le corps phénoménal*) is not necessarily "to know" as much it is "to act" (PP 105–06). It organizes its milieu by synthesizing its own actions with the sedimented or given world through which it lives (PP 232). Thus, the action of the body is the point of contact between the world already given and the world coming to be. As such, the phenomenal body reveals at any moment the manner in which we are existing in the world.

For Merleau-Ponty the appearance of the phenomenal body is already a "natural self" (*un moi naturel*) which is a "current of given existence" where we never know if we are the actors or merely acted upon (PP 171). It is only because the body is a natural self and remakes contact with the world that we rediscover ourselves (PP 206). Any notion of the self already presupposes the presence of a phenomenal body in communion with a prepersonal tradition (PP 254)[25] and "pre-human flux" (*un flux anonyme et pré-humain*) (PP 442).

On the other hand, a thematized or living self (*le moi vivant*) that we know ourselves to be with a name, a birthday, and a particular milieu only becomes possible as bodily presence presumes to transcend the natural world through acts of expression, especially language, which establish a situation for an incarnate subject or thematized self to appear (PP 364).[26] "The body is the general medium for having a world. Sometimes it is restricted to the actions necessary for the conservation of life, and accordingly it posits around us a biological world; at other times, elaborating upon these primary actions and moving from their literal to a figurative meaning, it manifests through them a core of new significance: this is true of motor habits such as dancing. Sometimes, finally, the meaning aimed at cannot be achieved by the body's natural means; it must then build itself an instrument, and it projects thereby around itself a cultural world" (PP 146).

Each of our perceptions is involved in a symbolizing activity which expresses, in however an unclear manner, a particular project of being-in-the-world; that is, each person has a distinct manner of signifying his or her intentions to others — which is that person's own particular "style" of being in the world (PP 183). Every human being is marked by a particular style just as he or she is marked by a particular fingerprint. These styles constitute a mute language from which all spoken language ultimately derives.[27] In short, language as gesture precedes language as word.

Consequently, only within a cultural world where "speech is able to settle into a sediment and constitute an acquisition for use in human relationships" (PP 190), can a thematized self take on the identity appropriate to its discovery in a linguistic community. It does not posit itself prior to language but realizes itself through language. For Merleau-Ponty, "man is a historical idea and not a natural species" (PP 170), and "speech itself *brings about* the concordance between me and myself, and between myself and others, on which an attempt is made to base thought" (PP 392). As a self matures, reads, listens, speaks, and observes, it learns various associations of words, situations, and objectivities until it acquires a linguistic style for its own expressive needs. In so doing, the lived body becomes the incarnate subject that takes up a position in the world of signs and meanings. The result is that we inhabit a signified "world" underpinned by our lived existence.[28]

But, the world as signified is never established once and for all. The body never stops "secreting in itself a 'significance' upon its material surrounding, and communicating it to other embodied subjects" (PP 197). Merleau-Ponty concludes, "We must therefore recognize as an ultimate fact this open and indefinite power of giving significance (*signifier*) — that is, both of apprehending and conveying a meaning (*sens*) — by which man transcends himself towards a new form of behavior, or towards other people, or towards his own thought, through his body and his speech" (PP 194).

Contrary to Husserl's transcendental ego, the incarnate subject always finds itself in a world that it did not constitute; that is, the self finds itself in a world in which the body is immersed and can never fully thematize. The reflective consciousness, or thematic intentionality, surfaces with respect to an unreflective consciousness or operative intentionality, which Merleau-Ponty alternatively calls the silent consciousness or tacit *cogito* (*un Cogito silencieux, un Cogito tacite*) (PP 402–04).

The tacit *cogito* is the presence of oneself to oneself where the silent consciousness "grasps itself only as a generalized 'think' in face of a confused world 'to be thought about.'" The tacit *cogito* or silent consciousness is an original opening in the world; both engender a precarious grasp (*une prise glissante*) upon a world in which a subjectivity finds itself "like that of the infant at its first breath, or of the man about to drown and who is impelled towards life" (PP 404).

This "precarious grasp upon the world" is a real equivocation for Merleau-Ponty and not a duality.[29] There is a prepersonal natural subjectivity that "penetrates" to the very heart of the personal, thinking subject such that the self recognizes in him or herself an anonymous element. This is an annoying anonymity since personal subjectivity can never turn fast enough to catch what is before it — the phenomenal body that forever plays "beneath" (*au-dessous de moi*) our personal existence (PP 254). Nonetheless, the "lived body," "habitual body," and "phenomenal body" are not a scale of being. They indicate, rather, various aspects of being-in-the-world for a perceptual subject that must first of all live in the world before making sense of it in some intellectual manner.

Hence, between the exigency of the natural self and the objective thought of the living self there is forever a gap.[30] What is lived is always one step ahead of what is understood objectively as living. "My voluntary and rational life, therefore, knows that it merges into another power which stands in the way of its completion, and gives it a permanently tentative look" (PP 346–47). What personal subjectivity intends to grasp but forever misses is not in the order of logic as would be the search for the middle term to a syllogism; the "precarious hold" to which Merleau-Ponty refers is, again, an irreducible tension or a fundamental ambiguity. For Merleau-Ponty, "ambiguity (*l'équivoque*) is of the essence of human existence." Such ambiguity cannot be resolved. It is ultimate (PP 169), "if we recapture the intuition of real time which preserves everything, and which is at the core of both proof and expression" (PP 394).

What lies at the heart of this ambiguity? In the case of the lived body, Merleau-Ponty's answer to this anonymous element is decisive — it is time. "This anonymous life is merely the extreme form of that temporal dispersal which constantly threatens the historical present" (PP 347). Stated in another way:

> My hold on the past and the future is precarious, and my possession of my own time is always postponed until a stage when I may fully understand it, yet this stage can never be reached, since it would be one more moment, bounded by the horizon of its future, and requiring, in its turn further developments in order to be understood. . . . Natural time is always there. *The transcendence of the instants of time is both the ground of, and the impediment to, the rationality of my personal history:* the ground because it opens a totally new future to me in which I shall be able to reflect upon the element of opacity in my present, a source of danger in so far as I shall never manage to seize the present through which I live with apodeictic certainty, and since the lived is thus never entirely comprehensible, what I understand never quite tallies with my living experience, in short, I am never quite one with myself. (PP 346–47; my emphasis)

As such, before coming to the matured linguistic realization that "I exist," I in fact already existed, such that as language aids me in acquiring a hold on myself, I discover myself as "already there." Each subject carries within him or herself a "prehistory" (PP 240). What is really apprehended in reflection is a self that is "already born" and "still alive" (PP 216). Both my life and its death are prepersonal horizons — I simply find myself in a time that I did not constitute. There is therefore a natural time that remains at the center of my history and surrounds me (PP 347). Reflection, as such, encounters time by discovering before itself the life of a natural subjectivity which for it is "already there." Any ambiguity that arises here arises in the order of time and not in the order of logic or a flaw in the laws of causality.

> What needs to be understood is that for the same reason I am present here and now, and present elsewhere and always, and also absent from here and from now, and absent from every place and from every time. This ambiguity is not some imperfection of consciousness of existence, but the definition of them. Time in the widest sense, that is, the order

of co-existences as well as that of successions, is a setting to which one can gain access and which one can understand only by occupying a situation *in* it, and by grasping it in its entirety through horizons of that situation. The world, which is the nucleus of time, subsists only by virtue of that unique action which both separates and brings together the actually presented and the present; and consciousness, which is taken to be the seat of clear thinking, is on the contrary the very abode of ambiguity. Under these circumstances one may say, if one wishes, that nothing exists and everything is "temporalized." (PP 332 — my emphasis)

In short, to the degree I live in a world that I did not constitute but suffer it through the presence of my body, I live in a present that is mine and no one else's but is never mine alone — it is a present with an original *"past that has never been present"* (PP 242).[31] It is here, in a temporal wave with a never presented past, that ambiguity finds its source and well-spring. It is here, under the sleight of time, that a reflection recognizes itself as body, being and world held forever in tension by the power of a temporal enigma alone. Consequently, "I," therefore, "know myself only in so far as I am inherent in time and in the world, that is, I know myself only in my ambiguity" (PP 345).[32]

In concluding on ambiguity, let us tally several of the aporias that have accumulated in this section. What, for instance, could a "past that has never been present" really mean for us? After all, what is the precedent in existential thought for remembering something as "past" in the life-world (the world of perception, no less) which itself did not endure time, that is, become temporalized? As will be explained in the following chapter, Ricoeur will put a great emphasis on the notion of the "trace" which is a present thing that stands for (*vaut*) an absent thing; it is one of three historical connectors between lived time and physical time. In having a recourse to such things as documents and monuments, Ricoeur's historical time is saved from an aporetic status in that it is not something like "an original past" that simply appears out of nowhere. Moreover, in Merleau-Ponty's case, how is it, if I am standing "in" time and "transcend its instants," that "everything" becomes "temporalized?" Is time, hence, "temporalized" as well? Obviously not in the light of an "original past that has never been present."

Unlike Bergson who refutes it in the beginning of *Time and Free Will*, or Husserl who brackets it, Merleau-Ponty allows physical time, or the ordinary concept of time, to be part of his own existential analysis. In referring to "time in the widest sense," or "I simply find myself in a time I did not constitute," ordinary time from the beginning exerts a sort of attraction-repulsion on Merleau-Ponty's entire existential analysis, forcing it to unfold, to distend itself, until it corresponds by an ever-increasing approximation, to its other which it cannot generate. This external aporia that develops in the concept of time, due to the disparity among perspectives on time, is what provokes, at the very heart of this analysis, the greatest effort at internal diversification. How else are we to explain the constant diversification·and distinctions within the fundamental categories of the body, self and time? How are we to understand the constant multiplication of designations of the body into its expression of being "a habit-body," "present body," "lived," "phenomenal," and so forth? The same can be asked about the self ("natural self," "living self," "personal subject," "incarnate subject," "tacit *Cogito*," "personal *Cogito*," "real *Cogito*") and time ("prepersonal time," "personal time," "natural time").

And yet, for the labor of language and all the linguistic precision in forging out the autochthonous territory of our prepersonal existence, what has Merleau-Ponty really expressed about the time of the self? Is there any such thing when — in one part of the text already quoted — we read "I am never quite one with myself," and "my possession of my own time is always postponed," while, in a later section, we are told that "I am not myself a succession of 'psychic' acts, nor for that matter a nuclear 'I' who brings them together into a synthetic unity, but one single experience inseparable from itself, one single 'living cohesion,' one single temporality which is engaged, from birth, in making itself progressively explicit, and in confirming that cohesion in each successive present?" (PP 407).

The fact is, up to this stage, the doctrine of autochthonous organization locates the ground of the unification required by the self in the phenomenal world. Unlike the transcendental ego of Husserl, phenomenal temporality does not take us into some supervenient activity of mind or *Nous* or *Geist*. The result is that the self is tied to the world of perception, the body and life. The most one can say at this point is that the time of the self, especially the natural self, if such a distinction is understandable, is that it exists as an original tension within the "density of being," (*l'épaisseur de l'être*) being mindful, of course, that it is not initiated by an instance of discourse but simply presumed to be (PP 196).

The Thematic Discussion of Temporality in Phenomenology of Perception

In the second chapter of the third part of *Phenomenology of Perception*, Merleau-Ponty directly confronts the topic of temporality, which has continually surfaced in his discussion up to this point but has never been systematically treated. The being of time is now examined explicitly so that we might better understand its role in the phenomenal world. The continuous conclusion of ambiguity on behalf of time now becomes a problem of seeing exactly how subjectivity is inherent in temporal relatedness; in other words, we must see *if* there is a phenomenologically proper side to Merleau-Ponty's thesis: "The problem is how to make time explicit as it comes into being and makes itself evident, having the *notion* of time at all times underlying it, and being, not an object of our knowledge, but a dimension of our being" (PP 415).

However, Merleau-Ponty's chapter on temporality contains glaring inconsistencies and contradictions that give the text over to confusion and misunderstanding. In such statements as "consciousness deploys or constitutes time," "constituted time . . . is not time itself" (PP 414–45), "we hold time in its entirety," and "time exists for me only because I am situated in it," as well as, "time *is* someone," and "subjectivity is not in time" (PP 422–44), the coherency of Merleau-Ponty's arguments becomes strained. Yet, are we not meeting here the ultimate contradictions of a thesis that refuses to distinguish cosmic time from mortal time? Let us see.

In *Phenomenology of Perception*, Merleau-Ponty employs Husserl's study of inner-time consciousness and attempts to give a better description of his mentor's analysis. In his phenomenological studies of time-consciousness, Husserl adopted a method that excluded every assumption, qualification, conviction, and all transcendent presuppositions concerning objective time since objective or world time is not a phenomenological datum. Husserl did insist that "what we accept, however, is not the existence of a world-time, the existence of a concrete duration, and the like, but *appearing*-time, *appearing*-duration as such."[33] Thus, as envisioned by Husserl, consciousness foregoes its interest and setting in cosmic or world-time. The time Husserl intended to analyze was not the time measured by either the sun, clock, or other physical means; rather, he was interested in the *immanent* flow of consciousness — that of a succession akin to the consciousness of a tonal process.

Merleau-Ponty, on the other hand, is interested in the time of the phenomenal body, in the "need to find a middle course between eternity and the atomistic time of empiricism, in order to resume the interpretation of the *cogito* and of time" (PP 374). In beginning his direct discussion of temporality, Merleau-Ponty rejects the prevalent metaphors of Husserlian internal time-consciousness such as "flow," and "succession," as well as the more common analogies of time as a stream, river, and line (PP 411). Instead, he begins his positive argument by distinguishing between "constituted time," that is, "the series of possible relations in terms of before and after," which "is a setting distinct from me and unchanging, in which nothing either elapses or happens," and the idea that "there must be another true time, in which I learn the nature of flux and transience itself" (PP 415).

Constituted time here is the time we have been referring to as ordinary time with its anonymous successions of "nows." Merleau-Ponty is clear to state that if these "nows" are not "present to anyone" they would have no temporal character, have no sequence, and lack any past and future. The objective world is too much a plenum for there to be time (PP 412). The plenum of being is only temporalized with the presence of subjectivity.

Accordingly, our primary experience in which time and its dimensions make their pure appearance "with no intervening distance and with absolute self-evidence" is in our "field of presence." It is here that we see a future sliding into the present and on into the past. In the sense that Merleau-Ponty speaks, time is not a line but a network of intentionalities. These intentionalities do not run from a central "I" but from our perceptual field itself which draws along in its wake its own horizon of retentions and bites into the future with its protentions (PP 416).

Merleau-Ponty employs a modified version of diagrams used by Husserl to understand the unity of time (PP 417).[34] When we pass from A to B, and then on to C, A is projected or outlined as A' and then as A". For A' to be recognized as a retention or *Abschattung* of A, and A" of A', as well as the transformation of A into A', there is a transitional synthesis linking A, A', A" and all other possible *Abschattungen*.

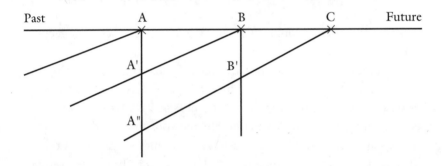

As such, the instances of A, B, and C are not successively *in being*, but *differentiate* themselves from each other, and correspondingly A passes into A' and thence into A". In short, the system of retentions collects into itself at each instant what was, an instant earlier, the system of protentions. "When we pass from B to C, there is, as it were, a bursting, or a disintegration of B into B', of A' into A", and C itself which, while it was on the way, announced its coming by a continuous emission of *Abschattungen*, has no sooner come into existence than it already begins to lose its substance" (PP 419). Such synthetic unity as this is not an activity on part of the subject. It is a synthesis that is properly termed transitional (*Übergangssynthesis*). "Once again, time's 'synthesis' is a transitional synthesis, the action of a life which unfolds, and there is no way of bringing it about other than by living that life, there is no seat of time; time bears itself on and launches itself afresh" (PP 423).

Such a synthesis is not to be conceived as something imposed upon a previously atomized collection of moments. Time is not a succession of synthetically joined moments but rather a unity phenomenon of lapse: "The fresh present *is* the passage of future to present, and of former present to past, and when time begins to move, it moves throughout its whole length," such that there is "not a multiplicity of linked phenomena, but one single phenomenon of lapse (*écoulement*)" (PP 419). Borrowing from Heidegger, Merleau-Ponty states that "there is an *ek-stase* towards the future and towards the past which reveals the dimensions of time not as conflicting, but as inseparable" (PP 422).[35]

But from whence comes this time? If the subject does not effect the transitional synthesis, what is the subject's role in and experience of time? Should we be satisfied with the reply that time "is nothing but a general flight out of Itself" where the *ek-stase* is the one law governing these centrifugal movements? (PP 419). Merleau-Ponty has consistently avoided making concrete allusions to a purely phenomenologically constituted time which would confound his thesis on the primacy of perceptual consciousness. However, can he really avoid differentiating the role of subjectivity from its immersion in the perceptual life-world? What is the role of subjectivity and time? Does subjectivity constitute the time of the self?

For Merleau-Ponty, "time, in our most primordial experience of it, is not for us a system of objective positions, through which we pass, but a mobile setting which moves away from us, like the landscape seen through a railway carriage window" (PP 419–20). There is only one single time which is "self-confirmatory" and which establishes itself at a stroke. Both past and future spring forth when I reach out toward them. The past, therefore, *is* not past or the future. "It exists only when a subjectivity is there to disrupt the plenitude of being itself, to adumbrate a perspective, and introduce non-being into it." As such, the passage of one present to the next is not a thing which I conceive or observe as an onlooker. Rather, I effect it; I am already at the impending present as my gesture is already at its goal. I am myself time, a time which "abides" (*demeure*) and does not "flow" or "change" (PP 421).

Further we read that "time *is* someone," (*le temps est quelqu'un*) or that temporal dimensions collectively express that "one single explosion or thrust which is subjectivity itself." At this level, primordial temporality is not a juxtaposition of external events; it is a subjective "power" (*puissance*) which holds these events together while keeping them apart. To this Merleau-Ponty warns that "ultimate subjectivity is not temporal in the empirical sense" in that we do not need to posit yet another consciousness to be conscious of the successive states of consciousness. "Ultimate consciousness is, therefore, 'timeless'" in the sense that it is not intratemporal. Subjectivity, finally, is not in time because it takes up or lives through time and merges with the cohesion of life (PP 422).

As such, the subject does not constitute time. "The fact that even our purest reflections appear to us retrospective in time, and that our reflection on the flux is actually inserted into that flux, shows that the most precise consciousness of which we are capable is always, as it were, affected by itself or given to itself, and that the word consciousness has no meaning independently of this duality" (PP 426). But, despite "this ceaseless welling up of time" (PP 427), I am not mercilessly submitted to its tutelage. Rather, I am constantly centered in a present, an "unbroken chain of the fields of presence" (PP 423) that provide situations with access to a past where I can find myself and act out of myself and be "wholly active and wholly passive" because I am "the upsurge of time" (*le surgissement du temps*) (PP 428).

In summary, time is a dimension of subjectivity and not a feature of the objective world. But subjectivity does not constitute time, and time is not simply an attribute of the self. The past and the future appear in the present as an expression or excrescence of a being that is temporal. Yet, how are we to understand the subject that does not constitute time yet is the upsurge of time?

Let us look more closely at Merleau-Ponty's concern for the present. Contrary to Heidegger, the thesis of *Phenomenology of Perception* finds the dimension of the present at the phenomenal level more vital than the future (PP 427). In his chapter on temporality, Merleau-Ponty repeatedly asserts that the present is the primary dimension of time. But why this pronounced focus on the present?

For Merleau-Ponty, the present is never self-constituted or identical to an anonymous instant. It simply is: "time exists for me because I have a present" (PP 424). The primacy of the present is weighted in regard to the subject being first and foremost a phenomenal body. In fact, Merleau-Ponty's entire analysis of time is skewed toward protecting the primacy of a unique presence of time open to perceptual consciousness alone. This unique presence is, in fact, an original disruption in the natural order of events to which the body belongs and is not determined by it. More broadly, this unique presence only makes sense in regard to a plenum or "density of being" that it cannot constitute. The present of the phenomenal body stands in contrast to the horizon of being, and not, like Augustine, between a self-constituting present and eternity. In speaking about eternity, Merleau-Ponty states that our only recourse to it "is necessitated solely by an objective conception of time" (PP 374) and that "eternity feeds on time," and merely belongs to dreaming, which refers back to waking life from which it borrows its structures (PP 423). Eternity, at best, is relegated to the thematized or acculturated world of meaning; it remains the "other" of objective time but not phenomenal time. The present of phenomenal time, therefore, is always held in a tension *with* ordinary time and a purely phenomenological time. "It is of the essence of time to be not only actual time, or time which flows, but also time which is aware of itself, for the explosion or dehiscence of the present towards a future is the archetype of the *relationship of self to self,* and it traces out an interiority or ipseity" (PP 426).

We should not be surprised by a homonymy, on the one hand, between unbroken successions of "nows" in ordinary time and the "unbroken chain of the fields of presence" of phenomenal time, and, on the other, a homonymy between an absolute temporally constitutive flux of consciousness (Husserl) and a phenomenal truism that "we are the upsurge of time." To remove the possibility of reducing the phenomenal body to a mere object, it had to be endowed with a minimum amount of temporal tension such that "primordial temporality" is "a power" which holds external events together while holding them apart. In other words, the primordial time of the phenomenal body is simply the present ecstatically understood. For Merleau-Ponty, there is only one time, the time of the body in the phenomenal world at present.

But in what way can we say this present time really exists? Are we really the upsurge of time in the present? Is identifying subjectivity with time an idealistic presupposition of time?

The charge of idealism is not new within Merleau-Pontyean scholarship. Some have questioned the degree to which Merleau-Ponty really "existentialized" the original Husserlian inspiration of a transcendental philosophy. *Phenomenology of Perception* can be judged on its success or failure to provide a compromise between Husserl's intention-constitutional analysis and existential philosophy. At one point Merleau-Ponty seeks to provide a new definition of the transcendental that is no longer centered on the transcendental ego but, instead, on the bodily subject, or, more precisely, perceptual, prereflective, *lived experience*. Is it not true to some degree to say that what was transcendental in the intellectual consciousness of Husserl has simply been transplanted into the perceptual consciousness or the lived experience of Merleau-Ponty?[36]

Merleau-Ponty seems quite unaware that the mere substitution of a philosophy of experience for a philosophy of consciousness changes nothing in regard to the basic structures of this philosophy. What we find in *Phenomenology of Perception* is a philosophy of lived experience that operates with all the idealistic presuppositions of a philosophy of consciousness. For example, the world is still "subjectivized" while being is still defined as being-for-a-subject, even if this subject is now the phenomenal body and no longer the transcendental ego.[37]

The question raised here is whether the lived or phenomenal body falls prey to the same criticism that Merleau-Ponty levels against all objects of consciousness when, in *Phenomenology of Perception*, he states that "the whole life of consciousness is characterized by the tendency to posit objects, since it is consciousness, that is to say self-knowledge, only in so far as it takes hold of itself and draws itself together in an identifiable object. And yet this absolute positing of a single object is the death of consciousness, since it congeals the whole of existence, as a crystal placed in a solution suddenly crystallizes it" (PP 71).

Despite all the arguments that Merleau-Ponty could mount to defend the phenomenal body as being perspectival in nature or being our medium for having a world, he might not be able to defend it against being an object of consciousness as well. In fact, near the end of his life, this is the very criticism that Merleau-Ponty levels against his early endeavors in *Phenomenology of Perception* when he concludes that "the problems posed in *Ph.P* are insoluble because I start there from the 'consciousness' — 'object' distinction" (VI 200).

In this light, the lived present of the phenomenal world does not escape an accusation of being merely a presupposed time intellectually posited. But let us take our case to yet another court of appeal. Ricoeur makes a fundamental distinction between time without a present and time with a present, the former being found in ordinary time and the time of science with its anonymous instants while the latter refers to a self and is marked by the instance of discourse (TN3 91).

In reviewing much of what Merleau-Ponty has written about time at the level of the phenomenal body — "we are the upsurge of time," "I am myself time," "we hold time in its entirety," "it is always in the present we are centered," time is the "dehiscence of the present," we are "a field of presence," and time is an "unfolded series of presents" — one cannot help but note the presuppositional nature of these statements. Temporality, as such, is not constituted through an instance of discourse; it is merely stated as fact or, even worse, as an idealized presupposition. At the level of the lived body, Merleau-Ponty never decisively claims the present can be designated reflexively. In failing to make this clear, has Merleau-Ponty simply posited a time, identified it with subjectivity and embellished it with a Heideggerian *ecstasis* and a Husserlian flux? This is perhaps why, despite his great familiarity with Merleau-Pontyean scholarship, Ricoeur makes little if any use of

Merleau-Ponty's notions of time in *Time and Narrative*.[38] The former's idea of time remains too Husserlian and engenders the very aporias Ricoeur wants to avoid.

Just because Merleau-Ponty distinguishes a lived body from the density of being and uses perspective and a perceptual consciousness to situate the body, he has not critically distinguished between the time that passes and the self that reckons with the passage of time. There is very little difference between Merleau-Ponty stating that the lived body imbibes a phenomenal present and Bergson stating that intuition imbibes duration. Like Bergson's duration, Merleau-Ponty's phenomenal present is a form of "omni-temporality" that simply stands in contradistinction to all other forms of time.[39] Both are intellectual assertions. Like duration, the phenomenal present of Merleau-Ponty still needs to be embodied in ordinary time as a counterpoint to make sense of it. Stating that "we are the upsurge of time" posits a human subject that effects time; it is still another feat to say how a finite human subject situates itself meaningfully as a temporal being with regard to cosmic time. Does Merleau-Ponty not still need "a supplement" to distinguish his notion of phenomenological time; that is, can his phenomenal time really be understood other than by viewing it "from above" in the form of a Husserlian absolute consciousness or some other form of atemporal spectating?[40]

This conclusion is not a pronouncement of failure. While Merleau-Ponty's notion of the lived present can lead to confusion, his genius is in elucidating the uniqueness of our corporeal presence in the world. As Ricoeur remarks, it is from an analysis such as Merleau-Ponty's that we designate the lived body "as the most original mediator between the course of lived experience and the order of the world" (TN 3, 230–31). The lived body defies the dichotomy of the physical and the psychic, of cosmic exteriority and reflective interiority. The lived body is unique in that it precedes all the connectors at the historical level yet it is the very place where a truly historical present can take hold. It is only around this lived body that the world unfolds as a set of rebellious and docile potential utensils — a set of permissions and obstacles.

FREEDOM

The topic of freedom is the crowning chapter in *Phenomenology of Perception*. Unlike Bergson, who depreciates the presence of matter in hopes of describing a type of psychological freedom, Merleau-Ponty roots freedom in the phenomenal world. "The solution of all problems of transcendence is to be sought in the thickness of the pre-objective present, in which we find our bodily being, our social being, and the pre-existence of the world, that is, the starting point of 'explanations,' in so far as they are legitimate — and at the same time the basis of our freedom" (PP 433).

Merleau-Ponty sees temporality as pointing to freedom in so far as freedom is a project undertaken in time; it is an action. Because the subject is not a sheer self-conscious *cogito* but an embodied being like other human beings, any free choice takes place against a background of possibilities that have a kind of preliminary significance for it.

Here, freedom will be the occurrence of choice which, by its very nature, suggests the limits or situation of consciousness in which the choice is made. Freedom comes to function in the body phenomenon as a meeting of the inner and outer, of the subject with object, of the body with its other. There will always be a "field of freedom" and a "conditioned freedom" which are poles of the synthetic freedom that the body creates in the act of choice (PP 454). As such, freedom is not absolute. There are only situations or a field, with social spaces not of our own making. While we may think of freedom ideally, in reality we are limited to our capacities, knowledge, and social embodiment. In this sense, the notion of sedimentation, already invoked to explain the lived body, becomes a necessary ground of freedom: "it is by giving up part of his spontaneity, by becoming involved in the world through stable organs and pre-established circuits, that man can acquire the mental and practical space which will theoretically free him from his environment and allow him to *see* it" (PP 87).

Freedom, as Merleau-Ponty describes it, is determinate because existence is determinate (not determined). Freedom is not an unconstrained act of will; in fact it has nothing to do with the will. It is more a quality of action whether actively realized or not. Starting from his earlier work in *The Structure of Behavior*, where human beings were defined as having the "capacity of going beyond created structures in order to create others" (SB 175), the positive aspect of freedom for Merleau-Ponty is the freedom for the living being to create, innovate, and act rather than freedom from external compulsion. It is not freedom from something that a being in the world seeks, but the freedom to act, work and change a situation — to give situations new significances that is important. Freedom is "appropriating a *de facto* situation by endowing it with a figurative meaning beyond its real one" (PP 171–72, n. 1).

The attempt to endow situations with figurative meaning is not carried out deliberately as much as the milieu wherein life exists is challenged. In reflecting on Karl Marx, Merleau-Ponty states: "Thus Marx, not content to *be* the son of a lawyer and student of philosophy, *conceives* his own situation as that of a 'lower middle class intellectual' in the new perspective of the class struggle" (ibid.). In this sense, freedom starts from a limiting situation; I exist in a certain situation over which I may have little control. Beyond the situation, any choice is less conscious than it is existential, that is, preconscious. I am not free absolutely as my freedom does not appear from nothing. Any freedom exists only to interrupt a certain project in which I find myself engaged, and start another — given, more or less, the same predisposition of factors that precipitated the first project. This freedom is really a freedom to change or shift existing conditions and not to create radically novel ones.

In this light, history becomes of great importance to the human subject. History has a meaning that is not necessarily deterministic in a mechanical manner. Rather, history is "lived through" (PP 449). The individual is not the director of history, yet at a certain moment, an individual can take up and carry forward the meaning which has been maturing in social coexistence. Merleau-Ponty explains,

> I am a psychological and historical structure, and have received, with existence a manner of existing, a style. . . . The fact remains that I am free, not in spite of, or on the hither side of, these motivations, but by means of them. For this significant life, this certain significance of nature and history which I am, does not limit my access to the world, but on

the contrary is my means of entering into communication with it. It is by being unrestrictedly and unreservedly what I am at present that I have a chance of moving forward; it is by living my time that I am able to understand other times, by plunging into the present and the world, by taking on deliberately what I am fortuitously, by willing what I will and doing what I do, that I can go further. (PP 455)

On the other hand, we should not assume that the social world, as such, is all there is. Engagement in social time is not enough. Merleau-Ponty warns that we erroneously conceive of freedom as a choice that could be continually remade as long as we do not bring in the notion of a natural time. From previous discussions we know there is a preper-sonal time, a generalized time which is the perpetual reiteration of the sequence of the past, present and future; it is the cyclic time of our bodily functions and of nature upon which all existence is founded (PP 453). In other words, we cannot forget that there is an autochthonous significance to the world which is constituted in the dealings which our incarnate existence has with it, which provides the ground of every deliberate discovery or bestowal of meaning [*Sinngebung*](PP 441).

This double exposure of times is what allows Merleau-Ponty to claim that "the world is already constituted, but never completely constituted; in the first case we are acted upon, and in the second we are open to an infinite number of possibilities" (PP 453). This ambiguity mixes lev-els of meaning and understanding so that any clear concept of either freedom or time cannot be defined without the other: the living self both creates and finds meaning because he or she "belongs to" and "inhabits" time. While it is this ambiguity that allows for the time of acting, it prevents us from ever being truly original. Any creative endeavour is rooted in a given predicament so that the *absolutely* novel, unique and original never have human authors.

LANGUAGE, MEANING, AND THE UNFINISHED SELF IN *PHENOMENOLOGY OF PERCEPTION*

There are two levels of meaning developed in *Phenomenology of Perception*. One remains at the level of the phenomenal body and the other at the level of the incarnate subject or what can be called the unfinished or living self.

At the level of the phenomenal body there is the meaning explicit to intentionality. We have already made reference to "operative intentionality" as a type of prethematic patterning and unity that makes the world significant for a phenomenal body in it. As such, Merleau-Ponty separated himself from a more Humean model that sees perceptual experience built up from psychical elements and associated by both memory and judgement. As he argued in *The Structure of Behavior*, Merleau-Ponty understands our phenomenal fields in terms of meaningful wholes (*Gestalten*) with foregrounds and backgrounds trading predominance as perception shifts its focus. Using the analogy of a searchlight, we can imagine our perceptual life like a beam of light that is vectored in all directions, almost at once, accommodating the breadth and change in our perceptual perspectives in all directions. In other words, "[t]he life of consciousness — cognitive life, the life of desire or perceptual life — is subtended by an 'intentional arc' that projects round about us our past, our future, our human setting, our physical, ideological and moral situation, or rather which results in our being situated in all these respects. It is this intentional arc which brings about the unity of the senses, of intelligence, of sensibility and motility" (PP 136). This intentional arc is the thread that weaves together the disconnected moments of daily events that are filled with purposes and subpurposes mediated by the body. The intentional arc constitutes the subject as cognitively meaningful. The significance to the subject implied by the intentional arc is not a reflective knowledge but characterizes human existence and does not go outside what is felt and experienced by the phenomenal body. The phenomenal body is not yet a living self; consciousness remains simply "being towards the thing through the intermediary of the body" (PP 138–39), such that the phenomenal body is really a knowing-body (*corps-connaissant*) (PP 408). Hence, "consciousness is in the first place not a matter of 'I think' but of 'I can'" (PP 137); that is, I perceive a world that is not an aimless assemblage of inchoate matter nor chaos. Instead, I know certain ways of moving, working, and accomplishing tasks in the world because I have a body that gets defined in relation to a world that meaningfully exists for me.

Even from this aspect, time is central. The intentional arc reaches out into the future and back into the past of one's bodily experience. It manifests itself from a particular standpoint and projects itself from the present; it is the life of perceptual consciousness in the present. For the subject, in the preobjective sense, significations inherent to any operative intentionality exist prior to signs defining the world and any thetic intentions. This is so because the subject is foremost always a being-in-the-world and the world is the cradle of meanings (*le monde comme berceau des significations*), the directions of all directions (*sens de tous les sens*), the ground of all thinking (PP 430).

Merleau-Ponty's description of meaning here depends on his exploiting the different meanings of the French word *sens*: it simultaneously means sense (or meaningfulness) and direction (or vector of unfolding through space and time). "The meaning intrinsic to experience unfolds in the temporal running-off of phenomena."[41] This understanding of the original meaningfulness of experience is the basis of Merleau-Ponty's conception of autochthonous organization. In all uses of the word *sens* exists the fundamental notion of a being orientated or polarized in the direction of what the subject has yet to be with respect to time. "Our analysis of time has confirmed, initially, this new notion of significance and understanding. Considering it [the world] in the same light as any other object, we shall be obliged to say of it what we have said of other objects: that it has meaning for us only because 'we are' it. We can designate something by this world only because we are at the past, present and future. It is literally the tenor [*sens*] of our life, and like the world, is accessible only to the person who has his place within, and who follows its direction" (PP 430). As such, meaning is always present to the human subject. Perception anchors us in the world, which is the font of meaning. Yet, while perception is never fully complete, transparent, or fully understood because perceptual synthesis is fundamentally contingent (PP 221), there is always meaning in time. Our view of the world, our field, while always perspectival, is never an *a priori* truth or an absolute given in a nontemporal moment. The person who perceives is not spread out before him or herself as a consciousness already complete so much as he or she assumes a historical density, taking up a perceptual tradition that confronts him or her with a present. "In every focusing movement my body unites present, past and future, it secretes time, or rather it becomes that location in nature where, for the first time, events, instead of pushing each other into the realm of being, project round the present a double horizon of past and future and acquire a historical orientation" (PP 239–40). In this sense, meaning and time are inextricably tied in *Phenomenology of Perception*. Within phenomenal time the knowing body has intentional meaning by the very fact that it is a being-in-the-world.

But how and what meaning is expressed at the level of the incarnate subject or living self?

As just stated, the living self is born into a historical halo with an array of sedimented and possible meanings. The living self is not free to choose any frame of reference or cultural context for meaning and purpose because "the idea of situation rules out absolute freedom at the source of our commitments, and equally, indeed, at their terminus" (PP 454). To understand the meaning level appropriate to the living self we must recall that for Merleau-Ponty there are no received truths: "speech implants the idea of truth in us as the presumptive limit of its effort" (PP 190).[42] Behind language there is no immutable transcendent thought (PP 392). Rather, language is the "ever-recreated opening in the plenitude of being" held at bay by a formerly constituted linguistic and cultural world. "It might be said . . . that *languages* or constituted systems of vocabulary and syntax, empirically existing 'means of expression,' are both the repository and sedimentation of acts of *speech*, in which unformulated significance [*sens*] not only finds the means of being conveyed outwardly, but moreover acquires existence for itself, and is genuinely created as significance. Or again one might draw a distinction between *the word in the speaking [une parole parlante] and the spoken word [une parole parlée]*" (PP 196–97). For Merleau-Ponty, it is empirical language that allows us to inherit a world already structured by the expressive acts of others who incrementally established our conventional ways of speaking and organizing experience. In stating such a position, Merleau-Ponty separates himself from Husserl's eidetic theory of meaning where the thought behind the linguistic sign is quite distinct from the sign itself. There is no absolute, eidetic, or eternal meaning-structure separate from the external signs that convey it. We don't proceed into the world with our own meaning-bestowing acts, but find ourselves already in a world with a language, meaning, and words. The most I can hope for is to reconstitute such meanings when I confront them in an ideology, a text, or other artefact. Novel experience and growth in language take place in a creative or authentic moment in language (*une parole parlante*) wherein something is expressed for the first time. As such, it is language, "which is its own foundation, or which, like a wave, gathers and poises itself to hurtle beyond its own limits" so that any project of knowledge and meaning at the personal level is necessarily open-ended and incomplete (ibid.). Any finality that is posited would have to be strictly presumptive because the locus of meaning is not in the cultural world of language alone, but stems from the existence of a phenomenal body in a phenomenal world as well.

At the level of the phenomenal body, existence is lived and not conceived in thought through language. There is no one thought that adequately captures the essence of "being-in-the-world." Subsequently, meaning, like time and the self, finds itself under the scourge of ambiguity because "the lived is thus never entirely comprehensible," and "what I understand never quite tallies with my living experience, in short, I am never quite one with my self" (PP 347). Meaning, therefore, for the living self will always be ambiguous in that "everything we live or think has always several meanings (*sens*)" (PP 169). "All explanations of my conduct in terms of my past, my temperament and my environment are therefore true, provided they be regarded not as separable contributions, but as moments of my total being, the significance [*sens*] of which I am entitled to make explicit in various ways, without its ever being possible to say whether I confer meaning [*sens*] upon them or receive it from them" (PP 455).

In short, any meaning that the living self assumes and inherits is partially arbitrary and underpinned by the prepersonal realities and the operative intentionalities of the phenomenal body. Yet, it is only speech, of all expressive operations of the body, that seems capable of transcending itself as a bodily expression and allowing a double reflection — a reflection of itself as a natural reflection of the body on itself. As such, not only is speech able to bear witness to a natural power of transcendence that the lived body brings about in relation to natural being, but speech can creatively designate a plethora of meanings.

This active transcendence is driven by the gap that exists between the worlds of operative intentionality and thematic intentionality, between the tacit — silent — cogito and the incarnate subject or living self. This tacit cogito is an original opening in the world and only obtains a "precarious grasp" upon the world. This precariousness is the result of our inability to definitively capture our prepersonal and phenomenal existence: the incarnate subject fails to give a complete account of the subject of perception. This is why Merleau-Ponty characterizes human existence as essentially ambiguous and any meaning as contingent. In the end, "this ambiguity (*équivoque*) cannot be resolved, but it can be understood as ultimate, if we recapture the intuition of real time which preserves everything, and which is at the core of both proof and expression" (PP 394).

This fundamental ambiguity translates itself into a constant openness at the level of the incarnate subject: openness to the meaning of our perceptions and to self-understanding. It is only in a cultural world that "speech is able to settle into a sediment and constitute an acquisition for use in human relationships" (PP 191), such that a thematized self can take on an identity appropriate to its own discovery in a linguistic community. The thematized self does not posit itself prior to language but realizes itself through language. For Merleau-Ponty, "man is a historical idea and not a natural species," so that it is only "speech itself [that] *brings about* the concordance between me and myself, and between myself and others" (PP 392). While the self finds itself already situated in a world of signs, symbols, and texts, the self participates in "constitut[ing] a linguistic world and a cultural world" (PP 197). As a self matures, reads, listens, speaks, and observes, it learns various associations of words, situations, and objectivities until it acquires an identity and linguistic style for its own expressive needs.

Any signified "world" is an "unfinished work" and it is not established once and for all (PP 406). The body never stops "secreting itself a 'significance' upon its material surrounding, and communicating it to other embodied subjects" (PP 197) such that a voluntary and rational life is given "a permanently tentative look" (PP 346–47). As Merleau-Ponty concludes, "We must therefore recognize as an ultimate fact this open indefinite power of giving significance (*signifier*) — that is, both apprehending and conveying a meaning (*sens*) — by which man transcends himself towards a new form of behavior, or towards other people, or towards his own thought, through his body and speech" (PP 194). This openness finds itself realized over and over again by authentic acts of expression that shatter sedimented levels of secondary expression and description. Authentic speech interpenetrates the natural world and language, disavowing any fixed meaning given to one particular picture of the world and to ourselves. Thematized meaning, configured for a particular purpose, is thus contingent.

Even our identities are not fixed once and for all. "There is no privileged self-knowledge, and other people are no more closed systems than I am myself" (PP 198). We live in a tension between a generalized existence and individual projects which bestows both a situation and an openness to our identity. We are unfinished selves. Hence, "there is no case in which I am utterly committed" (PP 452) and each of us possesses the means "to transcend ourselves" (PP 456). Each act of authentic expression constantly makes and unmakes our identities, reestablishing them as our field of experiences are challenged and confronted by previous orientations and creative expressions. "From these gains other acts of authentic expression — the writer's, the artist's, or the philosopher's — are made possible. This ever-recreated opening in the plenitude of being is what conditions the child's first use of speech and the language of the writer, as it does the construction of the word and that of concepts" (PP 197).

THE NARRATIVE TENDENCY IN *PHENOMENOLOGY OF PERCEPTION* AND BEYOND

While Merleau-Ponty's preoccupation with the phenomenal realm and perception permitted him to inadvertently draw out an unfinished self— one that is quite antithetical to the stable substance of the Cartesian *cogito* — the actual dynamics of how expression, speech, language, and literature configure identity and inscribe meaning was never definitively established. Unlike Ricoeur, Merleau-Ponty never zeros in on the narrative function as *the* medium for the production of meaning, especially the meaning of time. As some have suggested, his phenomenological description of perception lacks a discussion of the relationship between the reader and the text.[43] This would have at least induced readers of *Phenomenology of Perception* to reflect, at the outset, on their own function in disclosing the phenomena that the text describes.

Regardless of this oversight, there is a nascent sense in *Phenomenology of Perception* that reading and the narrative function produce meaning. While Merleau-Ponty rarely speaks of "narrative" *per se* as much as he comments on literature or literary language in general, he is very aware that literary texts do not constitute simply a mere reminder of facts but bring "meaning into existence as a thing at the very heart of the text, it brings it to life in an organism of words, establishing it in the writer or the reader as a new sense organ, opening a new field or a new dimension to our experience" (PP 182). Ultimately, because they carry meaning within them, in a certain way, a telling utterance (*une parole importante*) or a good book imposes (*imposent*) its meaning (*sens*) on each of us (PP 388).

In one poignant example, Merleau-Ponty recognizes the subtle shift in meaning reading brings about especially with regard to philosophy. In reading Descartes, for example, "it is I who reconstitute the historical *cogito,* I who read Descartes's text, I who recognize in it an undying truth, so that finally the Cartesian *cogito* acquires its significance (*sens*) only through my own *cogito*" (PP 371). Here, it is the reader who puts closure to the horizon opened up by the text; it is the reader who now finds the notion of "*cogito*" in his or her world; and it is the reader who now finds him or herself in the Cartesian world of self-understanding, with its own sense of meaning, that prior to reading Descartes's narrative was never a possibility. In other words, where language establishes a situation for us, reading goes further and opens new thoughts, new dimensions, and new landscapes such that the significance carried into the reader's mind exceeds language and thought as already constituted and is "magically" thrown into relief during the *incantation linguistique* (PP 401)[44] to be reconstituted by us with a meaning that is specifically ours. In reading, the incarnate subject understands more "because he has the power to live, beyond his immediate experience, through the events described" (PP 133).

But beyond these early remarks, and when one stands back and reviews the entire philosophical corpus of Merleau-Ponty, what is readily apparent is the inconsistency in the nature and temperament of his works. Once readers leave the heavily crafted domain of *Phenomenology of Perception* they are confronted with a barrage of often free-floating commentaries and less-than-rigorous texts on various topics from literature to politics. This inconsistency might be summarized as the problem of trying to define the connection between "I am myself time" at the phenomenal level and the incarnate living self that lives through time.

In an early critique of Merleau-Ponty's phenomenology, Ricoeur once commented that it was difficult to understand how a "philosophical act itself is possible if man is so completely identified with his insertion into his field of perception, action, and life."[45] It seems to be such criticism that spurs Merleau-Ponty to engage in his diverse studies after *Phenomenology of Perception*. But this gap between the phenomenal world and the incarnate living self is never cohesively bridged in Merleau-Ponty for two reasons. First, underwriting all of Merleau-Ponty's writing is the explicit testament to ambiguity between what he called the verbal cogito (*un Cogito sur parole*) and the tacit cogito. As quoted above, it is ultimate and cannot be resolved. The verbal *cogito* does not put me into contact with my own life and thought unless the tacit *cogito* is encountered. But Merleau-Ponty equivocates on such a contact ever being possible.

Second is Merleau-Ponty's problem with language. In a post-*Phenomenology of Perception* work, Merleau-Ponty makes a clear distinction between "a critical, philosophic, universal use of language," and "the more true non-philosophical writing" (S 78–83). He indicates a rather deep prejudice about language use when he wonders if philosophic language does not better "recover the slippery hold on our experience that literature gives us" and thereby express the essence of language better than literature does (ibid.). This prejudice is reminiscent of Bergson's distinction between poetry and scientific language where he believed there existed two different language chains. Such a prejudice negates the possibility of Merleau-Ponty ever employing the category of "narrative function" as wide and broadly as Ricoeur endeavours to do so. While Merleau-Ponty will see the self as a being that searches for clarity more than it possesses it and creates truth rather than finds it, the means to pursue such searches are never squarely put on the shoulders of narrative (PrP 220).

But to say that Merleau-Ponty never puts the creation of meaning on the shoulders of narrative is not to say that narrative is unimportant. Quite to the contrary, as noted, while Merleau-Ponty does not employ the term "narrative," one does find a rich set of remarks that point to the importance of narrative with respect to time, self, and meaning. This is strikingly clear in an article published in the same year as *Phenomenology of Perception*.

In the opening pages of "Metaphysics and the Novel," Merleau-Ponty states quite clearly that the task of literature and a phenomenological or existential philosophy are one and the same (SN 26–28). Neither literature nor philosophy are assigned to explain the world or to discover its "conditions of possibilities," but, rather, to formulate an experience of the world, a contact with the world that precedes all thought *about* the world. In the interpenetration of literature and philosophy whatever is metaphysical in human beings will no longer be credited to something outside our empirical being, that is, either to a God or a Cartesian *Cogito*. Motivated by a common end, both philosophy and literature must strive to express the fact that human beings are metaphysical in their very being, including their loves, hates, and individual and collective history. Philosophical expression, therefore, will assume the same ambiguities of literary expression to the degree that perhaps the world can in no better way be expressed except in "stories" (*histoires*) (SN 28).

To reveal this radical intersection and common task between philosophy and literature, Merleau-Ponty rigorously reviews a novel by Simone de Beauvoir entitled *L'Invitée*.[46] In his review, Merleau-Ponty sensitively details how its characters experience time and where the self undergoes a change in self-understanding given a tragic situation of betrayed love. This is the case of Françoise who is described in the beginning as having no inner life but who coexists with other people and the whole world. This lack of personal identity was only reinforced by her complete involvement with her lover, Pierre, to the point that both could only be identified under an indistinguishable "we." A crushing reality awakes her from her metaphysical slumber when she finds out Pierre has abandoned her for Xavière.

> The pages in which Françoise witnesses the ruin of her artificial world are perhaps the most beautiful in the book. She is no longer at the heart of things as if this were a natural privilege of hers: the world has a center from which she is excluded, and it is the place where Pierre and Xavière are to meet. With the others, things retreat beyond her grasp and become the strange debris of a world to which she no longer holds the key. The future ceases to be the natural extension of the present, time is fragmented, and Françoise is no more than an anonymous being, a creature without a history, a mass of chilled flesh. She now knows there are situations which cannot be communicated and which can only be understood by living them. There was a unique pulsation which projected before her a living present, a future, a world, which animated language for her — and that pulsation has stopped . . . At the moment when all projects thus collapse, when even the self's hold on itself is broken, death — which one's projects traversed without even suspecting it up to now — becomes the only reality, since it is in death that the pulverization of time and life is consummated. Life has rejected Françoise. (SN 32, 34)

In contrast to Françoise, Merleau-Ponty describes Xavière as someone who never lent herself to any project; she does not work toward any social goals. She is tied to her own sense of private completeness; she is egoistical and never goes beyond herself or puts herself in another's place. Xavière "never sacrifices the immediate, never goes beyond the present moment. She always sticks to what she feels" (SN 35). The creativity of language, the exigency of others, and the need to change, are too much for Xavière; only the present can be managed.

In reading Merleau-Ponty's review of *L'Invitée,* one has the sense that Merleau-Ponty concentrates on de Beauvoir's depictions of temporal experience not so much to accurately describe what de Beauvoir had in mind as much as to grasp better his own position, his own personal configuration, and his own emerging interpretation of time and life. He summarizes the book as a study of existence between two limits — the immediacy of Xavière's life and the confidence and rationality of Françoise's attempt to transcend the mundane. For Merleau-Ponty, the novel only reinforces his conviction that between the fragments of time and eternity (that never transcends time), "there is an effective existence which unfolds in patterns of behavior, is organized like a melody, and by means of its projects, cuts across time without leaving it" (SN 40). But in this "cutting across time without leaving it," there is no prize, no magic, and no taste of euphoria. In accepting the present there is the tacit agreement that looking for a solution, an ultimate philosophical or a religious escape, is an error.

> There is undoubtedly no *solution* to human problems; no way, for example, to eliminate the transcendence of time, the separation of consciousnesses which may always reappear to threaten our commitments; no way to test the authenticity of these commitments which may always, in a moment of fatigue, seem artificial conventions to us. But between these two extremes at which existence perishes, total existence is our decision by which we enter time in order to create our life within it. All human projects are contradictory because they simultaneously attract and repel their realization. (SN 40)

Speaking in a more existential mode, Merleau-Ponty endows his readers with a certain power. Regardless of the inherent ambiguity of existence, they must plunge themselves into time — not in order to merely follow exterior rules of conduct and value but to live in "good faith" and to give loyalty to promises and have respect for others. In the end, in a voice so unlike his previous technical works, Merleau-Ponty concludes with almost a personal plea that there is value in life and that "it consists of actively being what we are by chance, of establishing that communication with others and with ourselves for which our temporal structure gives us the opportunity and of which our liberty is only the rough outline" (SN 40).

In contradistinction to *Phenomenology of Perception* with its ingenious uncovering of phenomenal time, Merleau-Ponty uses *L'Invitée* to narratively play with time, offering us the power to "create our life within it." In reading back to us *his experience* of *L'Invitée,* through his own philosophical point of view, Merleau-Ponty's philosophy takes on a form of narration that tells his story to his readers, his critics, his "accountants." His philosophy becomes the story of his critique of various fabrications about an attainable eternity inherited from religion, as well as his rejection of an objective time that his culture uses for the sake of science and a capitalist economy. His philosophy, as such, might be seen as a story — an intellectual narrative — in which he recounts to us his existential journey in life, his grappling with the forces of time, language, and politics before he died.

In discussion with Merleau-Ponty, the philosopher Émile Bréhier once remarked that, "I see your ideas as being better expressed in literature and in painting than in philosophy. Your philosophy results in a novel. This is not a defect, but I truly believe that it results in that immediate suggestion of realities which we associate with the writings of novelists" (PrP 30). What Bréhier might have gone on to say is that perhaps Merleau-Ponty is expressing more of himself than a depersonalized philosophical treatise would. As we will see in the next chapter concerning narrative identity, perhaps Merleau-Ponty's identity is intimately tied to his philosophical writing, and, perhaps no writer escapes this hermeneutical circle of self disclosure.[47]

But for Merleau-Ponty to equate philosophy and literature to the point that "perhaps the world can in no better way be expressed except in 'stories' and, as it were, pointed at" (SN 28), is he not giving more credence to the role of narrative than he is aware of? Many writings in his middle period would suggest precisely this.

In a paper published earlier in the 1950s, entitled "Indirect Language and the Voices of Silence," Merleau-Ponty draws out two relationships between literature and the unfinished self. First, the self naturally seeks for its meaning through literature because there is a historical imperative to account for our lives through what we have done and said that is most true and valuable in our particular situations (S 73). Literature, as such, is a history that we want to tell about ourselves, "an invocation of truth, which is never created by what is inscribed in history, but which, insofar as it is truth, requires that inscription" (S 74). It is this desire for expression of a truthful account of our lives that lies at the heart of the incarnate subject as a living self.

> Men borrow from one another so constantly that each moment of our will and thought takes flight from other men, so that in this sense it is impossible to have any more than a rough idea of what is due to each individual man. It is nevertheless true that this desire for total manifestation animates life as it does literature, and that beneath the petty motives it is this desire which makes the writer want to be read, which makes man sometimes become a writer, and which in any case makes man speak and everyone want to account for himself in the eyes of X — which means that everyone thinks of his life and all lives as something that can in every sense of the word be told as a 'story'. (S 74–75)

However, there is also a second relationship between the self and acts of expression that is related to accountability but goes beyond it. It is to understand situations other than my own and to create a path between my life and that of others. In doing so I express myself, but always in a new and creative manner. "Words, and even the act of prose, carry the speaker and hearer into a common universe by drawing both toward a *new signification through their power to designate in excess of their accepted definition,* through the muffled life they have led and continue to lead us" (S 75, my emphasis). In this sense, literature is a "search and acquisition," a creation of new meaning.

> A language which only sought to reproduce things themselves would exhaust its power to teach in factual statements. On the contrary, a language which gives our perspectives on things and cuts out relief in them opens up a discussion which does not end with the language and itself invites further investigation. What is irreplaceable in the work of art? . . . The fact that it contains, better than ideas, *matrices of ideas* — the fact that it provides us with symbols whose meaning we never stop developing. Precisely because it dwells and makes us dwell in a world we do not have the key to, the work of art teaches us to see and ultimately gives us something to think about as no analytical work can; because when we analyse an object, we find only what we have put into it. (S 77)

In other words, the identity of the self at the level of the cultural world is never immutably defined; the possibilities for defining the meaning that authenticates that identity is never fully exhausted by any one linguistic act. The possibility of achieving newer levels of signification through narrative is not in the command of language since ordinary language is often destroyed in the process; language, rather, is entirely *ready* to convert everything new the author stands for as a writer into an acquisition. "It is as if it had been made for him, and he for it; as if the task of speaking to which he had been devoted in learning the language were more deservedly he than his heart beat; and as if the established language called into existence, along with him, one of *his* possibilities" (S 79).[48] In this sense, the meaning of a novel, for example, is a type of *coherent deformation* where our image of the world is thrown out of focus, distended, and drawn toward a fuller meaning (S 78). Our life's center of gravity is displaced with the suggestion that we cross-check and resume our operations in terms of one another (S 82–83).

Finally, in a posthumous text, *Le Prose du Monde,* we read even more pointedly that language and speech bring meaning into existence;[49] that is, language as institution or sedimentation. Sedimented language is the language the reader brings with him or herself, the stock of accepted relations between signs and familiar significations without which he or she could never have begun to read. With the aid of signs agreed upon by the author and myself, because we speak the same language, a book makes me believe that we already share a common stock of well-worn and readily available significations. The author has come to dwell in my world. Then, imperceptibly, she varies the ordinary meaning of the signs, and like a whirlwind they sweep me along toward the other meaning with which I am going to connect, upon which I will think, and by which I may even live. It is as if through a certain kneading of language an author is able to raise new significations for the reader. "Reading is an encounter between the glorious and impalpable incarnations of my own speech and the author's speech. As we have said, reading projects us beyond our own thoughts toward the other person's intention and meaning, just as perception takes us to things themselves across a perspective of which we become aware only after the event. *But my power of transcending myself through reading is mine by virtue of my being a speaking subject capable of linguistic gesticulation, just as perception is possible through my body.*"[50]

The reference to "transcending myself" above might be read in the light of what Ricoeur will call "refiguration" in the next chapter. It concerns the creation of meaning and self-understanding in the fusion of horizons between the experiential-imaginative horizon presented in the text and the horizon of the reader's actual world. As we enter into both the historical and fictive texts of our present "world," the hardened understandings and perceptions of the practical field become open for revision; more importantly, our identities, with reference to these texts, become open for a reevaluation, and possibly are offered new strategies of engagement. In reading, we appropriate the author's horizon which, in turn, becomes an opportunity for self-description, a redescription that is foremost a rereading of oneself in the world. "Once I have read the book, it acquires a unique and palpable existence quite apart from the words on the pages . . . One may even say that, while I am reading the book, it is always with reference to the whole, as I grasp it at any point, that I understand each phrase, each shift in the narrative of delay in the action, to the point where, as the reader, I feel . . . as though I have written the book from start to finish" (PrP 11). The text, therefore, becomes the opportunity to imagine, in this or that way, different responses to acting and being in the world. Self understanding in this sense is never a closed circle of immediate knowledge but the transformative product of breathing new life into and transgressing the already sedimented layers of stock expressions we employ daily.

But what is the purpose behind "transcending myself" that narrative realizes? What is the point of assimilating other meanings and values through narrative? What is the reason for seeking new meanings in a world where freedom is always confined to a certain situation? If my life is nothing more than the continual task of trying to explain myself because I am rife with ambiguity, why not accept any meaning rather than be condemned to a treadmill of endless constructions? In other words, what is the drive behind the search for personal meaning in novels, poems, and art? What motivates the living self to search for more meaning to its existence than can be found in a common, stereotypic social identity?

The answer to these questions is not well formulated by Merleau-Ponty. For Merleau-Ponty there is no Bergsonian "profound self" and a pure duration to return to (PP 380). Yet, it is in a particular time and place or situation that every self finds its freedom to act and express itself in hopes of finding itself. This idea is succinctly elaborated upon in an essay published shortly after *Phenomenology of Perception,* entitled "Reading Montaigne."

Here we read of the constant illusion that surrounds any attempt at self-possession or the procurement of a final truth about the self. In commenting on Montaigne's theme that all truth contradicts itself, Merleau-Ponty states that "self-understanding for Montaigne is dialogue with self." This dialogue is "like 'essaying' or 'experimenting on' himself" in an attempt to evoke a response from the conscious but opaque being that he is (S 199). In the end, the question of the self is never answered. The search for the self becomes an inquiry without discovery, a hunt without a kill; "*the world is only a school for inquisitioners,*" as Merleau-Ponty quotes Montaigne (S 202). It is as if the only victory over the self lies in expressing the self as Montaigne did so copiously because "the self is not *serious,* it does not like to be tied down" (S 210). As Merleau-Ponty himself reflects, "in this ambiguous *self* (*le soi ambigu*) — which is offered to everything, and which he never finishing exploring — perhaps he finally finds the place of all obscurities, the mystery of all mysteries, and something like an ultimate truth" (S 198, my translation).

The "ambiguous self" should not be understood as a troubled character or a lost soul. The ambiguous self is one that is distilled from the labour of living, from our ability to use language and reconstitute meaning from the works and artefacts that surround us. It conforms to a model of a dynamic identity arising from the projection of a life lived and the need to give it expression because "everyone wants to account for himself in the eyes of X." But the account we give of ourselves is never finished in our conscious lifetime. This sense of the self as an unfinished project was to remain constant in the works of Merleau-Ponty.[51] But as I will comment in the concluding chapter, it is hard to be satisfied with "the ambiguous self" as a final conclusion on personal identity. Merleau-Ponty fails to prove why such an identity is meaningful. If ambiguity is the identifying ground of the self, then why is the expression of any meaning important at all?

In the end, we must be wary of the many fecund themes that erupt in Merleau-Ponty's thought but are never elaborated or expanded upon. The most we can say in regard to narrative is that we find many passages scattered throughout the works of Merleau-Ponty that indicate a sympathy for literature and narrative as a facet of human expression in general, but there is little dedication to a systematic understanding of the narrative function as Ricoeur would understand it, and even a lesser identity with narrative as a condition for temporal existence.

THE VISIBLE AND THE INVISIBLE

In his later works, Merleau-Ponty never took up the topic of time as rigorously as he had in *Phenomenology of Perception*. Unlike Bergson who wrote a last great work before retiring, Merleau-Ponty died while still *en route* in his philosophical quest, while still writing his own intellectual narrative. His latter works, especially the unfinished text, *The Visible and the Invisible*, speaks of a continuing critique of his early works and a further interrogation of philosophy, especially with regard to language. In taking up new terms such as "depth," "silence," "flesh," and "the chaism," Merleau-Ponty entered into a serious meditation on language and mediation while working toward a new ontology.[52] His references with jungle tropes (jungle, wild, savage) are an attempt to come to grips with what is untamed by a philosophical interrogation of Being. Merleau-Ponty, in the end, was not uncritically seeking an unmediated sense of existence or a return to pure "Being." While criticizing language as being contradictory,[53] or even deceptive, he would never lose confidence in the lifeline that is language as expression. In this sense his philosophy never lost its proto-hermeneutical element.[54]

Having said this, it remains quite difficult to comment well on Merleau-Ponty's last work, *The Visible and the Invisible*. Left unfinished at the time of his death, the work, with only some 160 pages of organized text, is composed of a fragmented and incomplete set of "Working Notes." Some would argue that, given such meager materials, it is impossible to adequately reconstruct the philosophical integrity of the text as Merleau-Ponty envisioned it. As Gutting states, "there is no book titled *Le visible et l'invisible* by Merleau-Ponty (despite the published volume of that title, with his name on the cover)."[55] Besides these basic textual problems, there is the question of whether or not the work truly constitutes a decisive break from *Phenomenology of Perception*. In an unpublished text, Merleau-Ponty characterizes his work has a having two separate phases (PrP 6), yet some commentators argue that both major works have more continuity than Merleau-Ponty asserts.[56]

The most detectable shift in *The Visible and the Invisible* is an attempt to escape from any vestige of a philosophy of consciousness. As already quoted, Merleau-Ponty is fully aware that "the problems posed in *Ph.P* are insoluble because I start there from the 'consciousness'-'object' distinction" (VI 200). In other words, the early work remains dualistic in that it is shadowed by a thinker reflecting upon an external world of empirical objects and facts, separate from the cogitating subject. *The Visible and the Invisible* was to be a concentrated effort to move from a subject-based philosophy toward a more ontologically inclusive vision of existence. Leaving behind such alternatives as the classic Sartrean distinction between the for-itself and in-itself, Merleau-Ponty wanted to nuance the reciprocal seamless interplay — the reversibility — between self and world where meaning is neither posited by consciousness nor garnered from things outside of us.

In the shortest terms, *The Visible and the Invisible* tries to elaborate the real as a tension between perception and the creative act of expression and language. The work constantly reminds us of the ceaseless call to new acts of authentic expression — a vow of belief in our perceptual faith. To effect this call, Merleau-Ponty points to the intricate intertwining that perpetually endures between the sensible and the sensate, the body and the world, and the subjective and the objective with regard to the body. The body or, as he will refer to it, "flesh" (*chair*), is the chiasm or crossing over that permits the slippery inter-penetration (the reversibility) between subjective experience and objective existence. The flesh should not be understood as the third element between "me" and the "world"; it is also not a life force or an ethereal level of matter that subtends reality. Rather, it signals the reversibility that problematizes the notion of intentionality, the notion that lies, for Merleau-

Ponty, at the root of the subject-object dichotomy. The oft-quoted example is the one of touching hands. The body, in touching itself, enters into a kind of reversible reflection that is neither sheer identity nor nonidentity. As he states: "either my right hand really passes over into the rank of the touched, but then its hold on the world is interrupted, or it retains its hold on the world, but then I do not really touch *it*" (VI 148). Extending this example of the chiasm, the classical mind-body problem becomes transformed into looking at the creative moment between our perceptual faith and our articulation of it — the radical suggestion that world is no longer simply conceived as an object. The role of ambiguity that marked Merleau-Ponty's early works is now heightened to the level of paradox in these final reflections: "That the presence of the world is precisely the presence of its flesh to my flesh, that I 'am the world' and that I am not it, this is no sooner said than forgotten" (VI 127).

In light of these remarks and the problem of time, Merleau-Ponty revisits "the upsurge of time" that characterized the phenomenal time of *Phenomenology of Perception*. He reasserts the position that the upsurge of time could never be supplemental to the present presenting itself though the lived body. "Time must *constitute itself*— be always seen from the point of view of someone who *is of it*" (VI 184). What is decisively new in the later work is the dimension of depth; that is, in the intertwining of the perceiver and the perceived, time could never be an absolute series of events, a tempo. Continuity is replaced with "barbaric" flashes of reversals between the "ever new" and "the always the same." A point of time can be transmitted to the others without continuity and conservation, "without fictitious support in the psyche the moment one understands time as chiasm" (VI 267). As prosaically as possible, Merleau-Ponty attempts to express the body's sense as a fold in the flesh of the world where the "flesh" becomes an envelope for the past and present without distinction. This becomes for the philosopher "a sort of time of sleep" or "Existential eternity" (VI 267). For some, this "Existential eternity" marks the abolishment of time, not as a rejection of the temporal world, but for a fuller consciousness of it, a more profound wakefulness.[57]

In the course of *The Visible and the Invisible,* Merleau-Ponty twice quotes a telling passage from Paul Claudel's *Art poétique:* "From time to time, a man lifts his head, sniffs, listens, considers, recognizes his position: he thinks, he sighs, and, drawing his watch from the pocket lodged against his chest, looks at the time. Where am I? And What time is it? — such is the inexhaustible question turning from us to the world" (VI 103, 121). "Where am I? And What time is it?" are questions that appear several times in the course of *The Visible and the Invisible.* They appear frequently as if to emphasize the inexhaustible tensions that lie at the heart of the reversibility of perception in a philosophy that no longer abides by the oppositions of being and nonbeing, subject and object, the one and the many, identity and nonidentity. As embodied beings, we are enfolded in the flesh of the world in a non-dualistic fashion. Consequently, at the "zero point of Being," I may very well have "a mysterious tie with locality and temporality," but, on the other hand, in the inexhaustible field of experience, I am just as justified in asserting that I am everywhere and nowhere, always (VI 113). In a philosophy that sees embodied perception radically enmeshed with temporality, there lies a "secret knowledge of space and time as beings to be questioned, a secret knowledge of interrogation as the ultimate relation to Being" (VI 121). This interrogation, mediated by language and expression, never permits a level of signification that would be transparent to Being, that is, both timeless and universal.

Our attempts at understanding, Merleau-Ponty contends, should not aim to coincide with the immediate or "Being" but to deal with what is possible in our given horizon. The whole problem is to understand the relation between what is immanent and what is transcendent, as well as the mediate and immediate, without opposing them as mutually exclusive terms. For Merleau-Ponty, there is indeed something "*given*" but it is never completely or exhaustively given (VI 159). Whatever is given is not something we are called to coincide with. In commenting on the "given" in Bergson, Merleau-Ponty states that: "What is given, then, is not the naked thing, the past itself such as it was in its own time, but rather the thing ready to be seen, pregnant — in principle as well as in fact — with all the visions one can have of it"

(VI 124). What is "ready to be seen" is what is not yet caught in speech but something that will only come into our horizon as being once expressed. All conceptual constructions find their genesis in the temporalizing expressions arising from our embodied perceptions, governed as they are by the "barbaric Principle" where the "ever new" and "always the same" intertwine unceasingly in experience. This is why, noted in the final chapter, human time must be essentially creative because "Being is *what requires creation of us (exige de nous création)* for us to experience it" (VI 197).

It is difficult to encapsulate succinctly the philosophical nuances Merleau-Ponty envisioned for *The Visible and the Invisible.* To continue an exegesis of the text would take us too far afield. However, I would like to sketch in, in my own terms, two very broad summary statements describing Merleau-Ponty's overall project to serve as an introduction to Ricoeur's remarks, which follow in the next chapter.

First, in terms of time, Merleau-Ponty never wavered in his belief that our bodies and time are irrevocably intertwined. Time arises because we have very particular bodies, particular in the sense that they are mortal. If our bodies were not mortal, then the question of time would hardly raise a philosophical eyebrow. Since we can perceive the inevitability of our own deaths, time becomes our way of dealing with its opposite, eternity. Perhaps, if our bodies didn't know death we wouldn't know time, but, rather, be concerned with the rhythm of nature or the cycle of the seasons but not time *per se*. Mortality is the very tragedy of time that Simone Weil comments on in the introduction. Everywhere we sense eternity but cannot affect it; our bodies continue unceasingly in their aging and diminishment given the passage of time. The tragic sense is made more poignant in that our symbol systems offer us the categories of the infinite and the endless, neither of which adds a stitch of time to our mortal lives.

Second, since our embodied present does fall into some locality of time and space, we are always already part of a prereflective domain where natural phenomena are part of our body's ability to act. In a prereflective manner, we are sonorous beings using the natural materials of vocal cords, the medium of air and energy, to call out and ultimately communicate. Where, bioacoustically, nonhumans are restricted to various calls, human beings articulate. By use of signs and symbols, we articulate experiences that seem often to include more than the immediate and the pragmatic. Such articulations uncover the creative capacity of our ability to act. As Merleau-Ponty remarks, "Philosophy, precisely as 'Being speaking within us,' expression of the mute experience by itself, is creation. A creation that is at the same time a reintegration of Being. . . . It is hence a creation in the radical sense: a creation that is at the same time an adequation, the only way to obtain an adequation" (VI 197).

In anchoring his philosophical project in the embodied subject and the problem of perception, Merleau-Ponty went to lengths to explore how we adequately bring embodied perception to expression. As many of Merleau-Ponty's essays point out, this "adequation" takes form in the various products of literature, art and film. Where Ricoeur will argue that narration is the privileged mediation (adequation) among all signs and symbols, especially regarding our dealings with the tragedy of time, Merleau-Ponty will be much more tentative and see this adequation or mediation spread over all the expressive arts. Yet, in a telling description of Bergson's philosophy, Merleau-Ponty reveals something universal about all philosophical endeavors, even his own, that identify narrative as the primary means to approximate understanding.

> The genesis which the works of Bergson trace is a history of ourselves which we tell ourselves; it is a natural myth by which we express our ability to get along with all the forms of being. We are not this pebble, but when we look at it, it awakens resonances in our perceptive apparatus; our perception appears to come from it. That is to say our perception of the pebble is a kind of promotion to (conscious) existence for itself; it is our recovery of this mute thing which, from the time it enters our life, begins to unfold its implicit being, which is revealed to itself through us. (IPP 17)

We now turn to Ricoeur to make the argument that it is the narrative function, ultimately, by which we express "the natural myths" that permit this recovery not only of inanimate objects, but of our very self in time.

Four

The Historical Present and Narrative Identity

Canst thou that art the Lord of all eternity,
be ignorant of what I say unto thee?
Or dost thou see in relation to time, that which passeth in time?
Why then do I lay in order before thee so many narrations?
— St. Augustine, *Confessions,* Book 11

LINKING NARRATIVE AND TIME

For Bergson, a specifically human time was differentiated from ordinary time by concentrating on the immediate data of consciousness; his thesis was decisively psychological. By way of intuition, Bergson thought he had discovered a characteristic of human existence (pure duration) that could not be determined by empirical science and hence pointed out an irrefutable argument for human freedom. In extrapolating his initial inspiration, the categories of intuition, duration, consciousness, and "life" were melded together and forever mounted a scale that ended in a type of universalization of this original human time. Subsequently, the self was given in two depictions — one superficial and one profound. The profound self enshrined the possibility of freedom in that, at this level, human experience was not to be identified with either the confounding elements of space or language. Unfortunately, the Bergsonian analysis, while internalizing a particular time to the self, an internalization that very clearly "temporalizes" the anonymous instant of objective time into a personal present, past, and future, is not a reversible analysis. The analysis cannot stand for "all" of time since ordinary time cannot be accounted for or constituted. Eventually, the category of duration is a time that simply takes us out of being "in" time; it is the "other" of ordinary time.

Bergson's last work, *The Two Sources of Morality and Religion*, added a narrative component to this analysis by distinguishing two levels of storytelling, one conventional and one personal, hinting that the self described by Bergson lives in a world configured by narratives. However, Bergson finishes his thought on a mystical note that once again takes us out of the realm of the signified world. In short, while Bergson provided novel insight into grasping a time specific to the self, a time fused with the necessity of memory and anticipation in line with human action, his arguments for such a time are direct intuitions and often reduce themselves to a type of hermeticism.

Merleau-Ponty posits a phenomenal time — the time of phenomenal body. For the phenomenal body there is already a prethematic existential experience of time as a network of operative intentionalites binding us to the world; this lived time is a single "upsurge" or thrust into the "density of being" where human projects carve out relations of "before" and "after" in the world; this time is at once an "unbroken chain of fields of presence" that anchors me to an environment. At each stage of his analysis, Merleau-Ponty seeks out an ambiguous middle ground between the objective and the subjective, between the *en-soi* and *pour-soi*, that situates all of us as specifically "being-in-the-world." However, the "world" spoken of here is always the phenomenal one, the one I know foremost because I have a body. The price of defining the "world" through the phenomenal body as the locus of meaning is the radical production of distinctions within the categories of the body and self founded on disparate time perspectives — time of the present and an "original past" that has never been present. The result is aporetic; I find myself "belonging to" a time I did not constitute, yet "I am myself time." In terms of the self we find that "I am never one with myself" because ambiguity is "ultimate" — "I am inherent in time and in the world, that is, I know myself only in my ambiguity."

In the end, while providing invaluable insights into the phenomenal body, Merleau-Ponty's preoccupation with the lived present is a preoccupation with a phenomenal "omni-temporality" that is no less contrived than Bergson's duration. The lived present becomes the "all" of time yet never generates ordinary time. Meanwhile, within the acts of expression cogent to the lived body, language arises and with it the possibility of narrative. However, narrative is never seen as an ultimate condition of our temporal being. It can never refigure Merleau-Ponty's ultimate referent to time — the present of the phenomenal body. Despite numerous and consistent references to narrative, the theme is treated as an act of expression and less as the act of being that Ricoeur, to some degree, insists that it is.

The aporia that sabotaged the human time of both Bergson and Merleau-Ponty was the mutual occultation of finite lived or mortal time and the seeming infinity of cosmic time. It is difficult for any one theory of time to reconcile the autonomy of time *per se* and a purely phenomenological time. Neither pure duration nor the lived present of the ambiguous self expresses all there is to tell about time; they cannot act as ultimate sources for time in general or complete our thinking about time as such. When a phenomenology of time reaches those aspects of temporality that are most deeply hidden, even though they are closest to us, it discovers its external limit. Typically, this limit is overcome by either, like Bergson, multiplying the sources of inner time (intuition-consciousness-"life"), or, like Merleau-Ponty, insisting on an inherent and vicious ambiguity. Neither strategy adds to our thinking about time as a whole.

This chapter sketches out Ricoeur's response to this impasse through his discussion of historical time and the narrative self. As stated in my first chapter, Ricoeur is intent not on solving such impasses, or aporias as he calls them, but on uncovering how the narrative function plays with the aporias of time in the production of meaning.

In the course of *Time and Narrative*, Ricoeur makes two responses to these aporias; the first, covered in the first volume of *Time and Narrative,* presents the configuration of time under the formal elements of narrative composition. Ricoeur refers to this as the miniature version of his major thesis. It analyzes the concrete process by which narrative (a textual configuration) mediates between human action (prefiguration in the practical field) and our ability, through the reception of the work, to think and to act differently (refiguration). Ricoeur's second response expands the first over the course of two more volumes in a three-way dialogue between historiography, literary criticism, and phenomenology.

To unpack these responses calls for some preliminary remarks with regard to Ricoeur's indebtedness to Merleau-Ponty and Ricoeur's larger hermeneutical project.

First, having shared the common terrain of existential phenomenology, it is not too difficult to see why the philosophical trajectories of Merleau-Ponty and Ricoeur crisscross in light of common themes like language, freedom, and the body. In the literature, this convergence is well noted.[1] However, there is much less commentary on Ricoeur's indebtedness to Merleau-Ponty. The issue is made all the more obscure by the fact that, like many thinkers, Ricoeur never openly acknowledges his major inspirations, including Merleau-Ponty.

Ricoeur once remarked that Merleau-Ponty was "the greatest of French phenomenologists."[2] This has to be balanced with the severe critiques he often levelled at the project found in the *Phenomenology of Perception*.[3] Just to what extent Ricoeur is indebted to Merleau-Ponty is open for a broader discussion than can be undertaken here, yet there are several key instances that are important to acknowledge. First, Ricoeur's early phenomenological works on the will drew their inspiration from Merleau-Ponty, whom he greatly admired. By his own admission, Ricoeur hoped that his early *La Philosophie de la volonté* would rival Merleau-Ponty's *La Phénoménologie de la perception* — the former wanting to do for "the will" what the latter did for "perception."[4]

Further, Ricoeur's desire to formulate a hermeneutics of the self may have found some if not its seminal inspiration in remarks made by Merleau-Ponty with regard to the archaeology of the subject found in the preface to Hesnard's *L'Oeuvre de Freud et son importance pour le monde moderne*.[5] Here Ricoeur adapts the vision that basic philosophical problems such as the body, time, intersubjectivity, and consciousness cannot be addressed as objects given to a Cartesian mind.[6] Instead, the labor of reflection, interpretation and decipherment must replace the erroneous idea that answers to such ageless philosophical questions are somehow transparent to the rational mind. As Ricoeur will later argue, knowledge of the self is not rooted in the mind but in existence, desire, and effort. "The dependence of the Cogito on the positing of desire is not directly grasped in immediate experience, but interpreted by another consciousness in the seemingly senseless signs offered to interlocution."[7] In short, all truths, even of the self, will be hermeneutical ones, wrestled from the interpretations of dreams, fantasies, myths, texts, and monumental objects. This is because "a hermeneutic method, coupled with reflection, goes much further than an eidetic method."[8] Merleau-Ponty himself clearly moved in this direction near the end of his life without formally embracing the terms of hermeneutics as we understand it today thanks to Gadamer and Ricoeur.

The third area of indebtedness revolves around the topic of action. In Ricoeur's later works such as *Oneself as Another, Time and Narrative,* and *From Text to Action,* one finds a hermeneutics of action embedded in his wider philosophical task to elaborate a hermeneutics of the self. These later works repeatedly refer to Merleau-Ponty's notion of the "I can" from *Phenomenology of Perception* (PP 137). Following Merleau-Ponty, Ricoeur refers to the "I can" as a *fait primitif* (primitive fact) (OA 101–11).[9] This fact refers to the body's essential characteristic, namely, its motility or the fact that the body can effect action. It is because we act that we become conscious, temporalize ourselves, and experience the consequences of our actions as freedom or constraint. Without this essential characteristic, Ricoeur's "petite ethics" in *Oneself as Another* would fail since action is the linchpin to the ethical triple thematic of describing, narrating, and prescribing (OA 20). In paying homage to Merleau-Ponty shortly after his death, Ricoeur spoke so movingly about how Merleau-Ponty linked perception, action, and moral behavior together, something that Ricoeur would attempt to achieve over the next 40 years.[10] While one could argue that Ricoeur already had a theory of action premised in his very early *Philosophy of the Will,* the Merleau-Pontyean perspective, noted above, motivated Ricoeur in that early work.

It is perhaps important at this juncture to make some general comments about Ricoeur's larger philosophical project to make clearer the vital link he sees between human action, narrative, and time. Taken as a whole, Ricoeur's philosophical trajectory has sometimes been referred to as hermeneutical anthropology, or, more generally, as philosophical anthropology. This project should not be confused with classical anthropology and its concern with "man." Ricoeur's entire philosophical career, rather, has been devoted to revealing the limits of the capable person (*homo capax*), that is, to giving an account of our human capacity to act and to assume responsibility for those actions.[11]

In the 1950s, Ricoeur began his anthropology by studying human action in the tradition of existential phenomenology. This was followed by a methodological shift that demanded a delicate grafting of phenomenological description with the hermeneutic tradition.[12] The study of hermeneutics argues that knowledge and self-knowledge are not immediate to us. Knowledge does not originate in consciousness. None of us can grasp our own acting or existing except by interpreting the signs, texts, symbols, institutions, and monuments scattered in the world about us that objectify existence and mediate it. It is the case, rather, that we are born into a nebula of meaning that is already there in a prephilosophical manner much in the same way that each of us is placed in a language that exists outside of ourselves before we possess our individual selves consciously. For Ricoeur, there is no understanding, especially self-understanding "that is not *mediated* by signs, symbols, and texts" such that "in the final analysis self-understanding coincides with the interpretation of the mediating terms" (FT 15).

Unless one steps back from any one particular theme in Ricoeur, it is easy to lose sight of the link he forges between action, language, and, ultimately, time. Let us take each one in order.

In *Oneself as Another,* Ricoeur elaborates on how action can be understood philosophically in three modes. It can be described, which is the task of the human sciences and Anglo-American theories of action. Action can also be more informally and poetically narrated which gives rise to our vast archives of literature. Lastly, human action can be imputed with value and judged as good or bad. Description, narration, and prescription clearly describe the web of relations that must be determined to understand how we come to view practical actions as potentially ethical ones, that is, how we move from talking about human action in the practical field to speaking as moral agents in the ethical field (OA 20, 152).[13]

Thus, description, narration, and prescription are three modes of language that give action a certain intelligibility. Ricoeur's anthropology finds its originality here, at the intersection of the problem of language and the problem of action. He will describe the *mélange* of problems in bringing all these modes together under the phrase "poetics of action." The term poetics is borrowed from Aristotle. For Ricoeur it denotes the creative act of configuration that is in fact a creative reconstruction of experience in a literary mode. Such reconstructions have two important tasks. First, each configuration helps us to orient ourselves in the world. We need to formulate various schemes (religious, political, ethical, philosophical, scientific, etc.) to get a hold on the world and to live as human beings in it. Second, no one scheme is reducible to an unalterably static program. Rather, the creative aspect of configurations of all sorts is driven by the interplay of imagination and language. Thanks to our creative capacity to plot and to metaphorically restate experience, we are prepared to look at our humanity and its limits in new ways (RR 84).

What changes for us in this interplay of imagination and language is our way of dwelling in the world. Each composition, or configuration, offers a new way to orient ourselves in how we understand the world. In this way, texts of many kinds are heuristic, that is, they have the capacity to open and unfold new dimensions of reality by means of inviting us, the reader, to suspend belief in an earlier description (FT 175). It is in understanding this typically human activity, of imagination's intrusion into our linguistic formulations, that Ricoeur can say we discover reality in the process of being created. Said in other terms, we never live a world of one interpretation but, more pragmatically, we live in a world where conflicts of interpretations abound on almost every subject. The positive aspect of this insight is that we begin to see reality in terms of potentialities and not in terms of actualities. "When language is itself in the process of becoming once more potential it is attuned to this dimension of reality which is itself unfinished and in the making" (RR 462). In light of Ricoeur's overall anthropology, action and language come together in this "poetic" dimension as a disclosure of the "not yet" and of the "possible" (RR 490).

To bring in the theme of time, it is important to realize that many forms of communication have one element in common. They attempt to take our heterogeneous experiences and make them intelligible to those around us. There is no one standard formula for expressing experience. Under the auspices of metaphor and imagination, we constantly invent novel ways of saying "what is," "what happened," and "who did that?" As will be reiterated many times, our novel attempts at expressing ourselves — at giving shape to our experience — issue from what Ricoeur calls "one vast poetic sphere." This sphere is driven by the combined forces of imagination, metaphorical utterance and narrative emplotment applied to the constraints provided by grammar and past meanings sedimented in the various texts of our cultural archives.

Yet, this sphere would be meaningless without our prior immersion in the action of life and hence, the felt passage of time. *Time's meaning is never found ready-made in our experience.* Rather, to organize the experience of our actions into expressions is to simultaneously organize our experience of time because action takes place in time. To recall Ricoeur's thesis, "My chief concern in this analysis is to discover how the act of *raconter*, of telling a story, can transmute *natural* time into a specifically *human* time, irreducible to mathematical, chronological 'clock time'. How is narrativity, as the construction or deconstruction of paradigms of story-telling, a perpetual search for new ways of expressing human time, a production or creation of meaning? That is my question" (RR 463).

We should not misconstrue the subtlety behind this formulation. Narrativity is not just a static mode of language being applied to human action in order to distil something called "time." Ricoeur's claim is broader and speaks to the creative nature of language to transform readers and speakers into seeing the world anew. Not only does time become human when articulated through a narrative mode, but, more radically, narrative itself only attains its full meaning when it becomes a condition of temporal experience (TN1 52). In other words, the link between narrativity and time, underpinned by human action, is not arbitrary but necessary. This link gives rise to what Ricoeur calls a hermeneutic circle, something which will be discussed shortly as the "circle of mimesis." Narrative and temporality, he will argue, have a reciprocal relationship similar to how Wittgenstein understood a language game and a form of life. For Ricoeur, temporality is the structure of existence that reaches language in narrativity, and narrativity is the language structure that has time as its ultimate referent.[14]

Until the appearance of *Time and Narrative,* Ricoeur had published nothing on time outside of his treatment of history. By his own admission, "I was able to write on time only once I had perceived a meaningful connection between 'narrative function' and 'the human experience of time.'"[15] To elaborate more finely this intricate connection between action, narration, and time, Ricoeur will speak in terms of configurations or the formal mechanics of narrative composition. It is to this topic that we now turn.

FORMAL ASPECTS OF NARRATIVE COMPOSITION

Ricoeur opens *Time and Narrative* with a clash of themes: Augustine's experience of time and Aristotle's discussion of composition in the *Poetics.* Where Augustine groaned under the existential burden of discordance in temporal experience, Aristotle discerned in the poetic act — the composing of the tragic poem — the triumph of concordance over discordance in the human ability to construct a plot from disparate human events. While Augustine was oblivious to how the construction of textual meditations gave meaning and structure to his battle with time, Aristotle was incognizant of the relationship between poetic activity and human temporal experience.

This clash lays the groundwork for Ricoeur's lengthy reply to the aporetics of time. By interpenetrating Augustine's struggle with temporal experience and how Aristotle describes poetic construction, Ricoeur sets the stage for showing how the construction of plots and narratives is "the privileged means by which we reconfigure our confused, unformed, and at the limit mute temporal experience" (TN1 xi). He thus moves away from more traditional strategies that ask the "what" of time to inquire how our experience of time is embedded in the textuality of our existence. Unlike Bergson and Merleau-Ponty, his move does not provide a speculative resolution to the inscrutability of time. Without suppressing either mortal time or cosmic time, Ricoeur's tactic will preserve the paradox of time and pursue a "poetic" resolution to the aporetics of temporality (TN3 4).

Ricoeur employs the term 'poetics' throughout his many works and the themes he covers. It is drawn from his understanding of what Aristotle meant by the art of *poiesis* in his discussion of tragedy in the *Poetics*.[16] Poetics (*poiesis*), as such, is the art of composing plots (47a2). It entails two dynamic processes — *muthos* and *mimesis* — that are elemental in any verbal composition that produces a story, a fable, or a narrative with a plot. Where *muthos* has been translated as fable, or plot, such a translation lacks — Ricoeur argues — the active sense of putting-into-the-form-of-a-plot rather than of plot. For this reason, Ricoeur always speaks of *muthos* as emplotment. Emplotment is the *active* organization or arrangement of events and actions recounted which makes the story or fable a whole with a beginning, middle, and end (50a15). It is the actual activity of organizing the events into a system — complementary to how we use the verb "to compose." In the meantime, the aim of the plot is *mimesis* — the imitation or representation of human action. Formally, *mimesis* is the active process of imitating or representing something, but not the mere copying of reality. *Mimesis* is not simply reduplication but a creative reconstruction (RR 134; HS 292). In following the model of a tragic play, for example, we are made to look at human beings, and indeed ourselves, "in a new way because human action is redescribed as greater, nobler, than actual life is" (RR 84). Like poetic figures in metaphor, the configuration of a narrative suspends reference to the actual world in order to refigure it in a more meaningful manner.

Vital in both definitions, Ricoeur stresses, is the dynamism of the adjective "poetic"; there is no static assemblage of parts in composing a poem or narrative but a real "art of composition." As Ricoeur states, "I shall speak in defence of the primacy of our narrative understanding, in relation to explanation (sociological or otherwise) in history and explanation (structural or otherwise) in narrative fiction, I shall be defending the primacy of the activity that produces plots in relation to every sort of static structure, achronological paradigm, or temporal invariant" (TN1 33).

The vital middle term between emplotment and mimesis is human action (*praxis*). This is action as the object of expression (*mimesis praxeos*) and is the correlate of the mimetic activity governed by the organization of the events into a system. Said in other terms, *praxis* is, to some degree, the noematic (signified) correlate of a practical noesis (signifier); action here is "the construct" of that construction that the mimetic activity consists of (TN1 35). Ricoeur clarifies what is essential to this three-way dialogue when he points out that if the stress is put on organization, then imitation or representation has to be of action and not human beings. In other words, "action takes precedence over the characters. It is the universalizing of the plot that universalizes the characters, even when they have specific names. Whence the precept: first conceive the plot, then add the names" (TN1 41).

Ricoeur takes these key terms and works through their usage in the already constituted genres of tragedy, comedy, and epic as understood by Aristotle. It is Ricoeur's intention to "lift out" the *muthos-mimesis* pair and extract from Aristotle's *Poetics* a model of emplotment and extend it to every composition called narrative. Why? He never ceases to remind his readers that, despite the disparate topics he may be discussing, his touchstone is time. Emplotment is what we do in order to organize our ordinary experience of time into meaningful wholes. Time can be organized into meaningful wholes because we act and suffer in time. To the degree we understand how we plot our acting and our suffering into stories, we will understand how the ordinary experience of time, borne by daily acting and suffering, is refashioned by its passage through the grid of narrative.

To uncover this intimate relationship between time and narrative, Ricoeur seeks to establish a mediating role for emplotment (the text) by situating it between the stage of practical experience that precedes it (events, actions, situations) and a stage that succeeds it (the eruption of meaning and the potential to act differently based on the reading of the text). To achieve this, the mimetic activity is differentiated into three moments, namely mimesis$_1$, mimesis$_2$, and mimesis$_3$ of which mimesis$_2$ is the most important. The role of mimesis$_2$ is one of mediation; it is to conduct us from one side of the text to another, transfiguring one side into the other through its power of configuration.

Ricoeur's adventure, therefore, is to bring to the foreground the *narrative arc,* that is, the complicated entanglement of operations by which practical experience finds itself provided with works, authors, and readers that mediate the experience and potentially endow it with new meaning.[17] He wants to unveil the concrete process by which textual *configuration* (text) mediates between the *prefiguration* of the practical field (action) and its *refiguration* through the reception of the work (reader). Ricoeur's aim is not a mere repetition of Aristotle but what Aristotle did not address — the central importance of emplotment in dealing with the human experience of time. In short, Ricoeur wants to show that there exists a necessary connection between the activity of telling a story and our ability to give time, and, hence, human existence, meaning. Let us look closer at the three mimetic modes.

Prefiguration: Mimesis$_1$

Mimesis$_1$ is the entire set of presuppositions required for the possibility of any kind of narrative at all. The possibility of emplotment, of constructing a story, is rooted in our preunderstanding of the world of practical action. This preunderstanding is threefold — structural, symbolic, and temporal. Firstly, human life is unlike that of an animal or the existence of a mineral. Humans, rather, possess a "semantics of action." "We understand what action and passion are in virtue of our ability to utilize in a meaningful way the entire network of expressions and concepts which the natural languages supply us with in order to distinguish 'action' from simple physical 'movement' and from psycho-physiological 'behavior.' Similarly, we understand the meaning of project, goal, means, circumstances, and so on" (RR 433). Ricoeur emphasizes that our familiarity with the conceptual network of human action is of the same order as the acquaintance we have with the plots of the stories we know and tell. The same intelligence that guides the concepts of action (and passion) operates in the composition and narration of the story: "to understand a story is to understand both the language of 'doing something' and the cultural tradition from which proceeds the typology of plots" (TN1 57).

Another anchor point which the narrative proposition finds in practical understanding resides in the symbolic resources of the practical realm. Actions can be narrated because they are articulated in signs, rules, and norms; that is, human actions are always mediated symbolically. Given the descriptive context, we are always able to interpret a given gesture as having one meaning or another. A fling of the arm, for example, means different things in different contexts. Actions are always internally interpreted by symbols; that is to say symbolism confers on actions a first readability. This readability, however, is perhaps where narrative and life find their greatest interpenetration because this readability is not anonymous activity — someone must flesh out the action into a story, a narrative, an epic that is their life; this readability is not a projection of literature on life but a demand for a story (RR 434–35).

The third presupposition of narrativity is a grasp of the temporal character of action. Action in our daily lives is always temporally ordered in the sense we can never do everything possible at once. This gives way to the vast amount of temporal adverbs with which we describe our actions: *then, after, later, before, since, until, while, during, each time that, now that,* and so forth.

Configuration: Mimesis₂

Mimesis$_2$ is the ordering of events or the dynamic activity of emplotment (*muthos*). It is the narrative activity proper. This mimetic function lies between the two other functions because Ricoeur wants to understand its mediating role between what precedes narrative and what follows it. To understand what is important about the mediating role, we must look specifically at how a plot is mediating. First, it draws a meaningful story from a diversity of events or incidents and transforms them into a story (TN1 65). It is the pivot between action events and story. This is not just the enumeration of events in serial order; it is the creative and dynamic organization of an intelligible whole. Emplotment brings together the heterogeneous factors of agents, ends, means, interactions, circumstances, and unexpected results. By often incorporating pitiable and fearful incidents, sudden reversals, recognitions, and violent effects within the plot, the plot can be understood as a configuring act. It is the epitome of concordant discordance. "To make up a plot is already to make the intelligible spring from the accidental, the universal from the singular, the necessary or the probable from the episodic" (TN1 41).

The plot is mediating in a second manner through its temporal characteristics. The operation of emplotment engenders a paradox of time in that it combines in variable proportions two temporal dimensions, the episodic dimension (chronological) and the configurational dimension (nonchronological). Owing to the episodic dimension, events in narrative tend toward a linear representation of time in structuring the "then" and "and then" in order to answer the question "What next?" This allows a reader or listener to follow a story "in the midst of contingencies and peripeteia under the guidance of an expectation" (TN1 66). Such a dimension permits an open-ended series of "then" and "and then" while excluding what is not cogent to the dramatic whole. Moreover, episodes tend to follow one another in accordance with the irreversible order of time common to human and physical events.

The configurational dimension, on the other hand, elicits the pattern or plot from scattered events. This configurational arrangement that connects events into *significant* wholes is the correlate of the act of grouping together. The emphasis on "significant" points out the necessity of some reflective act that translates the plot into one "thought," which is nothing other than its "point" or "theme." Since judgement is involved, the configurational dimension displays temporal features that may be opposed to those of the episodic dimension because the correlation between thought and plot supersedes the "then" and "and then" of mere succession. This superseding of thought and plot is not the triumph of the a-chronological over the chronological. Rather, the time of the theme is the narrative time that mediates between the episodic aspect and the configurational aspect. Because configuration imposes a sense of ending on the open-endedness of succession, it constitutes an alternative to the representation of time according to the well-known metaphor of the arrow of time. "It is as though recollection inverted the so-called 'natural' order of time" (TN1 67).

Perhaps the most contentious element in Ricoeur's entire thesis lies here, in mimesis$_2$, with its emphasis on "synthesis of the heterogeneous" where "goals, causes, and chance are brought together within the temporal unity of a whole and complete action" (TN1 ix). In drawing manifold events into a unity of one temporal whole, the notions of "grasping together" and extracting a configuration from a succession are much akin to what Kant calls judging in his Transcendental Logic, where judging consists in placing an intuitive manifold under the rule of a concept (TN1 66). The trouble is that Kant understood this to be a transcendental operation and for him the transcendental dimension is atemporal. This raises the question of whether or not Ricoeur's thesis is itself grounded in an atemporal transcendental operation.

The answer, of course, would be yes if Ricoeur were proposing a speculative solution to time using a type of rationality based on foundations. Ricoeur's advance is, however, a hermeneutical one (postfoundationalist) with "poetics" and imagination as its very center. Unlike Kant for whom imagination was a "mysterious force,"[18] for Ricoeur the creative element in imagination is not located in images but in the emergent meanings in our language (RR 318). Ricoeur distances himself from Kant's "depths of the human soul" or a "'scene' unfolding in some mental 'theatre' before the gaze of an internal 'spectator'" (FT 171). Ricoeur's entire take on imagination lies in the realm of human discourse.[19] He believes that it is more productive to relate imagination to an aspect of semantic innovation characteristic of the metaphorical use of language. In this way, imagination becomes studied more as method than content (FT 173).

In the introduction to *Time and Narrative,* Ricoeur states that metaphorical utterance and narrative discourse belong to "one vast poetic sphere" (TN1 xi). He contends that in studying the creative capacity of language, one discovers its ability to reveal various aspects of reality, including time. "Language in the making celebrates reality in the making" (RR 462). The nature of the relationship between language and reality and emergent meaning is encapsulated in the unique role of metaphor. It is our linguistic-tropic ability that permits an eruption of meaning in the wake of a mutual shattering between language and reality. "My conclusion is that the strategy of discourse implied in metaphorical language is neither to improve communication nor to insure univocity in argumentation, but to shatter and to increase our sense of reality by shattering and increasing our language . . . With metaphor we experience the metamorphosis of both language and reality" (RR 85). The same sense of innovation that drives metaphorical utterances is present in narrative constructions where temporal unity is created out of a diversity of goals, causes, characters, and events. In other words, narrative and metaphor are vehicles through which imagination works. It is by looking closely at both metaphor and narrative creation that "human creativity is to be discerned and to be circumscribed within forms that make it accessible to analysis" (FT 8). As such, the labour of imagination is neither born from nothing nor atemporal. It is, rather, continually deployed between the two poles of servile application and calculated deviation within a linguistic tradition. Ricoeur has not overlooked or forgotten the temporality of the configurational act, the creative act of configuration is first and foremost a linguistic activity that engenders its own verbal time.[20]

Refiguration: Mimesis₃

Mimesis₃ completes the narrative arc and comprises "the crucial moment of the entire analysis" (TN1 75). It is concerned with the relation between the text and the reader. Ricoeur is adamant in arguing that the process of composition, of configuration, does not realize itself in the text but in the reader, and under this condition configuration makes possible reconfiguration of a life by way of the narrative. A text for Ricoeur is not an entity closed in upon itself. He unequivocally rejects the static and closed conception of a text that opposes an "inside" and "outside" as two unrelated states of the work (TN1 33, 76). A text is the projection of a new universe, different from the one in which we live. Appropriating a work through reading is to unfold the implicit horizon of the world which embraces the action, the personages, and the events of the story told.

The result is that the reader belongs to both the experiential horizon of the work imaginatively and the horizon of his or her action concretely. This results in the often-quoted "fusion of horizons" that Ricoeur repeatedly invokes from the thought of H.-G. Gadamer.[21] As such, the act of reading becomes the crucial moment of the entire analysis. On this act rests the ability of the story to transfigure the experience of the reader. To follow a story is to reactualize the act of configuration that gave rise to it. Readers interpret in the text the proposing of a world that they may enter and project their own-most powers. As such, composing a narrative resignifies the world in its temporal dimension, to the extent that narrating, telling, reciting is "to remake action" following the work's invitation (TN1 81). In other words, human praxis, as it is ordered by this or that plot of a text, offers us a possibility — a refiguration of a previous configuration of the temporal features in which action took place.

This refigured time is often referred to by Ricoeur as either "narrated time" or "human time." In figuring action, time is given shape, a voice, or face. Time as such becomes historicized. It is given a human dimension. This is the very disruption or intrusion into cosmic time referred to in the introduction where the distinction was drawn between "time given" and "time as giving." In the configuration of action, time's passage becomes the recognizable birth, life, and death of someone in which both tragedy and triumph might occur. It is the time wherein the search for meaning erupts and the demand to recall the past and to anticipate the future takes on force in a human lifetime. As we shall see, *narrated time is the historical present of someone.* As human life becomes narrativized and read, the possibility to act and to think differently arises.

The "fusion of horizons" offers the reader or listener the opportunity to refigure his or her motives, actions, and ends. To recall Ricoeur's central aim: "How is narrativity, as the construction or deconstruction of paradigms of storytelling, a perpetual search for new ways of expressing human time, a production or creation of meaning? That is my question" (RR 463).

As such, while preserving the paradoxes of time, the text, seen as one particular configuration of time, almost becomes a set of instructions that the individual reader or the reading public executes in a passive or creative way (TN1 77). It is only in this light that we understand Ricoeur's thesis as a "poetic" solution to how we reckon with time as opposed to the multiplications of befuddlements that have plagued previous "speculative" studies of time in the past. This means that by telling stories and writing history we provide "shape" to what remains chaotic, obscure, and mute in our lived experience. What he suggests is at work here in shaping our configured time is something akin to productive imagination.

A privileged role is given to metaphor and narrative in the works of Ricoeur because in both cases innovation is produced in the milieu of language, and reveals something about the imagination. Throughout *Time and Narrative* Ricoeur constantly reminds us that the production of the configurational act of narrative is comparable to the work of the productive imagination as formulated by Kant in his first *Critique*. This is not a psychologizing faculty but a transcendental one. It is the productive imagination as a synthetic function that schematizes the categories of understanding. It is not only rule-governed but constitutes the generative matrix of rules. It therefore stands at the intersection of understanding and intuition and engenders syntheses that are intellectual and intuitive at the same time. Moreover, this schematism is constituted within a history that is bounded by tradition. The labor of imagination, Ricoeur reports, is not born from nothing. It is bound in one way or another to the tradition's paradigms. Narrative configuration is imaginatively deployed between the two poles of servile application and calculated deviation to this tradition (TN1 ix–x, 68–70).

Ricoeur's discussion of the narrative arc is not an attempt to demonstrate that narrative alone can impose a reliable order (concordance) to the discord of human events, or that narrative is superior to the often contradictory musings of philosophers about the nature of time. Nor does Ricoeur believe that narrative ways of emplotting time take precedence over linear or cosmological methods of delineation. He is least of all interested in hypostatizing time. Rather, the discussion is only a prelude to Ricoeur's larger hermeneutical aim, namely, the role of narration in human understanding, especially our understanding of time. But the hermeneutical importance of narration can only be uncovered if all forms of narrative are implicated. This means showing that all narrative activity (historical and fictional) *jointly* provide not only "models of" but "models for" creatively articulating in a symbolic way our experience of time. This is why Ricoeur will expend enormous effort in *Time and Narrative* addressing the intentional modes of history and fiction on their own terms and together. He is interested in portraying the complexities that are involved in the interactions of these various modes that can never capture or control the entities they depict. Foremost as a hermeneutist, he is interested in showing that only interpretation can deepen our appreciation of these complexities since "the hermeneutic circle of narrative and time never stops being reborn from the circle that the stages of *mimesis* form" (TN1 76).

Only by bringing to light the role of narrative in both historical and fictive expression can Ricoeur implicate narrative *per se,* as the poetic solution to the aporetics of time. This is a daunting task because the referential relationship between text and world is complicated by the truth-claims between historical works and works of fiction. Unless Ricoeur can show that both historical narration and fiction, at some point, do not exclude each other in adequately accounting for the "reality of the past," he will be unable to sustain his claim for the pervasive ability of the narrative function *in general* to refigure the temporal experience of the reader. It is to this larger discussion we now turn.

HISTORICAL TIME

The Techniques of History

The existential import of Ricoeur's central aporia of time centers on the brevity of human life in comparison to the immensity of time. On a cosmic scale our lives seem insignificant, yet it is within this brief span of time that all meaningful questions arise. Herein lies the source of so much human misery and angst. This great disproportion drives both artist and scientist alike to distraction over the questions of life, time, and purpose. As mortals, our destiny seems condemned to consciousness of this fissure between the cosmic span of time and the limited existential duration of a mortal life. To contend with the impossible as best we can, we throw a bridge across the chasm which separates cosmic time from lived time. Ricoeur calls this bridge historical time. Such a time is the *tertium quid*, or third time, where, by means of certain procedures, we are able to negotiate, ever so imprecisely, some form of mediation between mortal time and the immensity of cosmic time. Historical time is the space where human beings use connectors — including the calendar, succession of generations, archives, documents, and traces — to inscribe lived time on the time that escapes us (astronomical time, biological time, etc.). Of these connectors, I will detail calendars and the trace.

Calendars. The time of the calendar for Ricoeur is an important one since it was the first bridge constructed by historical practice between lived time and universal time (TN3 105). It is a creation that does not stem from either of these perspectives on time. What makes calendar time a third form of time between limited human time and cosmic time is its universal constitution. As Benveniste notes, "In every form of human culture and in every epoch, we find one method or another that attempts to objectify time. This is a necessary condition for societies, and for individuals in society. This social time is the time of the calendar."[22]

The computation of this chronicle time for calendars has three necessary common features: a) identification of a founding event such as the birth of Jesus or Buddha, which acts as an axial moment or a zero point to which every other event is dated; b) this axial moment allowing our own life to be part of events that our vision passes over in going from the past to the present and vice versa, thus allowing every event the possibility of being dated; c) the determination, usually through astronomy, of a set of units of measurement that serve to designate the constant intervals between the recurrence of cosmic phenomena (TN3 106).

In these three distinctive features, we recognize the explicit relationship to physical time as well as the implicit borrowings from lived time. At the core, however, we recognize the borrowing that occurs between the phenomenological notion of the present and the idea of an instant in general, derived from the segmentable character of physical time and its definition as a uniform, linear, and infinite continuum. If the phenomenological notion of the present were absent, the present, as the "today" in terms of which there is a "tomorrow" and a "yesterday," could not be differentiated, thereby negating the idea of a new event that breaks with the previous era and inaugurating a course of events wholly different from what preceded it. There is simply no present as long as some instant is not determined as "now" or "today." Here we see the necessity for instituting some notion of habit and memory in every discussion of phenomenological time. As Augustine so well described, measurement is grafted onto experience as the shortening or lengthening of memory; Husserl returns to this theme with the help of metaphors such as falling away, flowing, and receding, which convey the qualitative differences between near and far away.

The one abiding necessity, nonetheless, for the real institution of the present is that someone must speak. The present is indicated by the coincidence between an event and the discourse that states it. To rejoin lived time starting from chronicle time, therefore, we have to pass through linguistic time, which refers to discourse. Any date, no matter how explicit or complete, cannot be said to be future or past if we do not know the date of the utterance that pronounces it (TN3 109).

In short, calendar time remains external to either physical time or lived time and expresses the specificity of chronicle time in its mediating role between these two other times on the lexical plane. A calendar must be seen as the neutral instrument that cosmologizes lived time and humanizes cosmic time thereby opening up the possibility of reinscribing the time of narrative into the time of the world.

The Trace. The notion of a trace constitutes, for Ricoeur, a new connector between time perspectives that a phenomenological understanding of time originally dissociates. What is so special about a trace?

To outline his answer, Ricoeur begins with a discussion of archives. An archive has an institutional character that produces, gathers, and conserves documents. The institutional element ensures that any deposit made becomes an "authorized deposit." However, if archives can be said to be instituted, and their documents are collected and conserved, this is so on the basis of the presupposition that the past has left a trace, which has become the monuments and documents that bear witness to the past. But what does it mean "to leave a trace?"

The notion of a trace can be linked to a "vestige" that a human being or an animal has left on the place where it passed. More generally, it is any mark left by a thing. What is important to note is that something is "left behind." This however engenders the paradox that, on the one hand, this trace is visible here and now as a vestige or mark and, on the other hand, there is a trace (or track) because "earlier" a human being or animal passed this way. Something did something and there remains evidence of that action. The trace indicates the passage of time from an action to our evidence of that action. Subsequently, the trace invites us to follow something back to another point in time. The trace orients the hunt, the quest, the search, or the inquiry (TN3 120).

As such, the significance of the trace consists in our being able to effect the mediation between the *no-longer* of the passage and the *still* of the mark. The trace forces us to recognize that the past is never something over and done with in a negative sense. As a present remnant, the trace demands we deal with what no longer exits — people, institutions, actions, or passions.

The trace as a present mark standing for an absent past was not well established in Heidegger's ontology of Dasein. While Heidegger recognized that "remains, monuments, and records that are still pre-sent-at-hand, are *possible* 'material' for the concrete disclosure of the Dasein which has-been-there,"[23] he failed to elaborate that it is only the operations proper to the historian's practice relative to monuments and documents that contribute to forming the notion of "the Dasein which has-been-there." There is simply no other way for *Dasein* to interpret its having-been-there if not by relying on the autonomy of marks left by the passage of former humans.

> This bringing about of the convergence of a purely phenomenological notion with historiographical procedures, all of which can be referred to the act of following or retracing a trace, can only be carried out within the framework of a historical time that is neither a fragment of stellar time nor a simple aggrandizement of the communal dimensions of the time or personal memory; this is a hybrid time, issuing from the confluence of two perspectives on time — the phenomenological perspective and that of ordinary time, to use Heideggarian terminology. If, however, we are to give equal rights to the time of Care and to universal time, we have to renounce seeing in the latter a "leveling off" of the least authentic forms of temporality. (TN3 122)

Heidegger's failure to understand the phenomenon of the trace, Ricoeur argues, reflects the failure of *Sein und Zeit* "to give an account of the time of the world which has no care for our care" (RR 346). It is only in the trace that we see the necessity of dealing with time within heterogeneous temporal orders. The trace is akin to the inscription of lived time upon astronomical time, from which calendar time comes, and it also kindles the founding of lived time on biological time from which the sequence of generations come.

In terms of the aporetics of temporality, the trace is key. It opens a space between the existential and empirical elements of our sense of time where these elements can overlap and converge. First, to follow a trace is a way of reckoning with time. Following back a trace requires that time be calculated and dated. We have to situate the search in an already established grid of chronicled time. Second, in retracing a trace we put into relief the "stretching-along" of time. The trajectory of the passage, like the tracing of the trace, is relentlessly linear.

Last, the trace, visible to everyone, projects our preoccupation with its origins and significance into a public time that makes our private durations commensurate with one another on the existential level (TN3 124).

This overlapping of the existential "now" and the empirical passage of time is for Ricoeur the opening up of *historical time;* it is only reflecting on this overlapping of temporal orders that we see a specifically new order of time emerge. It is here, in the historical present, that the problem of the trace arises and puts before us its demand for signification and interpretative understanding. In this mode of time, human discourse is a fundamental prerequisite, and narration, from the strict viewpoint of the narrative formation of discourse, makes an appearance. A trace forces us to speak of the past. To recount the past is to narrate it. By every act of recounting, of narration, the trace is given a voice.

Reality and Writing History

The presence of traces of various types (documents and material evidences of all sorts) signals a dividing line between history and fiction. Unlike fictional novels, the account given by historians purports to be a "true" recounting of the past. The role of narrative is contentious in twentieth century historiography. Positivist philosophers of history argue that a causal explanation of past events should model itself on the causal explanation employed in science. The implication is that to capture the past, a rigorous level of discourse is called for, one asymmetrical to any narrative mode that would easily confuse the reality of the past with the unreality of fiction. Carl Hempel (1905–1997), for example, argued that historical explanations have a uniformity to them that make them subject to general covering laws.

Ricoeur takes issue with such nomological models, reminding historians that even in their most truculent desire to forensically recount the past, that they too employ something of a narrative competence. Emplotting a diverse set of incidents and events into a whole is not like fitting numerals into the variables of an algebraic equation. Such events as the Hundred Year War or the American Revolution are rarely depicted well by just the chronology of events. While there is certainly a logic at work as a historian tries to piece together the various "facts" to render a coherent and truthful account of the events, Ricoeur suggests this "logic" is really a form of narrative understanding (TN1 93; 159; 228). Such understanding does not operate on the basis of laws but utilizes what above was summarized as the episodic and configurational dimension of emplotment.

At the heart of the matter, a historian emplots actions and events in order for them to be followed discursively by a reader. To follow a historical account is the same as following a story where we are pulled forward by "the sequence of actions and experiences done or undergone by a certain number of people, real or imaginary" (TN1 150). To be sure, history, while tied to narrative, is more than just a story. There is naturally the demand for evidence, argument, and proof. "It is for this reason that historians are not simply narrators: they give reasons why they consider a particular factor rather than some other to be the sufficient cause of a given course of events" (TN1 186). In short, it is taken for granted that historians refer to something "real" because the "having-been" about which they write was observable to witnesses in the past. The difficulty is that "having-been" is never observable in the present; it is only memorable. To overcome the enigma, Ricoeur elaborates the concept of standing-for or taking-the-place-of, signifying by this that the constructions of history are intended to be *re*constructions answering the need for a *Gegenüber (vis-à-vis)* (TN3 143).[24] For Ricoeur, the past is the *Gegenüber* to which historical knowledge tries to correspond in an appropriate manner. This prime category, however, of standing-for or taking-the-place-of, is ultimately irreducible to the category of reference as it functions in an observational language and in an extensional logic. This is confirmed by the fundamentally dialectical structure of the category of standing-for as it is employed in historical writing.

To explain this dialectical structure in historical writing, Ricoeur employs the Platonic categories of the Same, the Other, and the Analogue. Under the sign of the Same, Ricoeur groups those historians whose historical aim is defined by "reenactment" — the reeffectuation of the past in the present to the point that reenactment is numerically identical with what is initially thought. Under the sign of the Other, Ricoeur places the variants of what he calls "a negative ontology of the past" (TN3 147). Such historians take for their model of the past the alien consciousness, and the model for understanding of the past is the need to enter into such a foreign consciousness. Common to both historical endeavors is the reduction of, or forgetting of, temporal distance; both schools try to reenter the historical past on abstract models that are fully detemporalized.

As a counter, Ricoeur prefers to place the pastness of the past under the sign of the Analogue. Here, initial thinking to describe the past starts from thinking "*Wie es eigentlich gewesen.*" What is important is the metaphorical value of the *wie; as* this was, in fact. To say *what* things were *as*, is to *see* them *as*. In other words, if we are going to take seriously historians' claims that they describe "the past as it actually happened," then one cannot fail to make note of the metaphorical *as*. To say what things were *as* is to see them *as* — much in the same way a metaphor encourages "seeing as." In other words, tropology becomes a very important historical tool in attempts to prefigure the quotient of standing-for. The function of the Analogous is not really a counter to the Same and the Other. All three relations ultimately act together as a tropological filter to the reality of the past. It is only when we see the correlation between the "being-as" of the past event, correlative to the "seeing as" in which the work of metaphor on the plane of language may be summed up, that the reality of the past is brought to language (TN3 147–55).

In short, to grasp what "really" happened in the past, the historian must first *pre*figure *as* a possible object of knowledge the whole set of events reported by the documents. The point of this poetic function, much like creating a "tropological map of consciousness," is to outline possible itineraries within the historical field to give shape to what must be known (TN3 153). In short, history as iconography figures the past *as* it had been, with direct emphasis on the oblique *as*. Description is really redescription. In order to give shape to what can be known about the past, a historian makes something of a model or an icon of the past in order to represent it.

Historical writing cannot be taken lightly because the historian, often privileged to documentary proof, has a debt to the past, that is, to all those who have suffered and died (TN3 143). In fact, the art of historical reference is animated by this indebtedness. But this debt is never paid by a mere enumeration of facts or some form of genealogy. Here, the historical fact must elicit the assistance of imagination if the debt is to be adequately paid. In a moving description, Ricoeur states that

> when the expression of our debt to the dead takes on the colour of indignation, of lamentation, or compassion, the reconstruction of the past needs the help of imagination that can place it "right before our eyes," according to a very striking expression of Aristotle in speaking of metaphor. I would like to mention here those horrible events which we must not forget. It is true that there is something like an individuation in the horrible as well as in the admirable. Help with this comes from no where more than from the quasi-intuitivity of the imaginary. Fiction gives eyes to the horrified narrator. Eyes to bear witness as much as to weep. The present state of the Holocaust literature verifies this. (RR 353)

In bringing both metaphor and imagination into the historical mix, Ricoeur argues that despite this sense of indebtedness and allegiance to any number of traces, a historian's narrative is still a creative imitation. Inventing and discovering become indistinguishable as both become underwritten by the productive imagination. This is evident in those great historical works whose reliability may have been eroded by documentary progress and advances in research, but remain valuable in the tastefulness of their poetic art with regard to their way of "seeing the past." One and the same work can thus be a great book of history and a fine novel. To be sure, the interlacing of fiction and history in no way undercuts the project of "standing-for" belonging to history but instead helps to realize it (TN3 186).

FICTIONAL NARRATIVE

Reality and Reading the Two Worlds

In the same way Ricoeur challenged the contention that history only deals with "the reality of the past," he equally challenges the naïve concept of "unreality" applied to the projections of fiction. The function of standing-for or of taking-the-place-of is paralleled in fiction by being poignantly revealing and transforming (TN3 158). Fiction is revealing in the sense that it brings features into the foreground that were concealed and yet already sketched out at the heart of our experience, our praxis. It is transforming in the sense that *a life examined* in this way is a changed life, another life.

There are two key points to understanding this revelation and transformation and Ricoeur's entire approach to fiction. First, there is his hermeneutical prejudice that a text cannot be reduced to a closed system of immanent relations. The text always points to an "outside," that is, it has reference. The referential world Ricoeur refers to "is the whole set of references opened by every sort of descriptive or poetic text I have read, interpreted, and loved" (TN3 80). Prior to his study of time and narrative, Ricoeur wrote extensively on the problem of discourse as an event of meaning and reference, especially with regard to texts. Under the terms "distanciation" and "appropriation," he showed how the interpretation of a text ends in a reinterpretation or reevaluation of events and purposes on behalf of the reader. This was premised on the more poignant argument that self-knowledge is borne through reflection (strictly opposed to immediate self-consciousness in the Cartesian tradition) that is necessarily mediated by the various signs and works scattered in the cultural work.[25] "What a reader receives is not just the sense of the work, but through its sense, its reference, that is, the experience it brings to language and, in the last analysis, the world and temporality it unfolds in the face of this experience" (TN1 78–79).

Second, as already emphasized, reading is not a passive event. Texts of all types, including fictional narratives, are not necessarily mere forms of information and entertainment. Reading involves, as Ricoeur liked to refer to it, "an aesthetic of reception." The term aesthetic denotes the fact that a work acts on the reader and affects that reader. We have already encountered this interaction when discussing Mimesis$_3$ above. There is a synergetic relation between the world of the reader and the world of the text. The dialectic between the reader and the text is at once an interruption in the course of action (emplotting it) and a new impetus to action (on behalf of the reader). This dialectic results directly from the confrontation of the imaginary world of the text and the world of the reader. This confrontation takes place in a space of "indeterminacy" that opens up in three ways. First, the act of reading is a response to a strategy of deception which frustrates the expectation of an immediately intelligible configuration and gives readers the responsibility of configuring the work for themselves. Second, indeterminacy is a function of a work's surplus of meaning or polysemanticism. Every text is an inexhaustible mine of possible meaning. Last, the "right" reading of a text admits of a certain degree of illusion. The signals provided by the text "defamiliarize" the reader as the text "depragmatizes" itself from experience of the reader. The proper degree of illusion always remains on the fine line between the untenable and the irresistible (TN3 170).

Reading, hence, becomes a place, itself unreal, where reflection causes the reader to pause. In that pause it cannot be underestimated that "consciously and unconsciously" readers incorporate into their world the lessons of their reading. Reading, as such, is not a place where readers come to rest as much as it is a medium they pass through. In other words, what is considered by some to be "unreal" has the potential to move us into the realm of "the real." "To the extent that readers subordinate their expectations to those developed in the text, they themselves become unreal to a degree comparable to the unreality of the fictive world toward which they emigrate. . . . This fragile union can be expressed in the following paradox: the more readers become unreal in their reading, the more profound and far-reaching will be the work's influence on social reality" (TN3 179). The role of fiction for Ricoeur is something of shock treatment; it is to make reality problematic, demanding that readers see the world from the horizon presented by the story. In short terms, the world of the text and the world of the reader interpenetrate one another. Recalling mimesis$_3$, there is a "fusion of horizons" where the reader belongs to both the experiential horizon of the work imaginatively and the horizon of his or her own world concretely (TN1 77). As a fictional work suspends our belief in "the real," we are invited into a state of "non-engagement" where "we try new ideas, new values, new ways of being-in-the world" (RR 128). More broadly, our imagination is given to a free play of possibilities. Central to fictional writing is the mimetic activity of taking heterogeneous events, characters, and incidents and creating a whole. Narrative intelligence and the productive imagination work hand in hand in the creation and projection of "the world of the text." Fiction is not just fanciful literature but possesses the capability to shape the world of the reader. It offers configurations of acting and suffering that can be applied to actual human acting and suffering. "Fiction has the power to 'remake' reality and . . . to remake real praxis to the extent that the text intentionally aims at a horizon of new reality that we may call a world. It is this world of the text which intervenes in the world of action in order to give it a new configuration or, as we might say, in order to transfigure it" (FT 10).

But this ability of fiction to intervene and transfigure human experience is not devoid of all historiographical qualities. In the same way that history borrows aspects of fiction to recreate the past, fiction undergoes a certain "historization" in two senses. First, fiction deals with the "quasi-past" of actions "as if" they had taken place. Ricoeur sees events recounted in a fictional narrative as past facts for the narrative voice; it recounts what *for it* has taken place. Reading fiction demands a type of pact between the reader and narrative voice where the reader believes that the events related by the narrative voice belong to the past of that voice (TN3 190). Second, even though fiction is freed from documentary constraints and the need to work from historical traces of all sorts, it is nonetheless bound internally by the very thing it projects outside of itself. Creative freedom is a complex issue here. There is more to the liberation of fiction than just working outside the limitations of historical artefacts. Every writer attempts to express a vision or to articulate experiences of varying depth. "Free from . . . , artists must still make themselves free for . . ." the faithful expression of their deepest impressions. If this were not the case, Ricoeur asks, how could the anguish and suffering of artistic creation be explained as exemplified in the correspondence and diaries of a van Gogh or

Cezanne? The stringent law of creation, which is to render as perfectly as possible the vision of the world that inspires the artist, corresponds feature by feature to the debt of the historian and of the reader of history with respect to the dead (TN3 177).

The central paradox, however, is that the imaginative freedom of fiction can be communicated only by being cloaked in the constraining power of a particular vision of the world. The narrator's vision of the world is always caught in the tension of what is and what could be. The dialectic between freedom and constraint, internal to all creative processes, is thus transmitted throughout the hermeneutical process of reading mentioned above. It can be summarily characterized as *poiesis, aisthesis* and *catharsis*. The most important element here is catharsis and its complex set of effects. Catharsis sets the reader free for new evaluations that will take shape in reading. It engenders a process of allegorization which is an attempt to translate the meaning of a text in its first context into another context. "It is ultimately this allegorizing power, related to catharsis, that makes literary application the response most similar to the analogizing apprehension of the past in the dialectic of the *Gegenüber* and of indebtedness" (TN3 177).

Time in Fiction

But does fiction have the power to refigure our experience of time? The second volume of *Time and Narrative* is devoted to exploring how fiction plays imaginatively with the gap between cosmic time and mortal time. Like history, fiction is about human action in that narratives represent what human beings do. Unlike history, fiction suspends the constraints of documentary evidence and explores the various possibilities for a common temporal experience by playing with variations on different experiences of time.

> If these imaginative variations can be multiplied endlessly, it is because in the kingdom of fiction the specific constraints of historical knowledge have been suspended beforehand — this knowledge that is dependent upon the stringencies of calendar time, of the implacable replacement of the dead by the living, as a counterpart of this lifting of the restraint of reinscription, a greater freedom to explore the unexpressed modalities

of discordant-concordance or of the hierarchization of the levels of temporalization. The imaginary here *empowers* the common temporal experience, lightens the burden of the debt toward people of the past, and thus liberates in human acting and suffering the possibilities that were blocked or aborted. (RR 351)

In looking at authors where time is especially thematized, such as Virgina Woolf's *Mrs. Dalloway,* Thomas Mann's *The Magic Mountain,* and Marcel Proust's *Remembrance of Things Past,* Ricoeur argues that these "tales of time" do not so much solve the discontinuity of time as much as they sharpen it and make it productive. Such novels are poetic experimentations where truly human time is expressed: the works portray how living beings confront a discordance that lies at the heart of human existence. Fiction opens up "an unlimited career to the manifestations of time" and offers the reader a fictive experience of time that may very well lessen the paralyzing effect that such a discontinuity can have on our thinking about life and time. This is the very point of poetical solutions. We are presented with imaginative variations on the temporal experience of being-in-the-world proposed by the text. It constitutes what Ricoeur calls "a transcendence immanent in the text." Novels like those mentioned above have the potential to plunge the reader into a variety of temporal experiences "offering in each instance a different figure of recollection, of eternity in or out of time, and, . . . of the secret relation between eternity and death" (TN2 101). Given the mimetic arc noted above, each configuration of human time emplotted in a narrative is refigured in light of the reader's experiences. A narrative gives time a voice, or at least a shape, that helps us to render its passage more meaningful.

To show how a tale of time exacerbates an aporia, Ricoeur returns to the Husserlian "narrative" of temporal constitution. There we saw how a single temporal field is formed through the overlapping of the network of retentions and protentions stemming from the multiple quasi-presents into which recollection is transported. Is this a "real" discovery, Ricoeur asks, or perhaps an ideal solution that is just as contrived as any other tale of time? "What indeed do we mean when we state that a field of consciousness constitutes its unity through coincidence, if not that coincidence is the *eidos* under which phenomenological reflection places . . . the entire past in the comet-tail of the living present?" (TN3 139).

What Ricoeur suggests is that every phenomenological analysis that encounters an aporia in the beginning ends by covering it under an ideal resolution. In the various phenomenological treatises covered by Ricoeur and summarized in chapter one, we see the themes of "expansion of the present," memory, anticipation, and unity of constitution as *the* model for all the discordant concordances the different thinkers attempted to resolve. One can therefore move freely within the ideal resolutions posed from Augustine to Heidegger begging the question of whether or not we are just seeing so many ingenious variations of the same ideal type.

In terms of Augustine, for example, we saw the same "ideal" unity arise in regards to the recitation of a poem, as well as the unity of a vaster story extended to the dimensions of an entire life, and even to that of universal history. This is equally true in the case of Bergson and *la durée réelle* where the discordance between space and time dissolved under the concordance of duration. Did we not see one level of unity in the "intuition of duration" extrapolate itself to find that same unity arise under the title of "consciousness," and even later under "life?" Similarly, in regards to Merleau-Ponty, the discordance between scientific time and subjective time melded into "phenomenal time" with the continual assertion that we are only the continual "upsurge of time."

This same *eidos* of unity as an imaginative variation is found just as clearly in Heidegger's *Being and Time.* One only has to look at the second division of this work to see how many times the lacerating question of Being-a-whole (*Ganzsein*) arises. This demand for Being-a-whole is threatened by the potential for dispersion expressed by the ecstatic structure of temporality. This is why the conditions for authentic Being-a-whole, for truly primordial totalization, are perhaps never satisfied. While hermeneutic phenomenology distinguishes itself from Husserlian intuitive phenomenology in that the most proximate remains the most hidden, is the application of such an ideal type no less an imaginative ploy to wrest the conditions for totalization from their concealment?

HISTORICAL CONSCIOUSNESS

At this point the intersection of the two modes becomes a little clearer. Fiction seems to be as much quasi-historical as history is quasi-fictive. History is quasi-fictive once the quasi-presence of events are placed "before the eyes of" the readers by a lively narrative that supplements the elusive character of the past and assumes the responsibility for "standing-for." Fictional narrative is quasi-historical to the extent that the unreal events that it relates are past facts for the narrative voice that addresses itself to the reader. Equally important to remember is that both modes employ the universal character of emplotment that forges a "temporal synthesis of the heterogeneous" events that make up a plot or history.

Hence, in having dulled the sharp division between the "reality" of the historical past and the "unreality" of fictive narration, Ricoeur is now ready to ask the vital question: can the intentional aims of history and fiction be thought together as the poetic solution to the aporetics of time?[26] Is narrative time the place where historical time and the imaginative variations of fictional time meet to mediate between mortal time and the immensity of cosmic time?

In the end, both forms of narrative help us to give shape to and humanize the enigma of time. If we interweave the two, the result is what Ricoeur calls the historical present — the proper present, the authentic present to humankind. No one is born without being implicated in one story or another (be it the story of family, community, culture, nation, or religion). Each of us belongs to an entanglement or "living imbrication" of stories (TN1 75). This imbrication or enmeshment is a "pre-history" that binds every other story into a background or a tradition. The historical present is a hinge-point between accepting this background in a precritical manner and acquiring a historical consciousness. It is in the historical present that the past comes alive in that each member of a community, each storyteller, borrows from the past, and works with it toward the future.

The historical present, therefore, is neither the experience of a particular chronological moment nor a particular moment of invention and inspiration. Such a time is not presence but the moment of initiative. It is the time when the weight of history that has already been made and deposited is interrupted — awakened — by decision and action in the present (TN3 208). The verb "to begin" expresses the historical present better than all substantial forms, including presence. "To begin" is to be aware that the world is not fully actualized and that now is the moment *for me* to act. This historical present is the axial point where history both ends and begins — where initiative demands the making of history. It is within this consciousness that one realizes that the "established facts of history" are never irrevocably established. For Ricoeur, the future has priority over the past and the past in turn is never complete. It always remains unfinished so that its real efficacy lies in its indetermination and reinterpretation.

If we see tradition as the accumulation of stories that do not necessarily bestow an invariant form of knowledge on us, then we must accept the hermeneutical challenge that what history offers us is "a chain of interpretations and reinterpretations" (TN3 222). Knowledge of the past is not one of "mastery over" but always "being-affected." History is always "effective history" to the degree that we see that every expression of hope and expectation in the present reopens the past. For Ricoeur, we are never finished being-affected-by-the-past and in this sense, history should humble our pretensions in the present. We are not the creators of our world *ex nihilo*. "The hermeneutical approach shifts the problematic from the sphere of knowledge into that of being-affected by, that is, into the sphere of what we have not made" (TN3 228).

The historical present, as the touchstone of a hermeneutics of historical consciousness, is an attitude toward existence that does not blindly embrace a tradition but attempts to reconcile humanity to its tasks and challenges. Ricoeur's entire take on narrative has been to show how text and action interpenetrate one another. The situation of the reader is always influential. In *Oneself as Another,* the major work that follows *Time and Narrative,* Ricoeur talks about human agency. He is very clear that human agents, holding certain configurations of political and ethical beliefs are often compelled to change institutions and practices — not texts. In this sense, the debt of historians to remember and to account for the suffering and the victims of the past belongs to all of us. The power to listen, to speak, to read, and to act is the energy that drives our personal initiatives and interventions in the present on behalf of the past. Nonetheless, it is the narrative mode and the connection between the mimetic arc and human action that permits a subtle analysis of those momentous but complicated steps by which human beings encounter and transform a tradition.

NARRATIVE IDENTITY

The Narrating Self

Where Ricoeur opened *Time and Narrative* with the hermeneutical circle of narrative and temporality, he will close the work by unequivocally stating that "narrative identity" is the poetic resolution to the circle.[27] So important is this theme that Ricoeur says it "crowns" his analysis (TN3 305, n. 8; 321, n. 13).

The notion of "narrative identity" is a response to a query Ricoeur poses to himself, namely, whether there is *a fundamental experience* capable of integrating the two great classes of narrative — history and fiction — and how to apply this experience to self-understanding: "do we not consider human lives to be more readable when they have been interpreted in terms of stories that people tell about them? And are not these stories in turn made more intelligible when the narrative models of plots — borrowed from history or from fiction (drama or novel) — are applied to them? It therefore seems plausible to take the following chain of assertions as valid: self-understanding is an interpretation; interpretation of the self, in turn, finds in the narrative, among other signs and symbols, a privileged form of mediation; the latter borrows from history as well as from fiction, making a life story a fictional history or . . . a historical fiction" (OA 114, n. 1).

To make sense of these assertions, it must be recalled that the art of narrative lies in the construction of plots, the ability to take discordant events, characters, and histories and tie them together into a coherent temporal whole. The byproduct of creating such a whole is that the experience of time takes on a human shape with layers and shades of meaning that demand interpretation. But what has been left unanswered until now is the question of "who" time is meaningful for. "Who tells their story of tragedy, of hope?" "Who acts and suffers and fears not to tell his or her story?" In asking "who," a particular narrative category is recognized, namely, that of character. The source-point for any narrative is that someone once upon a time acted and that his or her actions found themselves emplotted and a particular meaning arose. It is Ricoeur's contention that in the same way, to reach the self, we must travel from actions through narrative to self, and accept a form of embeddedness in one tradition or another. It is only in the telling of our individual stories over time that a durable character becomes recognizable as belonging to a certain family, place, tradition, culture. The character that arises finds him or herself enmeshed in a complex web of prior stories that make up the narrative heritage of a community, nation, or race. One might say that our identities, in passing through the grid of narrative in order to give our lives readability, become like a text. And here we are returned to the virulent mix between the world of the reader and the world of the text.

The significance of a story finds its springboard of change in what the reader brings to it. The world of the text and the world of the reader interpenetrate one another as a "fusion of horizons." A text can break open the narrowed and hard categories that define the world of the reader, presenting possible levels of meaning not previously perceived. As we learned above concerning an aesthetics of reception in reading, a text invites us into zones of indetermination and the layers of meaning embodied in it. Each unity of awareness (time, meaning, self, morality, etc.) embodied by the reader and sifted through the horizon of the text becomes open for refiguration. Refiguration constitutes the "active reorganization of our being-in-the-world performed by the reader following the invitation of the text to become the reader of oneself."[28] Emplotting human actions and reading them through other accounts are not efforts to solve a riddle or accumulate a compilation of fixed facts. The stories we tell about ourselves are mediums that I, the reader, must pass through in search of an answer to the elusive question of "who am I?" The narrative function underpins what I can know about myself. It is the basis for "narrative identity."

Narrative identity is not some permanently subsisting substance (*idem*) but a reinterpreting identity (*ipse*) whose narrative is never a *fait accompli* (TN3 246). Unlike an egological identity based on an immutable substance, self-constancy of the narrative self will include change and mutability within the cohesion of one lifetime. The narrative identity is at once, therefore, the reader and quasi-writer of his or her own life — a life which is woven and refigured through a tissue of narrated stories (TN3 246). It is only in telling their stories that subjects recognize themselves. To reply to the interrogative "who?" is to tell one's story to the other.

Narrative identity is not a stable and seamless identity. Just as it is possible to compose several plots based on the same incident, it is just as possible to tell different, even opposed, plots about our lives. As the historical component of the narrative draws the plot toward a chronicled documentary fragment, the fictional component, with its imaginative variations tends to destabilize the narrative identity. "In this sense, narrative identity continues to make and unmake itself" (TN3 249). It becomes, in a certain way, as much a problem as a solution. Echoed in Augustine's query about time and its explanation we hear a similar query about narrative identity. What is the self? Surely I know what it is as long as you don't ask me to explain it, but if you should ask, I will tell you a story!

Queries about time and the self issue from the same voice. The two voices must echo one another because as sure as a self endures temporal passage, it must dignify its existence in taking up narratives that will become for it an actual history. Caught, therefore, between the time of our mortal bodies and the infinity of the cosmos, we find a meaning in the plot that unfolds as our own historical narrative finds various interpretations and refigured horizons in what we read and hear. In our reading and listening, the plot thickens, thereby allowing us to continually reestimate and reevaluate our actions, allegiances, beliefs, hopes, fears, joys, miseries, and desires.[29]

As such, neither mortal time nor cosmic time is destroyed, eliminated, or denied. As a narrator "glances back" over a particular history and hears the histories of others, a referential horizon is scanned that reckons with a present time that is unique and authentic to the person narrating. Two examples make the point clear. First, there is a strong narrative component in the "working through" (*Durcharbeitung*) process of a psychoanalytical experience. The possibility of a cure resides in the hope of substituting a coherent and acceptable story for the fragments of memories and facts that are unintelligible as well as unbearable. If we accept the premise that subjects recognize themselves in the stories they tell about themselves, then in psychoanalysis the story of one's life comes to be constituted through a series of rectifications applied to previous narratives. A second example is the close fit of identity and history based on the founding patriarchal narratives of biblical Israel. Here, in a communal sense, we see how, in the telling of narratives taken to be testimony about the founding events of its history, biblical Israel became the historical community called the Jewish people (TN3 248).

At this point we should perhaps clarify the stronger distinction being made in regard to narration. Where someone like Émile Benveniste expertly argues for the way language configures a place for the subject through grammatical forms such as personal pronouns and adverbs of location, absent in his linguistic account is the historical nature of the subject's identity.[30] For Ricoeur, on the other hand, while the self is inseparable from the life-story that it can narrate about itself through language, the self is more than what is depicted in the laws of language. In a work that followed *Time and Narrative* and centers narrative identity in his larger project of a hermeneutics of the self, Ricoeur makes this distinction quite clear: "To say *self* is not to say *I*. The *I* is posited — or is deposed. The self is implied reflexively in the operations, the analysis of which precedes the return toward this self. Upon this dialectic of analysis and reflection is grafted that of *idem* and *ipse*" (OA 18).

Identity as Idem *and* Ipse

The themes of *idem* and *ipse* are two concepts of identity. Together they become the conceptual frame within which Ricoeur intends to test the validity of and further flesh out the significance of narrative identity. Identity as sameness (Latin *idem*, French *mêmeté*, German *gliech*) and identity as self (Latin *ipse*, French *soi*, German *selbst*) are not equivalent in meaning even though they intend to designate the same entity. Neither of them alone captures the essence of narrative identity but in their overlap we see the uniqueness of a storied identity arise (OA 116).[31] We now follow Ricoeur's path to this intersection.

Identity-as-sameness (*idem*) concerns the problem of spatiotemporal selfsameness. It has traditionally been based on some recognizable substance through time. There are normally four possible criteria to define identity-as-sameness. First, numerical identity is when two occurrences of a thing are designated by the very same term in ordinary language. The opposite of such an identity would be a plurality. Second, qualitative identity arises in the case where two items are identical in appearance such that they can be mutually substituted. The opposite of qualitative identity would be difference. Third, identity through developmental change is the uninterrupted continuity of a being between the first and last stages of its evolution. The opposite of this identity would be discontinuity. Last, positing some principle of permanence through time is where we look for an invariable structure unaffected by time. This last criterion is irreducible to the first three; it is categorically different in that its opposite would not imply plurality, difference, and discontinuity *in the moment* but, rather, diversity over time. This dissymmetry in the determination of identity arises because the notion of uniqueness, threading the first three criteria together, does not thematically imply time. All problems of personal identity turn around this search for a relational invariant, giving a strong signification to permanence in time (OA 118).

Ipseity (*ipse*), on the other hand, implies the capacity of an agent to initiate an imputable action. It is not reducible to the determination of a substrate or invariant. The point of deployment of the notion of ipseity is searched for in the nature of the question where the self constitutes a response or a plurality of responses; this question is the question of *who* as opposed to *what*. It is because we begin with human action, searching for the agent and author of action, that we ask *who* does this or that? We call *ascription* the assignation of an agent to an action. By it, we attest that certain actions are the possession of those who perform them; that an action is someone and that it properly belongs to him or her. Onto this act, neutral from a moral point of view, is grafted an imputation which invests an explicitly moral signification in the sense that it implies accusation, pardon or acquittal, blame or praise — in short, an estimation of the "good" or the "just."

Ricoeur discusses the intersection of these two concepts of identity, elaborating on the link between what we mean when we remark about the "character" of a person and the ability of that character to keep his or her word or a promise.

> When we speak of ourselves, we in fact have available to us two models of permanence in time which can be summed up in two expressions that are at once descriptive and emblematic: *character* and *keeping one's word*. In both of these, we easily recognize a permanence which we say belongs to us. My hypothesis is that the polarity of these two models of permanence with respect to persons results from the fact that the permanence of character expresses the almost complete mutual overlapping of the problematic of *idem* and *ipse*, while faithfulness to oneself in keeping one's word marks the extreme gap between the permanence of the self and that of the same and so attests fully to the irreducibility of the two problematics one to the other. ... the polarity I am going to examine suggests an intervention of narrative identity in the conceptual constitution of personal identity in the manner of a specific mediator between the pole of character, where *idem* and *ipse* tend to coincide, and the pole of self maintenance, where selfhood frees itself from sameness. (OA 118–19)

Character for Ricoeur represents the stable pole of sameness. It is the ensemble of durable dispositions that have undergone innovation and sedimentation in the acquisition of habits that yields the constancy of what permits us to recognize that person as particularly that person. It answers the "what" of the "who" (OA 122). Unlike character, however, keeping one's word falls entirely into the dimension of "who?" Where the continuity of character over time is one thing, the constancy of friendship and enduring faithfulness are quite another. To keep one's word is a challenge to time and to the denial of changes to mood and feelings under the self-imposed cry of "I will hold firm" and "I am accountable for my actions to another." Self-constancy is essentially an ethical pole. It is the manner of one's behavior such that another can count on me. If someone is depending on me, I am accountable for my actions before that person. The term responsibility reunites the two significations that arise between "to depend on" and "to be accountable for." It unites them in adding the idea *of a response* to the question, "where are you?" which is posed by the other and to which I must respond. This response will be, "here I am!" — a response which indicates self-constancy. In keeping one's word the "who I am" is maintained regardless of change, yet it is not dependent on the criteria of sameness found in character (OA 124). The promise to keep one's word is fidelity to self linked to the presence of the other and not reducible to a form of *idem*-identity.

In opposing the sameness of character with the constancy of the self in a promise, a hiatus or a conflict of sense erupts that cannot be assuaged by choosing for either side. The conflict at hand is temporal, namely, which of two models of permanence in time — the perseverance of character or self-constancy in a promise — best addresses identity? For Ricoeur, the answer is to seek a mediation in the sphere of temporality. The likely candidate that mediates the interval is narrative identity. This type of identity oscillates between two limits, a lower one where the permanence in time expresses the confusion of *idem* and *ipse,* and an upper one, where the *ipse* poses the question of its identity without the assistance and support of *idem* (OA 124). It is little wonder that Ricoeur often refers to this form of self as "fragile" and that it is as much a problem as a solution: it flies in the face of what is commonly understood as "self," that is, a self-subsisting prelinguistic entity that exists behind our actions. This conventional prejudice of self is evident every time we employ such phrases as "I think," "I run," and "I read." This conventional prejudice assumes that somehow the self is ready-made prior to his or her actions and that the self is immediately given to itself by means of some transparent introspective intuition. Such prejudices are heavy with the Cartesian myth that the relation of self to self is nonproblematic. Yet the postmodern schools of hermeneutical phenomenology and poststructuralism rail against this traditional but naïve prejudice.

LIFE AND MEANING

In subsequent works to *Time and Narrative* already quoted, Ricoeur universalizes the role of narrative, making it fundamental to the emergence and reality of the self. "If it is true that fiction cannot be completed other than life, and that life can not be understood other than through stories we tell about it, then we are led to say that a life examined, in the sense borrowed from Socrates, is a life narrated" (RR 435). But what exactly is a life *narrated* and how is it meaningful? The question is crucial since we normally understand life as lived, not told.

Ricoeur puts a lot of emphasis on what he called mimesis$_1$, the prenarrative structure of experience. He argues that our pre-expressed and pre-thematic experience is already an implicit or quasi-narrative. In all of life's activity, we seem to understand how events and actions hang together. In applying a "semantics of action" to the multifarious incidents that we endure, there seems to be a precomprehension of how to emplot action in order to make it meaningful. Actions are made meaningful by the symbolic systems that mediate them. Every one of life's transactions is an incipient story. Indeed, Ricoeur argues, life is "*an activity and a desire in search of a narrative*" (RR 435). Under the auspices of a narrative intelligibility, this desire finds us taking incidents from the active flow of our life and creatively imitating them — turning the untold into the told assisted by what has already been told. This is how we derive meaning from the ceaseless parade of joyous occasions, chance situations, emergencies, and other affairs of a lifetime. Surfacing from this desire to narrate, there exists the equally constructive "attempt to recover (rather than impose from without) the narrative identity that constitutes us" (RR 436). It is here that we can begin to talk about the worked-up conscious narratives that ennoble our historical and biographical archives and become potential models for future readers to make sense of their own lives.

Moreover, life would never be more than a biological phenomenon if we did not attempt to interpret the events that make it up. Thanks to the surplus of meaning that overflows from the symbolic systems that mediate experience, there is "always *more* order in what we narrate than in what we have actually already lived" (RR 468). This order is further reinforced by the fact we are born into traditions that themselves have been built up from a plethora of epics, tragedies, dramas, and novels. This storehouse of narrative competence is "always already" there, often acting as a master narrative and providing us with patterns, schemes, genres, and myths in order to emplot our lives and therefore give shape to our identity. In the end, Ricoeur contends, we become our own narrator without becoming authors and assume the identity of a fictive *persona*.

> In this sense, it is certainly true that life is lived and the story told. An unbridgeable distinction remains, but it is, in part, abolished through our capacity to appropriate in the application to ourselves the intrigues we received from our culture, and our capacity of thus experimenting with the various roles that the favorite personae assume in the stories we love best. And so we try to gain by means of imaginative variation of our ego a narrative understanding of ourselves, the only kind of understanding that escapes the pseudo-alternatives of pure change and absolute identity. (RR 437)

Presently, authors from the various disciplines of philosophy, psychology, and literary criticism as well, argue for a notion of the human subject that takes acts of self-narration as fundamental to the emergence and reality of the self.[32] The central argument is that self-knowledge is ultimately a form of self-narration and that self-narration is an interpretative act. Each of us is involved in taking up the quasi-narrative structure of our experience and making it our own in a more explicit fashion — sometimes willingly, sometimes not. The argument is that the narrative function is not the reserved art of poets, dramatists, and novelists for mere entertainment. Narrative form is neither disguise nor decoration. Rather, it is the case that "we dream in narrative, daydream in narrative, remember, anticipate, hope, despair, behave, doubt, plan, revise, criticize, gossip, learn, hate, and love by narrative."[33] In this respect, one is always telling stories about oneself, not necessarily in a self-consciously autobiographical way; ultimately the unity of an individual life does not escape the necessity of a unifying narrative that underpins a single life.

To be clear, narrative identity is always spawned in the traditions of the historical present. To recall, the historical present is the axial point where history ends and begins. It is "an open-ended, incomplete, imperfect mediation, namely, the network of interweaving perspectives of the expectation of the future, the reception of the past, and the experience of the present, with no *Aufhebung* into a totality where reason in history and its reality would coincide" (TN3 207). This is precisely the present where narrative identity finds itself on the cusp of initiative — that is, the time when the weight of history that has already been made is deposited, suspended, and interrupted, and when the dream of history yet to be made is transposed into a responsible decision (TN3 208). Thus time, *per se*, is refigured within the human dimension of history.

It is therefore in the historical present, that is, in the duration of my lifetime and yours that the task of meaning lies. For Ricoeur, meaning is never given directly to consciousness. He is famous for his argument that immediate consciousness is always a false consciousness.[34] Any self-understanding and meaning is a form of recovery accomplished by the deciphering of and reflection upon the signs, symbols, and discourses deposited and scattered in the spatiotemporal world. Any constitution of the self, therefore, is contemporaneous with the constitution of meaning (HS 158). In this dual task, narration is the privileged mediation among all signs and symbols.[35]

Meaning, to be sure, is never invented or discovered in an absolute sense. In the course of time, it is always emerging. Meaning is a hermeneutical task. It is situated in the middle of a conversation that always *belongs* to a historical tradition where we find ourselves already in conversation with institutions, social roles, and communities (groups, classes, nations, races, etc.). Finding ourselves always already "belong-ing" undermines any pretensions we may have to absolute knowledge. One might say in a Ricoeurian fashion, that we appropriate and recover self and meaning one text at a time. We understand ourselves because what we appropriate from texts is a proposed world. The proposed world is not behind the text like some hidden intention but in front of it, as something the work reveals. "Henceforth, to understand is to under-stand oneself in front of the text" (HS 143). The reader, however, does not project him or herself but is invited to follow "the 'arrow' of mean-ing and endeavours to 'think in accordance with' it, [and] engenders a new *self*-understanding" (HS 193). The result is not something that becomes monolithic, static, and unchangeable. Rather, our sense of self and our actions involve us in an

> unending work of interpretation applied to action and to oneself [where] we pursue the search for adequation between what seems to us to be best with regard to our life as a whole and the preferential choices that govern our practices. . . . By the same token, our concept of self is greatly enriched by this relationship between interpretation of the text of action and self-interpretation. On the ethical plane, self-interpretation becomes self-esteem. In return, self-esteem follows the fate of inter-pretation. Like the latter, it provokes controversy, dispute, rivalry — in short, the conflict of interpretations — in the exercise of practical judgement. (OA 179)

Ricoeur's position does not simply advocate for each of us to become an essayist like Montaigne. The narrative nature of the self demands a double accountability. First, as I find my narrative voice and differen-tiate my story from its anonymous prehistory, I learn the full impact of the promises and covenants that I make in my name. The more fully I own my narrative voice, the more I realize the necessity for the other to tell the truth about her or himself. If there is no self to abide by its promises and covenants, ethical relations are impossible (TN3 249). Secondly, while Ricoeur might agree with Montaigne that the best way to find the self is to express it, Ricoeur goes further and accepts the hermeneutical task of understanding the formative narratives of the past as invaluable archives of human suffering, hope, and action. In this response to the past there is a refusal to accept the self as a mere heap of reified technique or commodified ideological illusion.[36] Rather, there is the ethical imperative for selves to tell their stories and encumber histories in order to hold one another accountable. "We tell stories because in the last analysis human lives need and merit being narrated. This remark takes on its full force when we refer to the necessity to save the history of the defeated and the lost. The whole history of suffering cries out for vengeance and calls for narrative" (TN1 75).

THE INSCRUTABILITY OF TIME

In the conclusions attached to the final volume of *Time and Narrative,* written one year after the final writing of the entire work, Ricoeur lists and discusses three aporias. They recapitulate in a more concise way the ones I listed and discussed in chapter one of this work. For the sake of an ending, I will briefly summarize these aporias. I say "for the sake of an ending" because it must be emphasized that narrative and the notion of narrative identity are not solutions to the aporias of time. The reply of narrativity to the aporias of time consists less in resolving these aporias than in putting them to work, in making them productive with regards to meaning. This is how thinking about history contributes to the refiguration of time. In recognizing these aporias we recognize not only the valid domain wherein narrativity can be effective but the limits that circumscribe this domain.

The first aporia of temporality, and the most visible in Ricoeur's view, is the occultation between phenomenological and cosmic time. Of all the aporias this is the one Ricoeur speaks to the most eloquently. The aporia reflects the conflict of knowing, from the cosmological tradition, that time surrounds us, envelops us, and dominates us without the soul, mind, or consciousness having the power to produce it. The essential character of this time is that change (movement) is its most primitive fact. Meanwhile the soul, mind, or consciousness, given the agency of its own distension, finds the presence of a present that is self-referential, attested to by the act of uttering a word. The very fact that we speak, therefore, makes each of us a "master of disruption" in light of the impersonal march of cosmic time. The spoken present, however, is not an anonymous one comparable to the simple succession of instants in physical time. This aporia is the sharp dichotomy between the time of the soul and the time of the world; the hiatus between the time which is fleeting and that which endures and remains. It is with this chasm that Ricoeur makes his clearest distinctions and where his notion of narrativity contributes most to what philosophical speculation separates.

The second aporia results from the dissociation among the three ecstases of time — the future, the past, and the present — regardless of the fact that time is conceived of as a collective singular. In other words, how do we explain our constant reference to the three ecstases of time and yet our overwhelming sense of time's totality and unity? Since Heidegger's phenomenological analysis failed to offer a response to this collectivity, Ricoeur's task was to see if the multiform unity of time would be rendered sensible and meaningful through the interplay of historical consciousness and narrative. His striking conclusion is that literary categories are ultimately inadequate to deal with what is at stake in thinking about history — inasmuch as there are multiple plots for the same course of events and they always get articulated in terms of fragmentary temporalities. For Ricoeur, the notion of plot gives preference to the plural at the expense of the collective singular in the refiguration of time. "There is no plot of all plots capable of equalling the idea of one humanity and one history" (TN3 259).

The last aporetic of temporality arises from the inability of our understanding of time to go beyond the bifurcation into phenomenology and cosmology and marks the limit to our ability to even "think" time. This last aporia comes into sharper relief when we realize that time, escaping any attempt to be constituted, "reveals itself as belonging to a constituted order always already presupposed by the work of constitution" (TN3 261). For this unresolvable question of origins Ricoeur defines time as inscrutable. Time's inscrutability, however, springs forth not so much from our failed thinking, but from our attempts to raise our thinking to posit itself as the master of meaning. Ricoeur notes that none of the conceptions of time in the authors he covered escaped being touched in one way or another by either the mark of an archaism or hermeticism. The thought of Aristotle and Augustine issue forth, for example, from two archaic currents, stemming from different sources — one Greek and one Hebraic—whose waters subsequently converged in Western thought. Meanwhile, the ideas of Kant, Husserl, and Heidegger face the charge of being hermetic by blindly seeking a time that surfaces in the course of analysis as an already presupposed ground.

As such, Ricoeur concludes, there is no reasonable escape from the disproportion between time that we deploy in living and the time that envelops us everywhere. His poetic resolution of the hermeneutical circle and the narrative function are not solutions to time but responses. But the mystery that time poses neither reduces to obscurantism nor prohibits language; it is rather an invitation "to think more and to speak differently" (TN3 274). It is a call, ultimately, with respect to the limits of an historical consciousness, for individuals and communities to search for their respective narrative identities.

Five

Creative Time

Time comes into it. / Say it. Say it. /
The universe is made of stories, not of atoms.
— Muriel Rukeyser, "The Speed of Darkness"

TIME AND SELF

This chapter consolidates the tripartite theme of time, self, and meaning by looking for the points of convergence and divergence throughout the thought of Bergson, Merleau-Ponty, and Ricoeur. The aim here is not to work toward a specific model but, rather, to understand how the three themes hold each other together in a bonded constellation centered around time.

As the chart below indicates, only in Ricoeur, under the ardour of narrative time, is any bifurcation of the self absent. This bifurcation of self in both Bergson and Merleau-Ponty is the result of their attempts to detail an authentic "human" time without reference to any time external to the human subject. Such analyses attempt to stretch, unfold, and distend as many levels of temporality as necessary in hopes of reaching, by way of approximation, that which temporality left behind and cannot produce, namely, the autonomy of time with respect to movement (cosmic time). What falls victim to this impossible task is a unified sense of identity. The self must continually be bifurcated to accommodate the internal disparity in time perspectives that erupts at the existential level. This problem can also be read backwards. In holding

	Time	Self	Meaning
Bergson	– durée réelle	– superficial self – profound self	– freedom
Merleau-Ponty	– phenomenal present	– phenomenal body – ambiguous self	– (freedom) – contingent
Ricoeur	– narrated or human time	– narrative self	– emergent within historical present

duration or the lived body as the source of time, the figures of temporality exclusive to the self become split or bifurcated. Hence, pure duration is understood in contrast to chronicle time, which it derides, just as phenomenal time is understood in contrast to empirical time, which it cannot produce.

In both the cases of Bergson and Merleau-Ponty, the result is not a mastery over the meaning of time, but the production of meaning at the level of world-time. We simply know more about ourselves in terms of freedom and the ambiguity of any meaning given their attempts to elucidate a specifically existential personal human time. For Ricoeur, Bergson, and Merleau-Ponty deepened the interpretative levels of time that can be described in any medium of narrative. This brings us back to the hermeneutical question of whose time we judge as the correct time of the self. For Ricoeur the answer is obvious — we must entertain the conflict of interpretations that will encourage the further production of meaning. The prize of a poetical solution to time through the auspices of narrative is our seemingly infinite creative capacity to generate meaning within the span of temporal finitude. This recognition is not theoretical as much as it is part of the wider historical consciousness that stands behind every writer in every generation who takes the initiative to explore and enlighten the mystery of our temporal passage.

The Present — The Link Between Time and Self

As we learned emphatically from Bergson, outside of clock-time, time is change. From Merleau-Ponty we learned that the lived body defies a strict dichotomy of the physical and the psychical, of change and non-change. Change can only be recognized from some point of "non-change." Meanwhile, Ricoeur taught us that to speak of change is to understand that there exists a narrator that can thematize the reality of change within a certain historical present. In the chain of natural causes, the only category totally peculiar to change is the temporal present of the self.

In Aristotle's *Physics,* the autonomy of time is dealt with in respect to movement. In light of *physis* and the need to protect the dimension of change from human interference, Aristotle concentrates on the anonymous "now" point, distinguishing the "before" and the "after," failing to recognize the necessity of a discriminating "soul" or a mediating functionary that employs the operations of perception, discrimination, and comparison.

While it is one thing to employ time for the measurement of motion, as Aristotle does, it is another thing to ask what precisely is being employed and to attempt its thematization. In reply to his plea, "What, then, is time?," Augustine recognizes the "present" as a fundamentally unique characteristic of human temporal existence. Human temporal observation occurs in the present, and the present is never simply instantaneous and anonymous. The anonymous "now" is temporalized when interrogated in the recognition of the present; that is, the present becomes the pivotal point (*intentio*) between a past (memory) and a future (anticipation). It was Augustine, perhaps more than anyone else, who first saw the necessity of accounting for the triple-present through some uniquely human capacity such as the *distentio animi.*

In trying to precisely delineate the human present, whether we take Augustine's triple-present, Husserl's "source-point" stretching protentively and retentively, Bergson's duration, or the present of Merleau-Ponty's phenomenal time, we see the same ideal in operation — the desire to distinguish a unifying principle that accounts for the temporal order in us as we stand in the midst of change or, as it has often been referred to by Ricoeur, a time that we did not effect. Whatever their designation, succession and change require a fixed point outside themselves as the basis for determining their order. At differing levels of discourse, this unifying principle may variously be referred to as a *distentio animi,* transcendental ego, durational consciousness, lived body, the self, *Dasein,* and narrative identity. Despite the radical differences in the origins of each of these terms, they aspire to one end — to find some original mediator between the course of lived experience (mortal time) and the order of the world (cosmic time); or, in other terms, they attempt to seek the optimum but always unkept balance of discord and concord between the two chains of time.

In the introduction, the terms "the present as giving" (lived experience) and the "given present" (cosmic time) highlight the vital necessity of a human being to "disrupt" the seemingly uniform and monotonous tyranny of cosmic time. In the case of Bergson, the experience of lived time as disruption is ordered internally from the material to the less material, from the extended to the least extended. Equally noticable in Merleau-Ponty is the constant distinction between natural or prepersonal time and personal time or time of the living self. Notably, in the cases of Bergson and Merleau-Ponty, an attempt to order temporal experience in contrast to world time always runs the risk of becoming an irreversible analysis. That is, while a phenomenological time may be established, this time cannot stand for the whole of time; hence, as Ricoeur so astutely asserted, phenomenological and ordinary time mutually occlude one another.

The decisive factor that divides, for example, both duration and phenomenal time from narrated time is the problem of origins: Bergson's notion of duration is an intuition of time and Merleau-Ponty's lived present is a presupposition. Neither is initiated by an instance of discourse. The danger of all such presumed times is their false universalization and subsequent ascent above the labor of history. On the other hand, for Ricoeur, the very notion of the present is defined by the instance of discourse that designates the present reflexively from whence a hold is taken in a tradition, and the problem of history cannot be transcended.

In short, time as mere change calls for its counterpoint. In the causal order of nature, the presence of a self *is* the intervention of the present. With the absence of a self, there would be no time as such. The self, as human attention to the present, creates time, wins time.

Therefore, with every assertion of the present there is the equal assertion of a self that lives that present. The self that is manifested in the assertion of the present depends on the notion of time employed. Bergson's superficial and profound selves are a result of duration's flight from matter and clock-time; Merleau-Ponty's ambiguous self surfaces from the tension of a phenomenal time that defies the dichotomy between objective or ordinary time and a purely subjective time. Meanwhile, Ricoeur's narrative identity develops from the worldliness of existence or human action *and* a textuality that manifests the meaning of action as oriented toward totality — a totality that has a narrative character. The narratives we tell about ourselves and one another always issue from a certain tradition manifested in a particular historical present that is both narratively configured and constantly open and enduring refiguration.

Yet, however stated by each of the three authors, in every case, time as change is probed more profoundly and the human experience of time as change is deepened and unfolded into so many "layers" of meaning. Whether the fundamental nature of the human experience of time begins in intuition, through a phenomenology of perception, or in narrative, the outcome can be summarized: *a notion of time begets a notion of the self which begets a notion of meaning that authenticates the self.*

Ricoeur and the Question of Meaning

Of all our themes, meaning is perhaps the most difficult to adequately breach. This discussion begins with Ricoeur because, of all our authors, his hermeneutical phenomenology has not been forged to refute one school of thought or another; rather, the central theme through his many works is to clarify both meaning and existence. In an earlier work, Ricoeur stated a philosophical agenda that found fruition in *Time and Narrative*. In "Existence and Hermeneutics," Ricoeur showed how it was possible to enter into the problem of existence through an ontology of understanding implied by the methodology of interpretation.[1] He explored this "truncated" ontology through a philosophical reflection on psychoanalysis. His aim in reflecting on this particular school of thought was twofold: first, to dismiss the classical problematic of the subject as consciousness; then, to restore the problem of desire as central to the question of meaning.

Ricoeur felt Freud vicariously challenged us to reevaluate the relationship between signification and desire, between meaning and energy, and, finally, between language and life. The result of Ricoeur's reflection is that existence becomes a type of continual "archaeology of the subject" where interpretation is the major tool. The path from interpretation to explanation becomes the key to deciphering the tricks of the desire at the root of meaning and reflection. Desire, however, cannot be hypostasized outside the process of interpretation; it always remains being-interpreted.[2]

The hermeneutical ground of the philosophical act is the prephilosophical experience. It starts with the questions that existence evokes. It reflects on the answers that have been given in a prephilosophical manner to these questions. Hence, in this sense, philosophy is never entirely original. Its source lies outside of itself, and it returns reflexively to this preunderstanding, in hopes of bringing to language the rationality and meaning that is implicit in it.

For Ricoeur, if life was not originally meaningful, understanding would be forever impossible. He takes it as his task to continually clarify the relationship between life as the bearer of meaning and the significance of meaning. Human existence for Ricoeur, therefore, is indeed meaningful to the point that despite the real existence of nonmeaning, necessity, and even evil, there is in existence a "super-abundance of meaning to the abundance of non-sense."[3] In conclusion to "Existence and Hermeneutics," Ricoeur writes, "It is the task of this hermeneutics to show that existence arrives at expression, at meaning, and at reflection only through the continual exegesis of all the significations that come to light in the world of culture. Existence becomes a self — human and adult — only by appropriating this meaning, which first resides 'outside,' in works, institutions, and cultural monuments in which the life of the spirit is objectified."[4] To a large degree Ricoeur has succeeded in formulating this theme of meaning in a nonmetaphysical fashion. This has been accomplished through his intensive research into textuality, history, metaphor, and interpretation theory.

We read in the preface to *Time and Narrative* that this voluminous work is in fact the twin of an earlier work entitled *The Rule of Metaphor*.[5] Starting from two different levels, both books converge on the topic of semantic innovation. In *The Rule of Metaphor* Ricoeur argued that in the destruction of literal meaning in a metaphor the possibility of new meaning arises. The innovation of metaphor lies in the production of new semantic pertinence through impertinent attribution, as in the phrase: "nature is a temple where living pillars . . ." (TN lxi). The poetic function of metaphor destroys its referential function by creating a new reference which describes and redescribes the world, or part of the world; it brings to language aspects, qualities, and values of reality that lack access to direct description and that can be spoken only by means of the complex interplay between the metaphorical utterance and the rule-governed transgression of the usual meanings of our words.

With narrative, on the other hand, semantic innovation lies in the invention of another work of synthesis — a plot. In the construction of a plot, goals, desires, intentions, events, causes, and chance are brought together within the temporal unity of a whole and complete action. It is this synthesis of the heterogeneous that brings narrative close to metaphor. "In both cases, the new thing — the yet unsaid, the unwritten — springs up in language. Here a living metaphor, that is, a new pertinence in the predication, there a feigned plot, that is, a new congruence in the organization of the events" (TN1 xi).

In the case of both metaphor and plot, the result is always the same. It is the possibility of saying or writing something new, that is, the surfacing of a new insight or meaning. Yet, the ultimate triumph is always a case of understanding something better.

> As a result, whether it be a question of metaphor or of plot, to explain more is to understand better. Understanding, in the first case, is grasping the dynamism in virtue of which a metaphorical utterance, a new semantic pertinence, emerges from the ruins of the semantic pertinence as it appears in a literal reading of the sentence. Understanding, in the second case, is grasping the operation that unifies into one whole and complete action the miscellany constituted by the circumstances, ends and means, initiatives and interactions, the reversals of fortune, and all the unintended consequences issuing from human action. (TN1 x)

In the end, for Ricoeur, metaphorical redescription and mimesis are closely bound up with each other, to the point that we can exchange the vocabularies and speak of the mimetic value of poetic discourse and the redescriptive power of narrative fiction. What Ricoeur purports to unfold before us is one vast poetic sphere that includes metaphorical utterance and narrative discourse in the continual production of meaning, of sense over non-sense.

What is the connection between meaning, narrated time, and storytelling? These connections are put into sharper relief by contrasting Ricoeur's ideas with another French thinker, namely Albert Camus (1913–1960). In his famous essay, *The Myth of Sisyphus,* Camus poignantly discusses how the impulse to seek meaning in irreducible diversity constitutes the absurdity of humankind's position. The dilemma of human existence stems from our insatiable desire to establish relations between phenomena, and ultimately to bring everything under one comprehensive system. This search for rational unity, however, is really a wish (*nostalgie*) to escape from uncertainty and contingency. But for Camus there is no escape. Our blunt awareness of time, of contingency and death, contrasted with the nostalgic hope of unity, purpose, and the eternal, condemn us to exist within the "walls of absurdity."[6] A philosophy of the absurd banishes hope as a form of escapism in this life. For Camus, therefore, temporal existence is a form of condemnation; time for *l'homme absurde* is devoid of a future and man is paralyzed by the fact that "he belongs to time, and by the horror that seizes him, he recognizes his worst enemy."[7] In other words, time is aporetic, a grand puzzlement in which we find ourselves without hope and meaning but under whose tutelage we must live stoically.

Yet, upon closer inspection, Camus's conclusions of absurdity in human existence belie a deep presupposition on how to account for meaning. They are the conclusions, in fact, of a disappointed idealist, based on his failure to attain certainty about meaning and personal identity.[8] When Camus asks about the purpose of life, he refuses any answer that attempts a "mere" interpretation. To avoid the conclusion of absurdity, Camus demands a brand of epistemological and metaphysical certainty reminiscent of Cartesian rationalism. Like most modern thinkers, he has something aptly criticized by Rorty, namely, a foundationalist concept of knowledge.[9] In short, since "true knowledge is impossible,"[10] absurdity reigns in Camus's world. Lacking certainty, it is easy to understand why the characters in his many novels gave in to despair — they are identities valued only as "knowing" beings, and once "knowing" is seen as uncertain, so is the knower's existence.

In the meantime, Ricoeur, who like Camus claims time is aporetic, does not find it to be absent of meaning; on the contrary, in hermeneutically uncovering the aporetics of time he believes there exists an excess of meaning. Meaning for Ricoeur is not a verifiable proposition but is tied to our ability *to seek meaning emergent in our interpretation of human experience,* which is the only meaning, as acting and speaking beings, to which we have access. Meaning is possible only as a hermeneutical task. Moreover, this task of understanding the self takes place within a cultural milieu that is a mixture of dominant and less dominant traditions that help to mediate this understanding. Undoubtedly, for Ricoeur, there is no aboriginal nucleus of the self that exists prior to its actions; the self arises and takes on existence as it acts, as it undergoes experiences. Crucial, therefore, to the emergent meaning that authenticates the self is time and the ability to bring the experience to language (narration), thereby giving the self both a reality and history.

If self is reduced to some form of substantialism — as defined, let's say, by Frondizi — then it easily becomes subjected to the laws of science and to ordinary time.[11] Its existence becomes observable data and its meaning defined by a particular interpretation of the structure of the natural world where both time and meaning are superfluous. Where time is merely a measure of magnitudes, meaning of the self falls to the mercy of a definition of natural entities found in the ideology of the historical tradition prevalent at the time when the question is raised.

However, disclaiming every appeal to some hidden or obscure substantial core, the narrative self that Ricoeur proposes depends upon what it does, has done, and proposes, or is able to do. His argument runs that without the function of narrative to tie all these latter requirements into a communicable story, the self would not exist as we know it. Narrative, therefore, is essential to the self in that it situates the self historically, rooting it in pregiven meaning, the fabric out of which the narrative self finds its own meaning. It is only within the historical present of narrated time that desire, as the root of meaning, can remain forever being-interpreted and be allowed to exert its full force through the excess of meaning in all human expression.

In volume 2 of *Time and Narrative,* Ricoeur details how fictive narration can play with the problem of time's unity, the theme of eternity, time's other, and the remythization of time by looking at the works of Virgina Woolf, Thomas Mann, and Marcel Proust (TN2 100ff.). Unlike Camus, Ricoeur cleverly shows how narrative variation offers a poetic solution of playing with and maintaining the aporias of both mortal and cosmic time, while preventing paralysis by either time. The narrative function offers the reader an opportunity to reveal covered-over traits operative in experience — experiences that can be transformed by the narrator in search of meaning to a lifetime.

At stake here ontologically is the realization that what we prejudicially call "the real" comes to resemble and depend on the fictive in so far as we recognize the same elements in play (time, imagination, tradition, emplotment) in the telling of our lives. In stating that narrative is the privileged medium of self-understanding, the very concept of an unchanging and immutable self which lays claim to ontological and epistemological priority becomes decentered. Apodictic certainty, consciousness as representation, and knowledge as correspondence are set aside in favor of the chronicle which emerges from our ability to coherently connect — and thus imbue with meaning — otherwise heterogeneous and disparate events. Knowing, meaning, and self become hermeneutical exercises that aim at consensus rather than the recovery of presupposed actualities. But to be sure, time has the upper hand. Narrative understanding does not cheat death and the finiteness of our biological existence. It does allow us, however, a choice of how we choose to signify temporal passage and find each of our lives meaningful. In this sense, there is something highly democratizing about narrative understanding and its role in ethical and political theory.[12]

BERGSON AND RICOEUR

Duration, The Profound Self, and Meaning

For both Bergson and Ricoeur, clock-time is derived for practical purposes. On the other hand, the duration of Bergson and the narrated or human time of Ricoeur are both expressions of temporal being original to the self that endures. Both of these times have no currency or relevance outside the human self. For Ricoeur, human or narrated time finds its genesis at the confluence of human finitude and language. It is discourse as narrative that offers the possibility to refigure time, thereby easing the paralysis caused by the aporias of both mortal and cosmic time. In Ricoeur's thesis, human time is engendered when selves as narrators begin to narrate their story and continue to do so. In Bergson's perspective, time as duration is by its very nature human because it is only through a conscious being that duration, "life," consciousness, and freedom find their fullest manifestation and greatest distinction from matter.

However, there are sharper and deeper distinctions to be made. Can we not say that Bergson's *durée réelle* is a temporality of consciousness which attempts to uncover pure inner experience, while Ricoeur's narrated time is a temporality of disclosedness that attempts to uncover meaning in its chaotic and disordered emergence?

Where the human time in Ricoeur's thesis erupts within the aporias he has intentionally set for himself in hopes of avoiding a mere intuition of time, Bergson's *durée* wants to overcome all aporias and is a direct but silent intuition of time. In fact, intuition lies at the very heart of Bergson's philosophy and his core *ur*-intuition — duration — begets all else that is to follow, namely the self and meaning. This is encapsulated in his already quoted phrase: "There is one reality, at least, which we shall seize from within, by intuition and not by simple analysis. It is our own personality in its flowing through time — our self which endures" (CM 162).

We know that "the one reality" of Bergson means the qualitative, heterogeneous, and unextended flow of inner life. This one reality represents both time as duration and the self as *le moi profonde*. The intuition of a specifically human time is therefore pregnant with an intuition of the self. But is there really a one-to-one correlation between time and self?

As already mentioned, some would argue that it is impossible to make a claim about the existence of the self without making reference, at least to some extent, to its constitutive nature.[13] The genius of Bergson in the late nineteenth century was to dramatically oppose the positivism of his era and to claim there is form of time specifically human and empirically unverifiable. The only grounds for this claim, however, are an intuition and some well organized presuppositions about the reality of time over that of space. The result is that time as duration becomes the ultimate constituent of the self. The profound self is the self where duration is felt to flow uninhibitedly; it is the self that acts freely and recovers possession of itself by getting back into pure duration. In fact, there is little error in stating that duration *is* the profound self and vice-versa.

Duration is really a temporality of the inner self, of consciousness. Its entire existence is based on its contradistinction from matter and the work of science. Duration is described as "pure change" not so much to idealize it but to make sure that it stands in the sharpest distinction to ordinary linear time as the measurement of local motions in discrete instances. The distinctions between duration and clock-time, between the superficial and profound self, issue from the heart of temporal experience, producing a hierarchy of levels of temporalization according to how close or how far a given experience approaches or moves away from the "other" of linear time. It is little wonder why Bergson's key metaphor to describe duration is something that is least material, least linear, and least intelligent, namely a melody.

Ultimately, because of the intuitive nature of duration, it exists as something already formed, complete beyond the evolutionary labor of history. It is also open to the many levels of universalization that Bergson desires. As already noted, once the durational nature of the intuition is presumed, its ever-expanding lines of dispersion include not only the "durationalization" of consciousness but of self and "life" as well. Given the absence of the historical and the strong urge to universalize, we can say that in Bergson's philosophy everything is already given in principle. There exists little room for interpretation. Either the person is profound or superficial, living durationally or chronometrically, free or unfree, depending on how one's attention deviates from a pure intuition of duration. It is very difficult to see how Bergson's notion of attention mediates between these poles. There is little room for imparting other meaning to duration and its accomplishment. All psychologically intuitive starting points are subject to the same danger in regard to the closure of meaning if they seek a "pure" moment while trying to exclude the necessity of language and interpretative analysis. Bergson's claim to be dealing with "pure" perception, "pure" memory, and "pure" duration is emblematic of this danger.

Here the problem of intuitionism and time strikes at our third theme, meaning. In the profound self, matter, finitude, and immobility are left behind in favor of duration, freedom, and eternity (immortality). Where Ricoeur speaks of the creation of meaning in the refiguration of time, Bergson will speak of creative freedom in duration. For Bergson, freedom *is* the meaning of the conscious life since our very essence is to be a center of action and indetermination; that is, meaning in humankind resides in the freedom to elude the snares of both materiality and the convention of language that work to "de-personalize" the profound self into the superficial self where real duration is replaced with clock-time. Meaning, like so many of Bergson's key terms, is reduced to another hybrid of durationalism. In Bergson there is the constant closure of meaning around the intuition of duration, and rightly so; it is his ultimate intuition, the source of his thought as well as its end-point. It is a circle without escape. But the lines of his entrapment are clear — time as duration becomes the defining moment for both self and a notion of meaning that authenticates the self.

Bergson's seminal error, however, is not that he unquestioningly believed in his own intuition. In an early critique of Bergson, Ricoeur remarks that from the beginning Bergson shared the same prejudice of his associationist opponents in that he believed the succession of states of consciousness was a natural phenomenon.[14] Bergson felt he could transcend the static elements of this succession, often described spatially, by diluting these states of consciousness and making them more flexible. In Bergson's analysis of freedom, a motive is not distinguished from a cause. This is achieved by reconstructing mental reality into a sort of interior space where alternatives and motives are juxtaposed as so many ways on an ideal map with the expressed aim of simply trying to reduce and eliminate any distinction among motives whatsoever.[15] But this in fact solves nothing; it is only a flight from the struggle of choice, intentions, and searching for rational alternatives.

As Ricoeur points out, the rediscovery of the intentionality of conscious acts provides a radical critique of psychological determinism, that is, distinguishing between acts and the correlates that they intend. Bergson conflates this distinction under the name of "states of consciousness." While Bergson may admit that a plurality of intentional motives arises within the infinity of continuous acts, he insists this is a mental plurality and not an intentional plurality. This serious confusion taints all Bergsonian psychology, which always seeks to elude the problem of clear conflicts and rationally grasped alternatives, taking refuge in the clear-obscure realm of organic metaphors that issue from the "purity" of his key notions.[16] In short, a notion such as freedom in Bergson is not a capacity or power but a type of determinate fact that substantiates the meaning of the self; it is a fact that eliminates other indeterminate actions or choices that might incur the doubt that the "mental" self is anything but absolutely free.

The Narrative Function in Bergson

In his last work, *The Two Sources of Morality and Religion*, Bergson identifies two specific roles narrative plays in society. Not only does he outline a narrative capability (*la fonction fabulatrice*) common to "everyone" but, as well, a second level of narrative employed by the "open soul" personality that encourages others to go beyond the mentality of a closed morality and religion. These two categories of narrative at first seem very striking in light of Ricoeur's notion of "the pre-narrative quality of experience," and narrative identity. However, the similarities are just that — similarities.

While Bergson may very well have sociologically recognized a narrative function working in society, his ideas remain far from linking narrative to time specifically. Regardless of the importance he gives to the story-making function in his last work, it is not central for Bergson because language in general is not thematized in his works. In fact, much more energy is put into telling us why the "ready-made" and inflexible concepts of representational language fail to obtain duration. After all, metaphysics begins by "dispensing with symbols" of all sorts. Instead, we read about pure contact or coincidence with the intuition of *durée*. In this sense, Bergson is consistent. His aim is not to have his descriptions of duration correspond to a real thing in a mode that distinguishes the knower and the known. He is much more interested in using language to recreate the movement of reality and thereby have us taste the reality of process and change. But his medium is still language all the way down, though he seems almost oblivious to his magnificent use of tropes to breathe life into his description of pure change. Bergson is a mimetic artist who recreates the sense of movement characteristic of duration, demonstrating that language is instrumental in lessening the distinction between mind and matter. His use of the linguistic medium goes beyond ornamentation and decoration and shows, unwittingly, how language can inform without becoming mired in spatialized and static concepts.

In this sense, isn't Bergson perhaps the best test case in showing how experience, sifted through the grid of narrative, reveals something remarkably novel about our experience of temporal passage, namely, the recognition of pure change? In reading Bergson, isn't his metaphorical description of duration an exceptional exercise in the power of narrative to refashion our experience of reality and time? The affirmative answers to these questions are lost on Bergson, who is suspicious of language except as a sociological tool. He is an artist who, immersed in the ways of imaginative variation, delivers us, his readers, to the realm of duration where we follow his lead without ever realizing we've left something behind.

THE TEMPORALITY OF MERLEAU-PONTY AND THE HUMAN TIME OF RICOEUR

For Merleau-Ponty, understanding time and the self revolve around a fundamental ambiguity, while for Ricoeur time and self revolve around a certain set of aporias. Positing a fundamental ambiguity and working within a certain set of aporias pose problems. By definition, something ambiguous (from the Latin, *ambiguus*) is doubtful, obscure, and indistinct — often capable of being understood in two or more possible senses. The lived body as defined by Merleau-Ponty is ambiguous because neither empirical nor intellectual elements can be totally disregarded in its discussion. Meanwhile, because we live with a tissue of sedimented meanings, there is no one meaning absolutely attributable to the lived body that is at once a body-subject and a living self. On the other hand, something which is aporetic (from the Greek, *aporia*) is a theoretical difficulty or puzzle. Such difficulties, such as time, are far more than ambiguous in the sense that a conceptual grasp cannot be reduced to a set of choices between one, two, or several possibilities. Time is a nonreductive conundrum, not reducible to "something" merely *conceptually* obscure or cleverly solved, or solved by merely saying it is intellectually ambiguous.

Ambiguity for Merleau-Ponty starts with the body; the aporias of Ricoeur start with a self in time. The ambiguity of Merleau-Ponty begins with an irreducible tension between the prepersonal/preobjective and the personal/objective of perception. The aporetic tensions of Ricoeur start with a prenarrative understanding of the self, the cleft between cosmic time and mortal time, and human action in general as understood both historically and culturally. The present for Merleau-Ponty is framed within a perceptual field while the present of Ricoeur is framed within a story or a history. It is to some of these fundamental differences that we now turn.

In which way does Merleau-Ponty's preobjective level of existence differ from Ricoeur's prenarrative level of experience? In Merleau-Ponty's view, the lived body or the phenomenal body are not living selves in the sense that there is a self who decides, chooses, and reflects. The *pre*-personal or the *pre*-objective is where the body is at once the

body of the moment and the habit body that exists as a margin of impersonal existence and plays anonymously beneath a personal identity (PP
82–84). This "*pre*-ness" is part of the organic interconnectedness that
defines a body as existing. It is the body's perspective upon the world,
the source of perceptual consciousness. While this "*pre*-ness" is not thematized, it is not without meaning. It is the autochthonous significance
of the world constituted by our bodily dealings with it. "Pre-ness" is
the basis for our incarnate existences, permitting us to know the world
the way we do. It is the ground of every deliberate *Sinngebung*. This
is intentional meaning — the meaning not proposed by "I think" but
by "I can" because we live in a certain fashion by way of our bodies.
This preobjective level is, therefore, not something that exists prior to
our body's expression but lies at the root of all expression.

Ricoeur's prenarrative quality of experience already presupposes
much of Merleau-Ponty's "I can." Where Merleau-Ponty's operative
word is "anonymous" at the preobjective level, Ricoeur's operative phrase
is "incipient story." Embodiment is not the issue for Ricoeur. The prenarrative issue is the unexamined life, that is, the state of awareness
that believes time's meaning is somehow ready-made, irrevocably
established and fixed. It is an awareness devoid of its historical instau-
ration and its potential to replace a conscious understanding with a more
conscious understanding of self. The prenarrative self is what ferments
through time given the textuality of our existence. Its ignorance is effaced
in entering the fusion of horizons that erupts between the world
of the text and the world of the reader. For Ricoeur, it is the reader
who completes the text in that reading "transforms it [the text] into
a reading guide with its zones of indetermination, its latent richness
of interpretation, its ability to be reinterpreted in novel ways within
historical contexts that are always new" (RR 432). The self of every
human subject emerges into a world that is already the product of
a narrative density. It recognizes itself through stories already told
and half-told and finds its enduring characteristics by acting and suffering through time. Yet such enduring characteristics are always open
to change. None of our lives are ever finished being examined or
interpreted.

Ricoeur would agree with Merleau-Ponty's statment that "Man is a historical idea and not a natural species" (PP 170) and that "speech itself *brings about* the concordance between me and myself, and between myself and others, on which an attempt is made to base thought" (PP 392). Their agreement would be based on the fact that the presence of the self to itself is a mediated presence (by language) and never an absolute self-presence. In this light, the self is never finished; it is never a substantial ego having ontological priority over communicative praxis.[17] Ricoeur's argument with Merleau-Ponty is that the latter's notion of self is always a layered self, a subject where underneath there is something else anonymously posited, regardless of its contemporariness with the living incarnate self. For example, Merleau-Ponty states that "since the lived (*le vécu*) is thus never entirely comprehensible, what I understand never quite tallies with my lived experience (*ma vie*), in short, I am never quite one with myself. Such is the lot of a being who is born, that is, who once and for all has been given to himself as something to be understood" (PP 347). Ricoeur's thesis, on the other hand, is that "Our own existence cannot be separated from the account we can give of ourselves. It is in telling our own stories that we give ourselves an identity. We recognize ourselves in the stories we tell about ourselves."[18]

If something cannot be tallied with lived experience, as Merleau-Ponty suggests, then in what way can it be narrated or historically accounted for? As Ricoeur insists, if narrative is meaningful to the extent that it portrays the features of temporal experience, how does natural time find itself taken up into a philosophical narrative? In very short terms, Merleau-Ponty leads us to believe that phenomenal time at the preobjective level is beyond description, while Ricoeur insists that the time delineated by Merleau-Ponty is one possible (narrated) interpretation among others of what a phenomenological description of time might look like.

Merleau-Ponty's notion of autochthonous organization, with its constant reference to "natural time," the "natural self," and the prepersonal world in general, negates a narrative account with its overemphasis on perceptual consciousness. Time for Merleau-Ponty's living self finds its source in the present, the phenomenal present or the field of presence at the preobjective level of existence. The lived body takes possession of time and brings into existence a past and a future for a present. Every present grasps by stages, through its *ek-static* horizon of immediate past and near future, the totality of possible time. In doing so it overcomes the dispersal of instants, thereby endowing a past with a definitive meaning that never closes upon itself, given the ambiguity of being-in-the-world as translated by the body. At the level of the incarnate subject, however, this phenomenal or lived present only becomes thematized through a collection of culturally sedimented significations which do not overcome the basic ambiguity that erupts between the preobjectivity of existence and subjective reflection on that existence.

It is very clear that for Merleau-Ponty the present of the lived body is an ultimate referent. Thematized discussions of time will always be derived from this nonrefigurable configuration of the phenomenal present. As stated earlier, this phenomenal present is foremost a presupposition of time that acts as a form of omni-temporality. It is a "prepersonal time" that flows "beneath the subject" (PP 84) much in the same way intentional acts surface from "beneath the flow of impressions . . . giving a form to the stuff of experience" (PP 121).[19] The phenomenal present for Merleau-Ponty is a type of inverted *durée* that may very well never exist for itself but still exists. The phenomenal present is placed between the finite perception of existence and the expression of this perception brought to language, creating a false hiatus between two different realms of being. Ricoeur's own critique of this time is instructive for us to note.

> Thus the finite perceptual intention, which gives me the fullness of the perceived at every moment, the present of the presence, is never alone and bare. In so far as this perceptual intention is saturated with presence, it is always enmeshed in a more-or-less complete relationship of fulfilment with regard to this other aim which penetrates it through and through, which literally passes right through it and to which the word is primordially linked. The mute look is caught up in discourse which articulates the meaning of it; and this ability to express meaning is continual transcendence, at least in intention, of the perspectival aspect of

the perceived here and now. This dialectic of signifying and perceiving, of saying and seeing, seems absolutely primal. *And the project of a phenomenology of perception, in which the moment of saying is postponed and the reciprocity of saying and seeing destroyed, is, in the last analysis, a hopeless venture.*[20]

While Ricoeur recognizes the preobjective "I can" of Merleau-Ponty as a "primitive datum" (OA 111), the self is not ultimately defined by its insertion into a mute preobjective world that silently shadows signification, intention, and expression. Rather, we find ourselves always already here, fully equipped to convert the "here" from an absolute placement into any place whatsoever, relative to all the others, in a social and geometrical space in which there is no privileged placement. Where Ricoeur structures the self on a narrative plot open to interpretation, Merleau-Ponty structures the self on perception. In the former, time is refigurable; in the latter, time has a nonrefigurable hold on the incarnate subject. With Ricoeur, we too can only wonder how reflection on the unreflected, and any narrative or "philosophical act itself are possible if man is so completely identified with his insertion into his field of perception, action, and life."[21]

In short, the present of which Merleau-Ponty speaks never expunges itself of somehow being an idealized present, that is, an indirect presupposition about the "other" of ordinary time. In discussion with Merleau-Ponty, another philosopher, Émile Bréhier, once remarked: "Thus your doctrine, in order not to be contradictory, must remain unformulated, only lived. But is a doctrine which is only lived still a philosophical doctrine?" (PrP 30). It is the charge of something "unformulated" that separates Merleau-Ponty's thesis from that of Ricoeur. It is because for Merleau-Ponty, the author of the *Phenomenology of Perception*, the lived present is lived and not interpreted.[22] Any interpretation would only be a superstructure informed by the infrastructure of the phenomenal present and the unreflected world of the lived body *as described* by Merleau-Ponty.[23] The effort of holding so close to an unreflected, mute instantiation of time — in order to exclude ordinary time — engenders constant dispersal and discordance. Consequently, "everything we live or think has always several meanings"

(PP 169) and "all human projects are contradictory" (SN 40). The phenomenal present of the lived body lacks a hermeneutical key. It is not open for interpretative activity. Where traditional philosophers identified an essential core in human beings that underlies cultural differences such as "Mind," "Reason," and the "Transcendental Ego," the lived body and lived time designate an equally elevated space that prevents the potential for difference and dialogue.

Despite these differences, there are asymptotic convergences between our two philosophers. Perhaps chief among these convergences is the necessity of communicative praxis. It should be obvious by now that Ricoeur centers this praxis in the medium of narrative. In stating that the subject "provides itself with symbols of itself in both succession and multiplicity, and that these symbols *are* it, since without them it would, like an inarticulate cry, fail to achieve self-consciousness" (PP 427), Merleau-Ponty acknowledges that self-knowledge arises from our linguistic-discursive practices. While this is certainly a move toward the Ricoeurian hermeneutical self, Merleau-Ponty's comments concerning interpretation are at best "oblique."[24] Moreover, at the time of his death, Merleau-Ponty did not leave behind a consolidated theory of language. As pointed out in chapter three, there are a large number of texts where language, literature, speech, and reading are addressed, but the entire field is never threaded together to create a whole.

More positively, both philosophers embrace a notion of the unfinished self and an unfinished world. Where Merleau-Ponty will say that the body never stops "secreting itself a 'significance' upon its material surrounding, and communicating it to other embodied subjects" (PP 197), Ricoeur will argue for an excess of significance issuing from the fusion between reader and text, as a type of surplus not only attributable to the polysemic nature of language, but to the interminable desire to account for our lives. Ricoeur's narrative identity and Merleau-Ponty's approximation of it under the guise of "the ambiguous self" are attempts to avoid the "pseudo-alternatives" of either pure change or absolute identity. Both suggestions replace, at the core of the self, a self-contained understanding of identity with one that makes and unmakes itself over the cohesion of a lifetime — a lifetime that will invite our identities to undergo many a "coherent deformation" and "reconfiguration" because there is no one algorithm or calculus to identity. Rather, our "personal life, expression, understanding, and history advance obliquely and not in straight lines towards ends and concepts" (S 83). Both thinkers are vitally aware of the communicative power of stories not only to weave our identities into a coherent whole over a lifetime, but to ever-recreate openings in the plenitude of being and draw it to fuller meaning.

Epilogue: Creative Time

While the central aim in this work has been to expose the triple themes of time, self, and meaning, a fourth has risen unbidden in each of the philosophers reviewed. All of the authors, in penetrating below an ordinary representation of linear time and seeking to describe the time that is authentic to our lived experience, revealed an essential characteristic of time through their analysis. It seems that no matter how one thematizes the time particular to the living self, the theme of creativity or novelty eventually appears. This is expressed vividly in the creative activity of duration in Bergson, present in Merleau-Ponty's remarks on creative expression through the lived body, and of course, in Ricoeur's narrative function as the continual creation of meaning.

Here we can recall Ricoeur's insistence on drawing a line between notions of change and evolution on one hand and history on the other. The natural world, despite all of its profound beauty, exhibits nothing of creative activity until we find the place where the self acts. Given the temporalisation of the anonymous "now" into a living present, the self does not merely foresee what will be but to some degree can determine what will be. While it is within the power of the self not to be totally at the mercy of natural forces, it becomes possible for the self to impose upon nature herself its own creations, sometimes creations of great and lasting significance. As Ricoeur pointed out, the narrating self is the arbitrator of time's meaning in the historical sense, for without narration there would only be the meaningless succession of things and no history at all. It is only within narrated time that we recognize and appreciate the creative and novel aspects of our human capability and potential.

Where animals can produce things of immense beauty, from spider webs to honeycombs, they are all produced by instinct and repeatedly reproduced. In some cases, the self can go one crucial step further; an act of human creation is never merely learned or inherited: "It is what a creative mind intends to be, something to which the notions of success or failure can apply, and sometimes something of such extraordinary originality that no other man or god, no one but its creator himself, could have foreseen. And if that creative mind possesses, in addition to this, the rare quality of creative genius, then what is wrought is not merely something that others could neither do nor foresee, it is something that others could not even imagine."[25]

But the act of human creativity could never have surfaced if, in the chain of natural causes, in the endless flow of before and after moments, a time with a human present did not intervene or erupt. In this sense, time is no longer something to be endured but engaged as a source of human creativity. "It is this capacity for creation that not only gives time its most fundamental meaning, but gives our lives whatever meaning they have, as well."[26] This is true at so many different levels of existence. Whether it be raising a family, writing a book, or finding a solution to tense political dilemmas, our creative capacities are engaged daily. As one of our "masters of disruption," Ricoeur reveals to us most fervently that, beyond the trotting and plodding of cosmic time over our mortal lives, *each of us* is capable of infusing this impersonal time with a personal story. In telling our story, the passage of time becomes historical, and this is precisely what gives our lives the possibility of being meaningful. Meaning arises as we reflect upon our story and examine our lives in light of the long tradition of stories that have preceded our own. All this is done for the price of telling a story — and then, only time will tell.[27]

There is a second, more diffuse theme that arose in the course of this study. It appeared in Bergson, who told us that each of us, "open soul" or not, has a story to tell and will do violence to language to tell our story. Merleau-Ponty remarks that perhaps none of us can better express who we are than in a story. But Ricoeur summarizes this amorphous theme the best in saying that "life is a story in search of a narrator." In these three authors, one sees more than just an appreciation of literature in general, and narrative in particular; rather, there is a command to heed the call of narration as an essential element in our humanity. As Ricoeur remarks in the beginning of *Time and Narrative*, we see coming into sight one vast poetic or creative sphere that mediates our existence, both personally and corporately. In this sphere one would like to believe there are many houses, some that novelists and journalists inhabit, some inhabited by philosophers and theoreticians of all sorts, and others yet, inhabited by poets and dreamers like ourselves. However, I do not believe Ricoeur has such subdivisions in mind. Implicit in his comment is the suggestion that language games aren't really the issue, that our neat parcelling of who writes what and what is written with various levels of anonymity may be unimportant.

This dispersion of the distinction between literary genres and levels of discourse is liberating to some and threatening to others. Philosophers are often the first voices to protest and defend their fastidious distinctions, technical vocabulary, and argumentative structure as being enlightened and worthy of uncritical respect. Yet, in the postmodern epoch, there is no elevated set of signifiers, no matter how eloquently construed, that defies critical appeal, interpretation and reevaluation. This leads me to believe that in this one vast poetic sphere in which we each participate, some more willingly than others, we may, as Ricoeur suggests, be forging our own identities, whether we are philosophers, journalists, letter writers, hacks, or the unlettered. Each of us is enmeshed in a narrative world that colors our understanding about who we are, how we are to live, and what we are to seek in life. The underlying assumption is that no text leaves our hands without some indelible mark of our identity imprinted on it. Time has done its work. If there is anything the "tricks of time" have taught us, then, it is that human identity is never ready-made. Identity is a process forged through time. Over the years, each of our identities must normally pass through the narrative grid of "what we used to be like, what happened, and what we are like now."[28] Passing through this narrative grid is never a solitary and isolated passage. In continually bringing the past to bear on the present, our story effects a perpetual reconfiguration of the self by the self *in relation to all* of the stories we've heard, read, and taken courage in. How important it is, then, to have such testimonies as Augustine's *Confessions* and Proust's *Remembrance of Things Past* that act as exemplars of the soul's struggle with the very time that forges identity.

Thus, despite their often impersonal and discursive nature, the works of our three "masters of disruption" are still narratives, and perhaps, even more, autobiographical. Have we read three philosophically astute theses on time or can we see such texts as autobiographical attempts to enframe the narrative identity of their authors? As Nietzsche once remarked, no matter how far a philosopher may extend his or her knowledge, and however objective the thinker may appear, what he or she reaps in the end is his or her own biography.[29]

Such a train of thought leads us into the larger postmodern debate about how intertextuality delimits the boundaries between philosophy and literature, and the more patriarchal debate over the superiority of one discourse over another. These metaphilosophical arguments are all worthy of a more extended discussion, but I would prefer to finish with some reflections on time and the self and their political implications. Let me begin with Julia Kristeva's "reading" of Hannah Arendt's (1906–1975) life.

Underlying Arendt's great philosophical works on totalitarianism, philosophy of mind, and political history is the "*theme of life.*"[30] In her works she decries the ratiocinating reason of capitalistic instrumentality of the present age that reduces persons into consumers and commodities and breeds a crass cult of individualism. In opposition to such currents, and in defence of what is unique to human life, Arendt places a narrative — shared with others — at the center of human existence as the essence of the human condition. "The chief characteristic of this specifically human life, whose appearance and disappearance constitute worldly events, is that it is itself always full of events which ultimately can be told as a story, establish a biography; it is of this life, *bios* as distinguished from mere *zoe*, that Aristotle said that it 'somehow is a kind of *praxis.*'"[31] The ends of narrative, therefore, are not merely personal but political. Narrating our lives grounds that life in what is specific to our humanity, beyond what is animal-like or just physiological. In doing so, the praxis of narrative links the destinies of life and the *polis* together, making each of our lives essentially a political life. Arendt, like Ricoeur, believes that it is through narrative and not the mechanics of language alone that politics is realized.[32] Narrative is the initial dimension in which we share our actions as political beings.

Narrated action serves several purposes. First, it saves governance from being ruled entirely by the latent tyranny of Platonic ideas applied to the human condition. Narrative, rather, permits authority to be based on the nature of differences rather than domination. What ensures this diversity under one collective domain is narrative's dependency on the role of memory.[33] Human stories are memories of actions that erupt in the public space that is, by its very nature, occupied by strangers with whom we must forge a set of shared meanings. In the attempt to preserve the paradoxical unity of "unique beings" in a collective setting, it is narrative that maintains a tension between *bios theoretikos* [contemplation] and *bios politikos* [action] in order to escape "the traps set by the wisdom of professional philosophers, and a chance to escape the utilitarianism of constructors of objects of art."[34] Another important aspect of narrative is its ability to keep "life" anchored in action, not in ideologies that devalue life by valuing it in and of itself, thereby putting a closure to meaning, memory, and history. Instead, Arendt argues for "the revelatory character of action as well as the ability to produce stories and become historical, which together form the very source from which meaningfulness springs into and illuminates human existence."[35]

Having said this, what is woefully missing in both Arendt's passionate plea for narrative, and Kristeva's account of it, is the role played by time. Memories take place in and grow over time. How we formulate the passage of time will have great impact on how we believe memory works and the importance we accord to it. As some have argued, modernity's love of linear temporality tends to obfuscate the role of memory and therefore alienate self-understanding.[36] For example, Kant's view of historical, teleological time — the one presented independently from his epistemology — favored a linear-progressive notion of time because it promoted an increasing and continuous distancing of the self from its past and from itself. In seeing history more as an abstract system, Kant denigrated the authority of inherited customs and practices. In the kingdom of ends that he propounded, he believed the distancing symbolized by linear time ensured "the construction of a homogeneous human space, without the divergences of exclusionary traditions and moral practices."[37]

The obvious danger of embracing such a disregard for the past is to become forgetful in the present and incur the bane of both purposelessness and alienation that leads each generation to repeat the moral horrors of the previous generations. It is for such reasons that Ricoeur discredits any fixation on future-oriented ideologies and, as detailed in chapter four, sees the historical present in which we live as a continual recovery of the past. Hence, his definition of historical consciousness is essentially one of "beginning." In the historical present, there are no universal, ahistorical truths attached to events. In bridging the distant moments with our interpretative activity, we attempt to redeem in hope the victims and lost voices of past atrocities. In Ricoeur's eyes, we attempt to safeguard our collective future against the repetition of such atrocities by paying this continual debt to the past. This sense of debt and reverence for the past, however, is constantly in danger of being eroded by modern forms of instrumentality applied to human life; such instrumentality breeds forgetfulness because time is reduced to the function of measurement alone where the past means nothing.

Every deployment of a particular understanding of time has its moral and political implications. Our various notions of time are the center that hold self and meaning in a tension open for both exploitation and loving cultivation. In time, all things are possible. Time's exigency is essentially creative but not determined, since time is a story not written in stone but in our daily actions, and hence, choices.

The force that through the green fuse drives the flower
Drives my green age; that blasts the roots of trees
Is my destroyer.
And I am dumb to tell the crooked rose
My youth is bent by the same wintry fever.

. . .

The lips of time leech to the fountain head;
Love drips and gathers, but the fallen blood
Shall calm her sores.
And I am dumb to tell a weather's wind
How time has ticked a heaven round the stars.

Dylan Thomas

Notes

Notes to Introduction

1. E. J. Craig, "Philosophy and Philosophies," *Philosophy* 58, no. 224 (1983): 189–201. See the various remarks in Christopher Phillips, *Socrates Café: A Fresh Taste of Philosophy* (New York: W. W. Norton & Co., 2001).

2. Lev Shestov, *In Job's Balance,* trans. Camilla Coventry and C. A. Macartney (Athens: Ohio University Press, 1975), 207.

3. Anthony Gottlieb, *The Dream of Reason: A History of Philosophy from the Greeks to the Renaissance* (Harmondsworth: Penguin Books, 2000).

4. Søren Kierkegaard, *Repetition: An Essay in Experimental Psychology,* trans. Walter Lowrie (Princeton: Princeton University Press, 1946), 114.

5. Simone Weil, *Lectures in Philosophy,* trans. H. Price (Cambridge: The Cambridge University Press, 1978), 197.

6. One could point out a plethora of literature on this topic. For the sake of brevity I cite one eloquent summary in Douglas Kellogg Wood, *Men Against Time: Nicolas Berdyaev, T. S. Eliot, Aldous Huxley, C. G. Jung* (Lawrence: University Press of Kansas, 1982).

7. Such questions are the stock and trade of the time-question. See, for example, Jan Faye, Uwe Scheffler, and Max Urche, *Perspectives on Time* (Dordrecht: Kluwer Academic Publishers, 1997). A classical summary of how philosophers have dealt with time is found in Eugene Freeman and Wilfrid Sellars, eds., *Basic Issues in the Philosophy of Time* (La Salle, Illinois: Open Court, 1971) and more recently Philip Turetzky, *Time* (London: Routledge, 1998). Yet, for a review of how ubiquitous the problem of time can be in various fields of research see J. T. Fraser, ed., *The Voices of Time: A Cooperative Survey of Man's Views of Time as Expressed by the Sciences and by the Humanities* (New York: George Braziller, 1966); J. T. Fraser, *Time as Conflict: A Scientific and Humanistic Study* (Basel: Birkhauser Verlag, 1978); and, G. J. Whitrow, *Time in History: Views of Time from Prehistory to the Present Day* (Oxford: Oxford University Press, 1988).

8. Renditions of the classical philosophical problem of human identity can be found in Brian Garrett, *Personal Identity and Self-Consciousness* (London: Routledge, 1998); Sydney Shoemaker and Richard Swinburne, *Personal Identity* (Oxford: Basil

Blackwell, 1984); and H. D. Lewis, *The Elusive Self* (Philadelphia: The Westminister Press, 1982).

9. I do not mean to insinuate here that there is but "one true meaning" to existence or that existence needs any recourse to foundationalism. I will return to the question of meaning in the course of this introduction.

10. This term and line of critique is borrowed from the clear exposition of the problem found in Marya Schechtman, *The Constitution of Selves* (London: Cornell University Press, 1996).

11. As Shaun Gallagher writes with respect to temporal experience: "I want to suggest that no one theory, no one paradigm, not even a hermeneutically enlightened one, will ever be able to account fully for temporal experience." See, *The Inordinance of Time* (Evanston: Northwestern University Press, 1998), 179.

12. For a comprehensive review of McTaggart's classical argument see Roger Teichmann, *The Concept of Time* (London: MacMillan Press, 1995).

13. Is Kant's rationalist program hopelessly bifurcated owing to his unclear and obscure definition of time(s)? For various discussions see Eyal Chowers "The Marriage of Time and Identity: Kant, Benjamin and the Nation State," *Philosophy and Social Criticism* 25, no. 3 (1999): 57–80; Amihud Gilead, "Teleological Time: A Variation on a Kantian Theme," *Review of Metaphysics* 38 (1985): 529–62; Charles Sherover, "Time and Ethics: How is Morality Possible?," in J. T. Fraser and N. Lawrence, eds., *The Study of Time II* (New York: Springer-Verlag, 1975), 216–30; Charles Sherover, *Heidegger, Kant and Time* (Bloomington: Indiana University Press, 1971). In a more contemporary example, Heidegger's description of the three temporal ecstases with his emphasis on the future demands Dasein's definition as a Being-towards-death. However, my point here is not to apply the dynamic configuration of time-self-meaning to every system but to make the argument that it exists and may well be applicable to every system that defines time in a particular fashion.

14. Norman Kemp Smith, *A Commentary to Kant's "Critique of Pure Reason,"* 2nd ed. (London: Macmillan & Co., Ltd., 1930), 137.

15. Vincent Descombes, *Objects of All Sorts: A Philosophical Grammar* (Baltimore: John Hopkins University Press, 1987), 4–5. With Decombes, I do not wish to imply that these isolated developments or trends were successive or cogent in French philosophy as much as they represent inconsistent movements of dialogue and experimentation within a philosophical community.

16. In this work, I will not provide a summary of Ricoeur's large and extensive philosophical anthropology. An expository summary can be followed in Mark Muldoon, *On Ricoeur* (Belmont, California: Wadsworth, 2002) and a more critical review can be found in Henry Venema, *Identifying Selfhood: Imagination, Narrative and Hermeneutics in the Thought of Paul Ricoeur* (Albany, New York: State University of New York Press, 2000).

17. Paul Ricoeur, introduction to *Time and the Philosophies*, UNESCO (London: The Benham Press, 1977), 13.

18. Ibid., 18.

19. See Anthony Kerby, *Narrative and the Self* (Bloomington: Indiana University Press, 1991); Donald Polkinghorne, *Narrative Knowing and the Human Sciences* (Albany: State University of New York Press, 1988); key essays are found in Lewis P. Hinchman and Sandra K. Hinchman, eds., *Memory, Identity, Community: The Idea of Narrative in the Human Sciences* (Albany: State University of New York Press, 1997). See references in note 32 of chapter 4.

20. Paul Brockelman, *Time and Self: Phenomenological Explorations,* AAR Studies in Religion 39 (New York: The Crossroad Publishing Company and Scholars Press, 1985); David Carr, *Time, Narrative, and History* (Bloomington: Indiana University Press, 1986). There are several other studies worthy of note. Genevieve Lloyd's *Being in Time: Selves and Narrators in Philosophy and Literature* (London: Routledge, 1993) develops the ways in which both philosophy and literature handle the relationship between time and selfhood but makes no attempt to show how notions of selves are in fact derivative of time — specifically omitting a discussion of the phenomenology of time (13). Sandra Rosenthal's chapter "The Temporal Self: A Restructuring of Mead and a Lesson in the Need for Vigilance," rigorously elaborates how any understanding of the self in G. H. Mead's work is inseparably interrelated with the way the self's temporal experience is characterised; see Sandra B. Rosenthal, *Time, Continuity and Indeterminacy: A Pragmatic Engagement with Contemporary Perspectives* (Albany: State University of New York Press, 2000), 93–108. With almost exclusive reference to Husserl's study of inner time consciousness, our theme is conspicuously alluded to in Gallagher's *The Inordinance of Time.*

21. Paul Brockelman, *Time and Self: Phenomenological Explorations,* 78, 1–2.

22. David Carr, *Time, Narrative, and History,* 184, 185.

23. Carr's chief contention with Ricoeur is that the latter sees life, action, and history as having narrative form because they acquire it from the literary products of our culture. For Carr, "full-fledged literary story-telling arises out of life," that is, historical and fictional narratives are extensions and configurations of reality's primary features (*Time, Narrative, and History,* 16–17). It should be noted that while both Brockelman and Carr acknowledge their debt to Ricoeur, they only made use of the first volume of Ricoeur's *Time and Narrative.*

24. Charles Taylor, *The Ethics of Authenticity* (Cambridge: Harvard University Press, 1992), 105–06.

25. Ibid., 31ff. and Charles Taylor, *Sources of the Self: The Making of The Modern Identity* (Cambridge: Harvard University Press, 1989), 27ff.

26. Charles Taylor, *Sources of the Self,* 47ff.

27. A more recent example is Corey Anton's *Selfhood and Authenticity* (Albany: State University of New York Press, 2001) where he readily acknowledges in the beginning that any "quest for self-fulfilment, requires or demands an adequate comprehension of the selfhood that is to be fulfilled. And yet, such a comprehension is sorely lacking" (8). It is only much later in the book that this gap is overcome with an extensive discussion on the temporality of the self based on Heidegger (115ff).

28. See Mike Sandbothe, "The Temporalization of Time in Modern Philosophy,"

in *Time in Contemporary Intellectual Thought,* ed. Patrick J. Baert (Amsterdam: Elsevier, 2000), 17–35.

29. There are many ways to read Derrida. When he argues that the goal of speech as a self-presence before and beyond time demands the temporalising play of writing and that such play undermines self-presence, deferring it *ad infinitum,* I do not infer from Derrida — as some do — that he ultimately disperses once and for all the epistemic-knowing subject and therefore intimates "the end of philosophy." See the various essays, especially *"Différance,"* in Jacques Derrida, *Margins of Philosophy,* trans. Alan Bass (New York: University of Chicago Press, 1982), 1–27. I am more inclined to see Derrida's employment of *différance* as yet another way in which philosophy makes explicit the radical instability of the self in the flux of time and why we should be suspicious of the classical approaches to the "self in time."

30. Gary Gutting, *French Philosophy in the Twentieth Century* (Cambridge: Cambridge University Press, 2001), 380ff.

31. Florian Rötzer, *Conversations with French Philosophers* (New York: Humanities Press, 1995), 7 (my emphasis).

32. As "masters of disruption," Bergson, Merleau-Ponty, and Ricoeur are unanimous in seeing the movement of the body as the "primitive datum" to any such disruption. In the causal chain of events in the natural order, our movement brings us to consciousness, that is, we are temporalized as we work toward self-consciousness of our actions through expression and language. As we work through each author, we will see that there is no one uniform unequivocal answer to how we think we are temporalized; it is open to numerous descriptions. In the end, we only have so many stories about time that are self-referential, telling us who we are (the self) and the significance (meaning) of our mortal lives. In short, self and meaning constellate around the story we tell ourselves about time.

33. James R. Mensch, *Ethics and Selfhood: Alterity and the Phenomenology of Obligation* (Albany, New York: State University of New York Press, 2003), 160.

Notes to Chapter 1

1. One of the consistent paradoxes of time is an ontological one concerning its being and nonbeing. Perhaps the earliest advocate of the argument against the existence of time was Parmenides of Elea (ca. 475 B.C.E.). For this Eleatic, the real was abiding and permanent while change and time were both an illusion. In one of the fragments attributed to him, Parmenides states: "To think is the same as the thought that It Is; for you will not find thinking without Being, in (*in regard*) which there is an expression. For nothing else either is or shall be except Being, since Fate has tied it down to be a whole and motionless; therefore all things that mortals have established, believing in their truth, are just a name: Becoming and Perishing, Being and Not-Being, and Change of position, and alteration of bright colour." Quoted in Hermann Diels, *Ancilla to the Pre-Socratic Philosophers,* trans. K. Freeman (Cambridge, Mass.: Harvard University Press, 1977), 44.

2. Peter Loptson, *Reality: Fundamental Topics in Metaphysics* (Toronto: University of Toronto Press, 2001), 142ff.

3. Plato, *Timaeus,* trans. H. D. Lee (Baltimore: Penguin Books, 1965), 37d4.

4. See Aristotle, "Physics," trans. R. P. Hardie and R. K. Gaye, in *The Complete Works of Aristotle,* ed. Jonathan Barnes, Vol. 1 (Princeton: Princeton University Press, 1984), 4.11. 219a34–35; 220a–222b29.

5. See Galileo Galilei, "On Naturally Accelerated Motion," in *Galileo Galilei: Two New Sciences,* trans. S. Drake (Madison, Wisconsin: University of Wisconsin Press, 1974), 153ff.

6. Isaac Newton, *Sir Isaac Newton's Mathematical Principles of Natural Philosophy and His System of the World,* ed. F. Cajori and trans. A. Motte (Berkeley: University of California Press, 1966), 6.

7. Paul Ricoeur, "The Human Experience of Time and Narrative," *Research in Phenomenology* 9 (1979): 18.

8. For an example of such argumentation see Peter Kroes, "Physics and the Flow of Time," in *Nature, Time, and History,* Part 2, Nijmegen Studies in the Philosophy of Nature and Its Science, No. 4 (Nijmegen: Catholic University of Nijmegen, 1985), 43–52.

9. Henri Bergson, *Duration and Simultaneity: with Reference to Einstein's Theory,* trans. Leon Jacobson (New York: Bobbs-Merrill Co. Inc., 1965), 48.

10. Milic Capek, *The Philosophical Impact of Contemporary Physics* (New York: D. Van Nostrand, 1961), 162.

11. David Hume, *A Treatise of Human Nature,* ed. L. A. Selby-Bigge (Oxford: The Clarendon Press, 1978). In stating that Newtonian thought had rather a substantial influence on Hume, I am following James Noxon, *Hume's Philosophical Development; A Study of His Methods* (Oxford: The Clarendon Press, 1975), 76ff., and, Antony Flew, *David Hume: Philosopher of Moral Science* (Oxford: Basil Blackwell, 1986), 7, 109; see also the introduction to Hume's *Treatise* in regard to his discussion between science in general and "the science of Man" (xv–xix).

12. Hume, *A Treatise of Human Nature,* 34. 35.

13. Ibid., 252, 251, 255, 252ff., 253.

14. Ibid., 253.

15. In the appendix to his *Treatise* Hume states: "upon a more strict review of the section concerning *personal identity,* I find myself involved in such a labyrinth, that, I must confess, I neither know how to correct my former opinions, nor how to render them consistent" (633).

16. In a work following *Time and Narrative,* Ricoeur criticizes Hume. How is it, Ricoeur asks, that "when I enter most intimately into what I call myself" and cannot catch myself, that I never ask "who" it is that enters into myself? "Was not Hume seeking what he could not hope to find — a self which was but sameness? And was he not supposing the self he was not seeking? Here, then, is *someone* who claims to be unable to find anything but a datum stripped of selfhood; *someone* who penetrates within himself, seeks and declares to have found nothing. With the question Who? — who is seeking, stumbling, and not finding, and who per-

ceives? — the self returns just when the same slips away." See *Oneself as Another,* 128.

17. This is the basic theme covered in the first two chapters of the first volume of *Time and Narrative.*

18. Edmund Husserl, *The Phenomenology of Internal Time-Consciousness,* trans. J. S. Churchill (Bloomington, Indiana: Indiana University Press, 1964), §1, 22.

19. Ibid., §34, 98.

20. For another summary of Ricoeur's treatment of Augustine, see John Protevi, "'Inventio' and the Unsurpassable Metaphor: Ricoeur's Treatment of Augustine's Time Meditation," *Philosophy Today* 43 (1999): 86–94.

21. The numbers refer to the chapter and line of the quote as found in book 11 of Augustine's *Confessions,* trans. R. S. Pine-Coffin (Middlesex, England: Penguin Books, 1964).

22. The numbers refer to the passages from Aristotle's "Physics" 4.11 found in *The Complete Works of Aristotle* ed. Jonathan Barnes, Vol. 1 (Princeton: Princeton University Press, 1984).

23. See Aristotle, "Physics," 2.1. 192b21–23; 3.1. 200b12–14.

24. Hermann Deils, *Ancilla to the Pre-Socratic Philosophers,* 19.

25. Aristotle, "Physics," 3.2. 201b25.

26. Ibid., 3.1. 201a10–11.

27. See 18 above. The German text, *Vorlesungen zur Phänomenologie des inneren Zeitbewusstseins,* was originally published in 1928 and edited by Martin Heidegger. Unfortunately it was not until the critical edition of Husserl's works that serious doubt was cast upon the value of the 1928 edition; see E. Husserl, "Zur Phänomenologie des inneren Zeitbewusstseins (1893–1917)," in *Husserliana,* vol. 10, ed. R. Boehm (The Hague: Martinus Nijhoff, 1966). Part A of this text contains the 1928 edition while part B comprises some 54 texts written by Husserl between 1893 and 1911. As Boehm points out, the original editorship of the 1928 edition is more attributable to Edith Stein (1891–1943) than to Heidegger. Stein's compilation is more of an impressionistic *Ausarbeitung* untamed by Husserl's vision and maturing logic. Consequently, Husserlian scholars are often faced with texts and notes which, even if they frequently contain detailed lines of argumentation, when taken as a whole, fall short of a thorough and systematically developed exposition. To ameliorate this, Rudolph Bernet's introduction to *Edmund Husserl: Texte zur Phänomenologie des inneren Zeitbewusstseins (1893–1917)* (Hamburg: Meiner, 1985) provides one of the most systematic descriptions (outside of the notes that make up the 1928 edition) of Husserl's texts on time.

28. By *hyletics,* Ricoeur understands Husserl to mean the analysis of matter (*hylê*) — or raw impression — of an intentional act, such as perception, abstracting from the form (*morphê*) that animates it and confers a meaning on it. See Ricoeur, *Time and Narrative* 3.281, n. 4.

29. The numbers refer to the pagination in *The Phenomenology of Internal Time-Consciousness* cited above.

30. There is a serious equivocation between the original French text of *Time*

and Narrative and the English translation of this particular passage. The French reads "le 'maintenant' ne se contracte pas dans un instant ponctuel, mais comporte une intentionnalité longitudinale," where the English reads, "the 'now' is not contracted into a point-like instant but includes a transverse or longitudinal intentionality." The addition of "a transverse or" is a confusing inclusion since the entire phrase, indicated later by the "lui-même" or "itself" describes what is properly the nature of the longitudinal intentionality only, and not the transverse intentionality distinguished by Husserl.

31. One commentator has argued that Ricoeur misinterprets Husserl's phenomenology of internal time-consciousness to make "time itself appear" as such, and, in fact, that Ricoeur's project in *Time and Narrative* is on shaky ground because it lacks the very description of such a consciousness; see Jane Chamberlain, "Thinking Ricoeur's Husserl in *Time and Narrative,*" *Minerva — An Internet Journal of Philosophy* 2 (1998): 15pp. December 2002, http://www.ul.ie/~philos/vol2/husserl.html. I will address this concern in chapter 4 in regard to Ricoeur's notion of mimesis$_2$.

32. Immanuel Kant, *Critique of Pure Reason,* trans. Norman Kemp Smith (New York: St. Martin's Press, 1965).

33. The numbers refer to the pagination in Kant's *Critique of Pure Reason* cited above.

34. Ricoeur makes special reference to this quote in that it seems to align Kant with both Augustine and Husserl. However as Ricoeur points out, in reference to Kant's early works, "the subject" Kant refers to (and elsewhere (A42)) designates no one in particular but the *humana conditio.* See Ricoeur, *Time and Narrative* 3.287, n. 39.

35. Martin Heidegger, *Being and Time,* trans. J. Macquarrie and E. Robinson (Oxford: Basil Blackwell, 1978). For other summaries of Ricoeur's treatment of Heidegger's analysis see Kim Atkins, "Ricoeur's 'Human Time' as a Response to the Problem of Closure in Heideggerian Temporality," *Philosophy Today* 44 (2000): 108–22 and Patrick L. Bourgeois and Frank Schalow, *Traces of Understanding: A Profile of Heidegger's and Ricoeur's Hermeneutics* (Amsterdam: Rodopi, 1990).

36. Numbers refer to the pagination in Heidegger's *Being and Time,* cited above.

37. See R. G. Collingwood, *The Idea of History,* ed. T. M. Knox (Oxford: Oxford University Press, 1946), 17–23.

38. For a more precise explanation of why the human present must be initiated by an instance of discourse see Emile Benveniste, "Subjectivity in Language," in *Problems in General Linguistics,* trans. Elizabeth Meek (Coral Gables, Florida: University of Miami Press, 1971), 223ff. For a more expanded discussion on the necessity of a speaking functionary in the causal chain of natural events see Antoine Vergote, "The Articulation of Time," in *In Search of a Philosophical Anthropology,* trans. Mark Muldoon (Amsterdam and Leuven: Rodopi and Leuven University Press, 1996), 265ff. Also, see note 20 in chapter 4.

39. Ricoeur, "The Human Experience of Time and Narrative," 33.

40. Paul Ricoeur, "History as Narrative and Practice," an interview with Peter Kemp in *Philosophy Today* 29 (1985): 214.

41. See Immanuel Kant, *Critique of Pure Reason*, trans. Norman Kemp Smith (New York: St. Martin's Press, 1965) where, in the light of his own philosophy, he states: "The concept of a noumenon is thus a merely limiting concept, the function of which is to curb the pretention of sensibility; and it is therefore only of negative employment. At the same time it is no arbitrary invention; it is bound up with the limitation of sensibility, though it cannot affirm anything positive beyond the field of sensibility" (272). Ricoeur is famous for the use of this notion of the "limiting concept" in many of his hermeneutical analyses. It is imposed as a regulative ideal to limit those sorts of claims to a final synthesis that one might be tempted to make in the course of a philosophical analysis.

Notes to Chapter 2

1. See R. C. Grogin, *The Bergsonian Controversy in France 1900–1914* (Calgary, Alberta: The University of Calgary Press, 1988), 168. Gabriel Marcel once remarked that "there is probably no idea less Bergsonian than that of Bergsonism" in "Bergsonism and Music," *Reflections on Art: A Source Book of Writings by Artists, Critics and Philosophers*, ed. Susanne K. Langer (Baltimore: John Hopkins Press, 1958), 142. By Bergson's own admission, "I do not have a system"; see Henri Bergson, *Mélanges,* ed. André Robinet (Paris: Presses Universitaires de France, 1972). Some have simply labelled Bergson "a process philosopher;" see "Bergson, Henri-Louis," *Routledge Encyclopedia of Philosophy,* (London: Routledge, 1998), 1:732–37.

2. Bergson's popularity ran the gamut from international fame at the turn of the twentieth century to near obscurity by the end of his life, despite receiving the Nobel Prize in 1927. Since then his influence has been reevaluated on several fronts. In terms of literature and art, assessments of Bergson's influence can be found in Thomas Quirk, *Bergson and American Culture: The Worlds of Willa Cather and Wallace Stevens* (Chapel Hill: University of North Carolina Press, 1990); Paul Douglass, *Bergson, Eliot, and American Literature* (Lexington: University Press of Kentucky, 1986). Mark Antliff, *Inventing Bergson: Cultural Politics and the Parisian Avant-Garde* (Princeton: Princeteon University Press, 1993); Donald Maxwell, *The Abacus and the Rainbow: Bergson, Proust and the Digital-Analogic Opposition* (New York: Peter Lang, 1999). For older, general assessments, see A. E. Pilkington, *Bergson and His Influence: A Reassessment* (Cambridge: Cambridge University Press, 1976); Thomas Hanna, ed., *The Bergsonian Heritage* (New York: Columbia University Press, 1962). While the works of Julien Benda (1867–1956) are legendary for their attacks on Bergson, perhaps the two most famous critiques of Bergsonism are: Fulton J. Sheen, *God and Intelligence* (Louvain: Université Catholique de Louvain, 1925) and Jacques Maritain, *Bergsonian Philosophy and Thomism*, trans. Mabelle L. Andison (New York: Philosophical Library, 1955).

3. Ilya Prigogine and Isabelle Stengers, *Order Out of Chaos: Man's New Dialogue with Nature* (London: W. Heinemann, 1984), 96. Prigogine elsewhere lauds Bergson when he states: "Again, of the changes that occur in nature, classical physics retained only motion. Consequently, as Henri Bergson . . . and others emphasized, everything is given in classical physics; change is nothing but a denial of becoming and time is only a parameter, unaffected by the transformation that it describes. The image of the stable world, a world that escapes the process of becoming, has remained until now the very ideal of theoretical physics." See Ilya Prigogine, *From Being to Becoming: Time and Complexity in the Physical Sciences* (San Francisco: W. H. Freeman & Co., 1980), 3.

4. For Bergson's influence on science see P. A. Y. Gunter's important introduction to *Bergson and the Evolution of Physics*, ed. and trans. P. A. Y. Gunter (Knoxville: The University of Tennessee Press, 1969); Milic Capek, *Bergson and Modern Physics; A Reinterpretation and Re-evaluation*, Boston Studies in the Philosophy of Science Vol. VII (Boston: D. Reidel Publishing Co., 1971); Andrew C. Papanicolaou and P.A.Y. Gunter, eds., *Bergson and Modern Thought: Towards a Unified Science*, Models of Scientific Thought, Vol. 3 (New York: Harwood Academic Publishers, 1988); and the various essays in David R. Griffin, ed., *Physics and the Ultimate Significance of Time* (New York: State University of New York Press, 1986); Philippe Gallois and Gérard Forzy, eds., *Bergson et les Neurosciences* (Lille: Institut Synthelabo pour les progrès de la connaisiance, 1997); Gregory Dale Adamson, *Philosophy in the Age of Science and Capital* (London: Continuum Press, 2002).

5. Elie During, "'A History of Problems': Bergson and the French Epistemological Tradition," *Journal of the British Society for Phenomenology* 35 (2004):4–23. This edition of the journal is entitled "Bergson Now" and is entirely devoted to Bergson's relevance in contemporary philosophy. Other current appreciations of Bergson's thought can be found in Philippe Soulez and Frédéric Worms, *Bergson, Une vie* (Paris: Flammarion, 1997); John Mullarkey, ed., *The New Bergson* (Manchester: Manchester University Press, 1999); John Mullarkey, *Bergson and Philosophy* (Notre Dame, Indiana: University of Notre Dame Press, 2000); and Leonard Lawlor, *The Challenge of Bergsonism: Phenomenology, Ontology, Ethics* (London: Continuum Press, 2003).

6. Gilles Deleuze, *Bergsonism*, trans. Hugh Tomlinson and Barbara Habberjam (New York: Zone Books, 1988); Gilles Deleuze *Cinema 1: The Movement-Image*, trans. Hugh Tomlinson and Barbara Habberjam (Minneapolis: University of Minnesota Press, 1986); Gilles Deleuze *Cinema 2: The Time-Image*, trans. Hugh Tomlinson and Robert Galeta (Minneapolis: University of Minnesota Press, 1989). As a companion text, see Keith Ansell-Pearson, *Philosophy and the Adventure of the Virtual: Bergson and the Time of Life* (London: Routledge, 2002). At the beginning of the twenty-first century, it is probably true to say that there are two readings of Bergson: Bergson as we read him in his classical works and the Deleuzian appropriation of Bergson. As Ansell-Pearson remarks, Deleuze is both profoundly Bergson and radically different from Bergson (Ansell-Pearson, *Philosophy and the*

Adventure of the Virtual, 3). What makes Deleuze Bergsonian is his profound appreciation of Bergsonian themes such as multiplicity, tension, and intuition. Deleuze sees Bergson as part of a counterhistory in philosophy that rejects Platonic idealism and dialectic logic, especially negation, as having any explanatory value in explicating the "what is" and our experience of it. Rather, Deleuze sees Bergson's philosophical intuition as the poststructuralist's tool par excellence for turning philosophy back upon itself, problematizing its own gaps, false dichotomies, and limitations. Intuition is not employed here in search of some ground or to constantly criticize. It is a method of disruption that makes us aware of our erroneous propensity to immobilize change and spatialize duration and thereby deny that there exists no ground against which we can represent differences. In reality, differences cannot be analyzed. More precisely, "duration divides up and does so constantly," such that "it changes in kind in the process of dividing up" (Deleuze, *Bergsonism*, 42). Elaborating this virtual "differing in kind," not just in degree, becomes a philosophical *tour de force* for Deleuze. See as well Dorothea Olkowski, *Gilles Deleuze and the Ruin of Representation* (Berkeley: The University of California Press, 1999).

7. On the similarity of analysis see the remarks of John M. Quinn, "The Concept of Time in St. Augustine," in *Studies in Philosophy and the History of Philosophy*, ed. John K. Ryan, (Washington, D.C.: The Catholic University of America Press, 1969), 4:117, and, Lezek Kolakowski, *Bergson* (Oxford: Oxford University Press, 1985), 17.

8. Regardless of the existential flavor of this statement, Bergson was hardly an existentialist as we now understand the movement. See P. A. Y. Gunter, "Bergson and Sartre: The Rise of French Existentialism," in Fredrick Burwick and Paul Douglass, eds. *The Crisis in Modernism: Bergson and the Vitalist Controversy* (Cambridge: Cambridge University Press, 1992), 230–44.

9. The first chapter of *Time and Free Will* is basically Bergson's critique of Wundt, Fechner, and Joseph Delboeuf (1831–1886).

10. Bergson felt Fechner's employment of a law formulated by E. H. Weber (1795–1878) was totally misguided. What has now come to be known as Weber's law states that, given a certain stimulus which calls forth a certain sensation, the amount by which the stimulus must be increased for consciousness to become aware of any change bears a fixed relation to the original stimulus. Bergson's doubt issues from the fact that such a law assumes one can easily jump from a category of the extended (objective measurement of stimuli) to the unextended (sensation) and back again. At the heart of Bergson's doubt lies the question: "how are we to pass from a relation between the stimulus and its minimum increase to an equation which connects the 'amount of sensation' with the corresponding stimulus?" See Bergson, *Time and Free Will*, 61.

11. C. U. M. Smith, in *The Problem of Life: An Essay in the Origins of Biological Thought* (London: Macmillan Press Ltd., 1976), chaps. 15–22, gives a succinct summary of how experimental psychology can be understood as an extension of the mechanical worldview.

12. Herbert Spencer, "Principles of Psychology," in *The Works of Herbert Spencer,* (Osnabrück: Otto Zeller, 1966), 4: 318–19.

13. Herbert Spencer, "First Principles," in *The Works of Herbert Spencer,* (Osnabrück: Otto Zeller, 1966), 1: 445–46.

14. Herbert Spencer, "Principles of Psychology," in *The Works of Herbert Spencer,* (Osnabrück: Otto Zeller, 1966), 5: 419.

15. Ibid., 208–09. Elsewhere Spencer states: ". . . if there exist certain external relations which are experienced by all organisms at all instants of their waking lives — relations which are absolutely constant, absolutely universal — there will be established answering internal relations that are absolutely constant, absolutely universal. Such relations we have in those of Space and Time." See "Principles of Psychology," 4: 467.

16. Spencer, "First Principles," 1: 128.

17. While many would call these polar opposites "dualisms," for Bergson I prefer the term "tensions" or "contrasts" in order to avoid any philosophical confusion with the substance dualism made famous by Descartes. Bergson's penultimate distinction, for example, between matter and spirit is one of degree, not kind. See Eric Matthews, "Bergson's Concept of a Person," in *The New Bergson,* 118–34.

18. Henri Bergson, "Lettre à Harald Hoffding; 15 mars 1915" *Mélanges,* 1148.

19. A. O. Lovejoy, in *The Reason, the Understanding, and Time* (Baltimore: John Hopkins Press, 1961), argued that Bergson's description of intuition adds up to nothing more than dreaming (68). But Bergson voiced his own hesitation at using such a term. Despite the confusion it might incur, he felt it was still the most appropriate notion; see Bergson, *The Creative Mind,* 30. Lawlor suggests that Bergsonian intuition really has three central aspects, namely, emotion, memory and imagination which permit intuition to be a type of "spiritual touching;" see Lawlor, *The Challenge of Bergsonism,* 63ff.

20. Here, Merleau-Ponty puts his finger on perhaps the most contentious issue surrounding Bergson's notion of intuition, namely, what does it mean to be in intuitive contact with things or becoming? Is this contact or coincidence mediated or unmediated? This will be the theme in the later part of the chapter as we reevaluate Bergson's evaluation of language in general.

21. Bergson uses the terms "ego," "personality," and "the self" interchangeably.

22. This passage is cited from Bergson's later works rather then the one I am following (*Time and Free Will*) since it much more concisely distinguishes *durée* from ordinary time; however, the same understanding of *durée* is stated more diffusely in *Time and Free Will,* 91–139.

23. Ordinary time often spoken of as analogous to a line indicates its highly visual bias. Yet the body does not structure its temporal experience by vision alone. In fact, there is no precedent to assume the human subject structures its temporal experience solely on the model of the visually biased linear metaphor. In continually employing a musical metaphor, Bergson thwarts this bias and indicates the time of the subject is other than physical time. Albert Einstein succinctly encapsulated this problem when he stated that "the order of experiences in time obtained

by acoustical means can differ from the temporal order gained visually, so that one cannot simply identify the time sequence of events with time sequence of experience;" see Albert Einstein, *Relativity: The Special and the General Theory,* trans. R. W. Lawson (New York: Bonanza Books, 1961), 140, n. 1.

24. See Marcel's comments in "Bergsonism and Music."

25. David Hume, *A Treatise of Human Nature,* ed. L. A. Selby-Bigge (Oxford: The Claredon Press, 1978), 253.

26. Elsewhere in *Matter and Memory,* Bergson states: "The whole difficulty of the problem that occupies us comes from the fact that we imagine perception to be a kind of photographic view of things, taken from a fixed point by that special apparatus which is called an organ of perception — a photograph which would then be developed in the brain-matter by some unknown chemical and psychical process of elaboration" (31).

27. In *The Challenge of Bergsonism,* Lawlor makes the strong argument in Bergson for "the primacy of memory" over "the primacy of perception," the latter being the signature thought for Merleau-Ponty. Unlike Merleau-Ponty and other phenomenological endeavours, Bergson does not define consciousness as consciousness of something and therefore Bergson in no way should be construed as a phenomenologist. Conscious perception is something for Bergson — it is already memory. Lawlor will go on to make the claim that the "past" Bergson defends can find its place in the more postmodern argument for the "a priori condition," that is, "a past that was never present" as discussed by various thinkers such as Merleau-Ponty, Derrida, Deleuze, and Levinas. This is because the unconscious or the past always conditions the present, that is, the past does not repeat the present but rather the present repeats the past (27–59).

28. "Bodily memory" is a term not consistently employed by Bergson. It emphasizes the fact that an aspect of memory is action oriented and not a repository of representations. Other commentators have used other designations; see E. S. Casey, "Habitual Body and Memory in Merleau-Ponty," in *Man and World* 17(1984): 279–97. Casey notes that Bergson's recognition of both a pure memory and a "habit" memory in *Matter and Memory* was a radical challenge to the standard theory of memory at the "fin-de-siècle." The orthodox understanding of memory was of some form of representation of past experience, usually via visualization. Memory as recollection through visualization can be found in rudimentary form in Plato and more concretely depicted in the mental, replicative representations of "ideas" as employed by Locke, Berkeley, and Hume (279).

29. In *The Two Sources of Morality and Religion,* Bergson states this tension extends as a continuity from organized small bodies to the huge "inorganic body" that "reaches the stars" (246–47).

30. In *Mind-Energy,* Bergson writes: "What happens when one of our actions ceases to be spontaneous and becomes automatic? Consciousness departs from it. In learning an exercise, for example, we begin by being conscious of each of the movements we execute. Why? Because we originate the action, because it is the result of a decision and implies choice. Then, gradually, as the movements become

more and more linked together and more and more determine one another mechanically, dispensing us from the need of choosing and deciding, the consciousness of them diminishes and disappears" (11).

31. For a wider discussion of "rhythm" and how it plays in both the thought of Bergson and Merleau-Ponty, see Alia Al-Saji, "Merleau-Ponty and Bergson: Bodies, Expression and Temporalities in the 'Flesh,'" *Philosophy Today* 45 (2001): 110–23.

32. Deleuze, *Bergsonism*, 32–33.

33. Giovanna Borradori, "The Temporalization of Difference: Reflections on Deleuze's Interpretation of Bergson," *Continental Philosophy Review* 34 (2001): 11.

34. Deleuze, *Bergsonism*, 106–07.

35. In *Time and Free Will*, Bergson states that the time employed in physics is at best "some spurious concept (*un concept bâtard*)" (98).

36. A. D. Sertillanges, *Avec Henri Bergson* (Paris: Librairie Gallimard, 1941), 37–40.

37. Henri Bergson, "The Problem of the Personality," *Les études bergsoniennes* 7 (1966): 75; this is a summary, in English, of a presentation given by Bergson in his Gifford Lectures in Edinburgh, Scotland, in 1914.

38. In "The Problem of Personality," Bergson states: "What we call our personality is a certain continuity of change" (77).

39. Bergson, "The Problem of Personality," 70–71.

40. In *Creative Evolution*, Bergson states that "everywhere but man, consciousness has had to come to a stand; in man alone it has kept on its way. Man, then, continues the vital movement indefinitely, although he does not draw along with all that life carries in itself" (266).

41. Bergson, *Duration and Simultaneity: with Reference to Einstein's Theory*, trans. Leon Jacobson (New York: Bobbs-Merrill Co. Inc., 1965), 51.

42. In *The Creative Mind* Bergson states that "no mixing of . . . concepts among themselves . . . would give anything resembling the person that endures" (176).

43. Criticisms of Bergson's ideas can be followed in A. E. Pilkington, *Bergson and His Influence: A Reassessment* as well as in the introduction to Fredrick Burwick and Paul Douglass, eds. *The Crisis in Modernism: Bergson and the Vitalist Controversy*, 1–11.

44. John Mullarkey, *Bergson and Philosophy* (South Bend, Indiana: University of Notre Dame Press, 2000), 150.

45. See Claudia Stancati, "Bergson et le langage de la philosophie: comment doivent parles les philosophes," in Claudia Stancati, Donata Chirico, Federica Vercillo, eds., *Henri Bergson:esprit et langage* (Liège, Belgium: Pierre Mardaga, 2001), 71–83. See Bergson's comments in *The Creative Mind*, 108–11.

46. Bergson, *Mélanges*, 999–1000.

47. Henri Bergson, *Le Rire: essai sur la signification du comique* (Paris: F. Alcan, 1900). Authorized translation by C. Brereton and F. Rothwell, under the title *Laughter: An Essay on the Meaning of the Comic* (London: MacMillan & Co. Ltd., 1911), 156. Elsewhere in the same text we read that "Poetry always expresses inward states" (108). Despite his affinity for poetry, Bergson could not have foreseen the

explosive interest in metaphor and its centrality in our linguistic practices. Much of the postmodern interest in metaphor erupted as a reaction to the structuralism of Saussure. See J. Noppen, S. De Knop, and R. Jongen, eds., *Metaphor: A Bibliography of Post-1970 Publications,* Amsterdam Studies in Theory and History of Linguistic Science, vol. 17 (Amsterdam: John Benjamen Publishers, 1985). See also W. Parotte and R. Dirven, eds., *The Ubiquity of Metaphor,* Amsterdam Studies in Theory and History of Linguistic Science, vol. 4 (Amsterdam: John Benjamen Publishers, 1985); Paul Ricoeur, *The Rule of Metaphor,* trans. R. Czerny and J. Costello (Toronto: University of Toronto Press, 1977), and M. Arbib and Mary Hesse, *The Construction of Reality* (Cambridge: Cambridge University Press, 1986).

48. Martin Heidegger, "poetically man dwells," in *Poetry, Language, Thought,* trans. Albert Hofstadter (New York: Harper & Row Publishers, 1975), 213–29.

49. Bergson, *Laughter,* 167. In the same text Bergson states that art, "whether it be painting, or sculpture, poetry or music, has no other object than to brush aside the utilitarian symbols, the conventional and socially accepted generalities, in short, everything that veils reality from us, in order to bring us face to face with reality itself," (157).

50. Paul Ricoeur, "The Power of Speech: Science and Poetry," *Philosophy Today* 29, no. 2 (1985): 59–70, 69. For an extended discussion of discovery, creation and truth mediated by different modes of language use (science and literature) with special reference to Bergson, see Donald R. Maxwell, *Science or Literature: The Divergent Cultures of Discovery and Creation* (New York: Peter Lang, 2000).

51. Martin Heidegger, *Being and Time,* trans. J. Macquarrie and E. Robinson (Oxford: Basil Blackwell, 1978), 60.

52. Edmund Husserl, *The Phenomenology of Internal Time-Consciousness,* trans. J.S. Churchill (Bloomington, Indiana: Indiana University Press, 1964), §36, 100.

53. While Bergson states his own position explicitly, it is questionable exactly how this latter work completes his earlier notions. For a concise discussion of the polemic see A.E. Pilkington, *Bergson and His Influence: A Reassessment,* 21ff.

54. In *The Two Sources,* Bergson suggests that we may never be able to escape the regard of the social ego even when the individual self is totally isolated. To some degree, but not absolutely, moral distress arises when the relations between the individual and social self are upset. The verdict of conscience is the verdict that would be given by the social self (7–8).

55. In the authorized translation of this particular work the French term "la fonction fabulatrice" is translated as the "myth-making function." In Deleuze's work on Bergson quoted earlier, the term has been rendered "the story-making function" which is an equally valid translation while still conveying the sense Bergson intended. See Deleuze, *Bergsonism,* 108–13.

56. While scholars spare no excess in emphasising such Bergsonian themes as the reality of time, possibility, freedom, and intuition, few, outside of Deleuze, give prominence to the story-making function. Philippe Sergeant in *Bergson, Matière à Penser* (Paris: E. C. Éditions, 1996) argues, however, that 'la fonction

fabulatrice,' along with the notions of indetermination and substitution, are the trilogy of themes that define Bergson's thought (30). Honorable mention of this function is made in A. R. Lacey, *Bergson* (London: Routlege, 1989), 211–13.

57. See Paul Ricoeur, *Freedom and Nature: The Voluntary and the Involuntary,* trans. Erazim Kohak (Evanston, Illinois: Northwestern University Press, 1966), 160.

Notes to Chapter 3

1. Perhaps the best summary of Bergson's influence on Merleau-Ponty is found in Patrick Burke's introduction to Maurice Merleau-Ponty, *The Incarnate Subject: Malebranche, Biran and Bergson on the Union of Body and Soul,* eds. Andrew J. Bjelland Jr. and Patrick Burke (New York: Humanities Press, 2001), 15–25.

2. Theodore F. Geraets, *Vers une nouvelle philosophie transcendantale; La genèse de la philosophie de Maurice Merleau-Ponty jusqu'à la Phénoménologie de la perception,* Phaenomenologica 39 (La Haye: Martinus Nijhoff, 1971), 5–7. For a more complete synopsis of Merleau-Ponty's early philosophical formation, see Robert M. Friedman, "The Formation of Merleau-Ponty's Philosophy," *Philosophy Today* 17 (1973): 272–79.

3. For the common theme of the body in Bergson and Merleau-Ponty see Albert Rabil, *Merleau-Ponty: Existentialist of the Social World* (London: Columbia University Press, 1967), 24ff.; see also Yuasa Yasuo, *The Body: Toward an Eastern Mind-Body Theory,* trans. Nagatomo Shigenori and Thomas P. Kasulis, ed. Thomas P. Kasulis (Albany, New York: State University of New York Press, 1987), 161ff.

4. Specific essays on Bergson appear in *In Praise of Philosophy* and *Signs.* For Merleau-Ponty's lecture notes on Bergson see Maurice Merleau-Ponty, *Nature: Course Notes from the Collège de France,* trans. Robert Vallier, comp. Dominique Séglard (Evanston, Illinois: Northwestern University Press, 2003). Also, see Merleau-Ponty's notes on Bergson in *The Incarnate Subject.*

5. Further in *In Praise of Philosophy,* Merleau-Ponty will summarize the internal movement of Bergson's thought as a development from a philosophy of impression to a philosophy of expression — the very same development that is more evident in Merleau-Ponty's own philosophical trajectory (IPP 28).

6. Alphonse de Waelhens, *Une Philosophie de l'ambiguité: L'existentialisme de M. Merleau-Ponty* (Louvain: Publications Universitaires de Louvain, 1951), 8–9.

7. For more extensive comparisons between these two philosophers, see Ben-Ami Scharfstein, "Bergson and Merleau-Ponty: A Preliminary Comparison," *The Journal of Philosophy* 52 (1955): 380–86; Antoon Burgers, "De Houding van Bergson en Merleau-Ponty t.o.v. de Wetenschappen," *Tijdschrift voor filosofie* 27 (1965): 262–97; and Augustin Fressin, *La Perception Chez Bergson et Chez Merleau-Ponty* (Paris: Société d'Édition d'Enseignement Supérieur, 1967).

8. See M. C. Dillon, "Merleau-Ponty and Postmodernity," *Merleau-Ponty Vivant,* ed. M. C. Dillon (Albany: State University of New York Press, 1991), ix–xxxv.

9. Hugh J. Silverman, "Between Merleau-Ponty and Postmodernism," *Merleau-*

Ponty, Hermeneutics, and Postmodernism, eds. Thomas W. Busch and Shaun Gallagher (Albany: State University of New York, 1992), 146.

10. Joseph Margolis, "Merleau-Ponty and Postmodernism," in *Merleau-Ponty, Hermeneutics, and Postmodernism,* 241–56.

11. See Edmund Husserl, "The Fifth Meditation," *Cartesian Meditations: An Introduction to Phenomenology,* trans. D. Cairns (The Hague: Martinus Nijhoff, 1960), 89–148.

12. Edmund Husserl, *The Crisis of European Sciences and Transcendental Phenomenology,* trans. D. Carr (Evanston, Illinois: Northwestern University Press, 1970).

13. Unlike Bergson, Merleau-Ponty did not authorize translations of his own work. Citations will be taken from the English version while noting weaknesses in and ameliorations to Smith's translation suggested by Monika Langer in *Merleau-Ponty's Phenomenology of Perception: A Guide and Commentary* (Tallahassee, Florida: The Florida State University Press, 1989).

14. Edmund Husserl, *Logical Investigations,* trans. J. N. Findlay, Vol. 1 (London: Routledge & Kegan Paul, 1970), 252.

15. Note the various references to "return" in *The Structure of Behavior,* 4, 137, 185, 209, 219, 220. See also *Phenomenology of Perception,* ix, xi, xx, 54, 57, 206, 362, 365.

16. While Merleau-Ponty denies all dualism in the human being he nonetheless still admits of a certain duality to that being; see *The Structure of Behavior,* 176, 210.

17. The preface was written after the body of the text had been completed for some time and was added by Merleau-Ponty upon the suggestion of Leon Brunschivcg.

18. Unfortunately there are equivocations in Merleau-Ponty's expressions to describe this "contact." In a series of oppositions between the unreflected and reflected, the preobjective and objective, and the immediate and the deduced immediate, the path of how one gains access to the preobjective, the immediate, and the unreflected is never clearly delineated. In *Phenomenology of Perception,* Merleau-Ponty neither betrays a bias to the primacy of the given nor to the primacy of reflection. This balancing act between the unreflective and reflection, and of thought and perception, is the "two-way relationship that phenomenology has called *Fundierung,*" which is "the founding term, or originator — time, the unreflective, the fact, language, perception — is primary in the sense that the originated is presented as a determinate or explicit form of the originator, which prevents the latter from ever reabsorbing the former, and yet the originator is not primary in the empiricist sense and the originated is not simply derived from it, since it is through it that the originator is made manifest" (394). The realization of this two-way relationship is grasped, however, not through objective thought but "radical reflection" (xiv) which is mindful and indebted to something that has preceded it.

19. "Correspondingly, my body must be apprehended not only in an experience which is instantaneous, peculiar to itself and complete in itself, but also in some general aspect in the light of an impersonal being" (*Phenomenology of Perception,* 82).

20. Elsewhere in *Phenomenology of Perception,* Merleau-Ponty states: "Habit has its abode neither in thought nor in the objective body, but in the body as mediator of a world" (145).

21. In *Phenomenology of Perception,* Merleau-Ponty goes on to say that: "The phantom arm is not a recollection, it is a quasi-present and the patient feels it now . . . The imaginary arm is, then, like repressed experience, a former present which cannot decide to recede into the past. The memories called up before the patient induce in him a phantom limb, not as an image in associationism summons up another image, but because any memory reopens time lost to us and invites us to recapture the situation evoked" (85). Merleau-Ponty's discussion of memory at the level of the prepersonal and the personal body is restricted to developing something closely resembling Bergson's bodily memory with no effort to develop either a pure memory or contemplative component. In fact there is a steady diminution of recollection's role in recapturing the past in *Phenomenology of Perception.* He never seems to compromise in his belief in the directly given character of the remembered past. But given what is developed, there still remains a lack of discussion on precisely how the habitual body incorporates memory. For a more extended discussion see E. S. Casey, "Habitual Body and Memory in Merleau-Ponty," in *Man and World* 17(1984): 279–97.

22. Jacques Taminiaux, preface to *Merleau-Ponty, The Incarnate Subject: Malebranche, Biran and Bergson on the Union of Body and Soul,* 11–12.

23. The Colin Smith translation of *Phenomenology of Perception* erroneously translates *un schéma corporel* as "body image" instead of "body schema."

24. Elsewhere in the *Phenomenology of Perception,* Merleau-Ponty writes: "Experience of one's own body runs counter to the reflective procedure which detaches subject and object from each other, and which gives only the thought about the body, or the body as an idea, and not the experience of the body or the body in reality" (198–99).

25. In *Phenomenology of Perception,* Merleau-Ponty states: "The natural world is the horizon of all horizons, the style of all styles, which guarantees for my experiences a given, not a willed, unity underlying all the disruptions of my personal and historical life. Its counterpart within me is the given, general, and pre-personal existence of my sensory functions in which we have discovered the definition of the body" (330).

26. As with the different terms Merleau-Ponty uses to designate various aspects of the prepersonal body, he employs several terms to designate the thematized self who makes decisions, choices, and reflections. These include the normal subject, personal subject, the incarnate subject, the personal *Cogito,* and the real *Cogito.* I prefer the term "living self" that Merleau-Ponty sometimes employs as it imparts a sense of the not-yet-complete and open-endedness in human development, growth, and change.

27. In *Phenomenology of Perception,* Merleau-Ponty goes on to say that "the spoken word is a genuine gesture, and it contains its meaning in the same way as the gesture contains its. This is what makes communication possible. In order that

I may understand the words of another person, it is clear that his vocabulary and syntax must be 'already known' to me" (183).

28. In *Phenomenology of Perception,* we read: "It [language] presents or rather it *is* the subject's taking up of a position in the world of his meanings. The term 'world' here is not a manner of speaking: it means that the 'mental' or cultural life borrows its structure from natural life and that the thinking subject must have its basis in the subject incarnate" (193).

29. In the first chapter of the last section of the *Phenomenology of Perception,* entitled "The Cogito," Merleau-Ponty makes an important distinction between a verbal *cogito* (*un Cogito sur parole*) and the tacit *cogito.* He states that the verbal *cogito* does not put me into "contact with my own life and thought" unless the tacit *cogito* is encountered (402). However, Merleau-Ponty throughout his thesis equivocates on this coincidence with the tacit *cogito.* In one place he speaks about "absolute contact with myself" (295) while in another he says that "nowhere do I enjoy absolute possession of myself" (240). This is further confounded when he states that we have "the primordial certainty of being in contact with being itself" (355) in contrast to "since the lived is thus never entirely comprehensible, what I understand never quite tallies with my living experience, in short, I am never quite at one with myself" (347). In one quote, Merleau-Ponty goes so far as to advocate a coincidence "with the act of perception and break with the critical attitude" (238), which negates not only the philosophical act but language as well, thereby making the natural self more significant than the social self. However, even this is contradicted when he advises that: "All that is required is that the coincidence of myself with myself, as it is achieved in the *cogito,* shall never be a real coincidence, but merely an intentional and presumptive one" (344). Merleau-Ponty will criticize himself on these very inconsistencies later in *The Visible and the Invisible* (175–76).

30. Elsewhere in *Phenomenology of Perception,* Merleau-Ponty remarks: "Objective thought is unaware of the subject of perception. This is because it presents itself with the world ready made, as the setting of every possible event, and treats perception as one of these events. . . . There can be no question of describing perception itself as one of the facts thrown up in the world, since we can never fill up, in the picture of the world, the gap we ourselves are, and by which it comes into existence for someone, since perception is the 'flaw' in this 'great diamond'" (207).

31. The full quote reads: "Hence reflection does not itself grasp its full significance unless it refers to the unreflective fund of experience which it presupposes, upon which it draws, and which constitutes for it a kind of original past, a past which has never been a present." See note 27 in chapter 2.

32. Elsewhere in *Phenomenology of Perception,* it reads: "the question is always how I can be open to phenomena which transcend me, and which nevertheless exist only to the extent that I take up and live them; *how the presence of myself (Urpräsenz) which establishes my own limits and conditions every alien presence is at the same time depresentation (Entgegenwärtigung) and throws me outside myself*" (363).

33. See Edmund Husserl, *The Phenomenology of Internal Time-Consciousness*, trans. J. S. Churchill (Bloomington: Indiana University Press, 1964), §1, 23.

34. See Husserl, *The Phenomenology of Internal Time Consciousness*, §10, 49; §43, 121.

35. Earlier in *Phenomenology of Perception*, Merleau-Ponty had remarked that the awareness of human existences lies in *ek-stase*, that is, "the active transcendence of the subject in relation to the world" (70) that is underpinned by a perceptual faith we each have in our primordial experience of existing in the world.

36. See G. B. Madison, *The Phenomenology of Merleau-Ponty* (Athens, Ohio: Ohio University Press, 1981), 271–72.

37. Ibid.

38. Ricoeur will repeatedly note his appreciation for Merleau-Ponty in *Time and Narrative* (230–31) but it is not for the latter's notion of time. The significant passage will be quoted on the following page.

39. Reminiscent of Bergson's idea of duration, John F. Bannan, in *The Philosophy of Merleau-Ponty* (New York: Harcourt Brace, 1967), in reference to the phenomenal world, states that the "present has an enduring central position — an omni-temporality — which, if it is not outside of time, nonetheless endures through time and gives rise to it" (133).

40. This is precisely the problem Merleau-Ponty pinpoints in his own self-critique of "the upsurge of time" when he states: "The upsurge of time would be incomprehensible as the *creation* of a supplement of time that would push the whole preceding series back into the past. That passivity is not conceivable. On the other hand every analysis of time that views it from above is insufficient. Time must *constitute itself* — be always seen from the point of view of someone who *is* of *it* . . . . time is not an absolute series of events, a tempo — not even the tempo of the consciousness — it is an institution, a system of equivalences" (*The Visible and the Invisible*, 184). The continual assertions of time as being an "upsurge," "an institution," or "a system of equivalences," all indicate a struggle to escape an aporia that he had planted years ago in presupposing a *silent but bodily phenomenal time*. The positing of a particular category of time does not lead to a clarification of time but only to further assertions to reinforce the original presupposition. See the arguments in Stephen Priest, *Merleau-Ponty* (London: Routledge, 1998), 131–37.

41. M. C. Dillon, "Apriority in Kant and Merleau-Ponty," *Kant-Studien* 78 (1987): 415.

42. In *The Visible and the Invisible*, Merleau-Ponty will argue that there is no finalism because there is always what he called in *Phenomenology of Perception* dehiscence (265).

43. Monika Langer, *Merleau-Ponty's Phenomenology of Perception: A Guide and Commentary*, 169.

44. Elsewhere in *Phenomenology of Perception*, Merleau-Ponty states: "This book, once begun, is not a certain set of ideas; it constitutes for me an open situation, for which I could not possibly provide any complex formula, and in which I

struggle blindly on until, miraculously, thoughts and words become organized by themselves" (369).

45. Paul Ricoeur, *Husserl: An Analysis of His Phenomenology,* trans. E. Ballard and L. Embree (Evanston: Northwestern University Press, 1967), 210.

46. Simone de Beauvoir, *L'Invitée,* (Paris: Éditions Gallimard, 1943), translated as *She Came to Stay* (Cleveland: The World Publishing Co., 1954).

47. I will return to this topic in the last section of the final chapter entitled "Creative Time," where I suggest that philosophers' works might be seen as partly their own self-narrative — that is, as a creative act in time to give their temporal existence the meaning they sought in it.

48. In *Primacy of Perception,* Merleau-Ponty writes, "Every incarnate subject is like an open notebook in which we do not yet know what will be written. Or it is like a new language; we do not know what work it will accomplish but only that, once it has appeared, it cannot fail to say little or much, to have a history and a meaning" (6).

49. Maurice Merleau-Ponty, *La Prose du monde,* ed. Claude Lefort (Paris, Gallimard, 1969). Translated by J. O'Neill as *The Prose of the World* (Evanston, Illinois: Northwestern University Press, 1973), 141.

50. Ibid., 11–14; my emphasis.

51. In *The Visible and the Invisible,* we read: "we ourselves are one sole continued question, a perpetual enterprise of taking our bearings on the constellations of the world, and of taking the bearings of the things of our dimensions" (103).

52. For a current summary see Fred Evans and Leonard Lawlor, eds., *Chiasms: Merleau-Ponty's Notion of flesh* (Albany: State University of New York Press, 2000). With regard to Merleau-Ponty's development of an ontology see M. C. Dillon, *Merleau-Ponty's Ontology* (Bloomington: Indiana University Press, 1988).

53. In *The Visible and the Invisible,* Merleau-Ponty writes, "We see the things themselves, the world is what we see: formulae of this kind express a faith common to the natural man and the philosopher — the moment he opens his eyes; they refer to a deep-seated set of mute 'opinions' implicated in our lives. But what is strange about this faith is that if we seek to articulate it into theses or statements, if we ask ourselves what is this *we,* what *seeing* is, and what *thing* or *world* is, we enter into a labyrinth of difficulties and contradictions" (3).

54. For how a contemporary hermeneutic position might be read back into Merleau-Ponty, see James Risser, "Communication and the Prose of the World: The Question of Language in Merleau-Ponty and Gadamer," in Patrick Burke and Jan Van der Veken, ed., *Merleau-Ponty in Contemporary Perspective* (Dordrecht: Kluwer Academic Publishers, 1993), 131–44.

55. Gary Gutting, *French Philosophy in the Twentieth Century* (Cambridge: Cambridge University Press, 2001, 185.

56. M. C. Dillon, *Merleau-Ponty's Ontology,* 85.

57. G. B. Madison, "Merleau-Ponty and Postmodernity," in *The Hermeneutics of Postmodernity* (Bloomington: Indiana University Press, 1988), 67.

Notes to Chapter 4

1. See Burkhard Liebsch, "Archeological Questioning: Merleau-Ponty and Ricoeur," in Patrick Burke and Jan Van Der Veken, eds., *Merleau-Ponty in Contemporary Perspectives* (Dordrecht: Kluwer Academic Publishers, 1993), 13–24 and Thomas W. Busch, "Perception, Finitude, and Transgression: A Note on Merleau-Ponty and Ricoeur," in Thomas W. Busch and Shaun Gallagher, eds., *Merleau-Ponty, Hermeneutics, and Postmodernism* (Albany, New York; State University of New York Press, 1992)·

2. Paul Ricoeur, *The Conflict of Interpretations: Essays in Hermeneutics* ed. Don Ihde (Evanston: Northwestern University Press, 1974), 247.

3. See Paul Ricoeur, *Husserl: An Analysis of His Phenomenology*, trans. Edward Ballard and Lester Embree (Evanston: Northwestern University Press, 1967), 209, and the opening chapters of Paul Ricoeur, *Fallible Man; Philosophy of the Will*, trans. Charles Kelbley (Chicago: Henry Regnery Company, 1965).

4. Paul Ricoeur, "De la volonté à l'acte: Un entretien de Paul Ricoeur avec Carlos Oliveria," in Christian Bouchindhomme and Rainer Rochlitz, eds. *Temps et récit de Paul Ricoeur en débat* (Paris: Les Éditions du Cerf, 1990), 17.

5. Angelo Hesnard *L'Oeuvre de Freud et son importance pour le monde moderne* (Paris: Payot, 1960); an English translation is found in Keith Hoeller, ed., *Merleau-Ponty and Psychology* (Atlantic Highlands, New Jersey: Humanities Press, 1993).

6. See Paul Ricoeur, *Freud and Philosophy: An Essay in Interpretation*, trans. Denis Savage (London: Yale University Press, 1970), 417–78.

7. Ibid., 458. Elsewhere, Ricoeur will call this suggestion from Merleau-Ponty for an "archaeology of the subject" an "adventure of reflection." It will result in "a *cogito* which posits but does not possess itself, a *cogito* which understands its primordial truth only in and through the avowal of the inadequation, the illusion, the fakery of immediate consciousness;" see Paul Ricoeur, *The Conflict of Interpretations*, 243.

8. Paul Ricoeur, *Freud and Philosophy*, 458.

9. With the regard to the "I can," Merleau-Ponty states that "our bodily experience of movement is not a particular case of knowledge; it provides us with a way of access to the world and the object . . . which has to be recognized as original and perhaps as primary (PP 140).

10. Paul Ricoeur, "Hommage à Merleau-Ponty," *Esprit*, 296 (1961): 1115–120.

11. Paul Ricoeur, in *Paul Ricoeur and Narrative: Context and Contestation*, ed. Morny Joy (Calgary University Press, 1997), xv.

12. For a summary of Ricoeur's philosophical agenda see Mark Muldoon, *On Ricoeur* (Belmont, California: Wadsworth, 2002).

13. For a discussion of Ricoeur's place within contemporary moral philosophy see John Wall, William Schweiker, and David W. Hall, *Paul Ricoeur and Contemporary Moral Thought* (New York: Routledge, 2002).

14. Paul Ricoeur, "Narrative Time," *Critical Inquiry* 7 (1980): 169–90.

15. Paul Ricoeur, *The Philosophy of Paul Ricoeur*, ed. Lewis Edwin Hahn (Chicago: Open Court, 1995) 39.

16. Aristotle, *Aristotle's Poetics*, trans. James Hutton (New York: W. W. Norton & Company, 1982).

17. Some of the basic presuppositions found in *Time and Narrative*, such as the narrative structure of life and the completion of a text through reading, have their antecedents in Ricoeur's early scholarship. In *The Conflict of Interpretations*, Ricoeur stated that the reflecting subject "can be recovered only by the detour of a decipherment of the documents of its life" (18). Ricoeur's second presupposition concerning the interaction of the text and the reader is found predominately in works dating from the mid-1970s. See Ricoeur's various studies in *Interpretation Theory: Discourse and the Surplus of Meaning* (Fort Worth, Texas: The Texas Christian University Press, 1976) and *Hermeneutics and the Human Sciences* (HS 274–96). I shall return to this topic in a later portion of this chapter.

18. Immanuel Kant, *Critique of Pure Reason*, ed. Norman Kemp Smith (New York: St. Martin's Press, 1965), A118.

19. For a summary of Ricoeur's notion of imagination see Mark S. Muldoon, "Reading, Imagination and Interpretation: A Ricoeurian Response," *International Philosophical Quarterly* 40 (2000): 69–83.

20. Émile Benveniste, in *Problèmes de linguistique générale, II* (Paris: Éditions Gallimard, 1974) states that "Language manifests the human experience of time and linguistic time appears to be irreducible to either chronicle time or physical time. . . . This time has its center — both a generating and axial center – in the *present* instance of speaking. Each time a speaker employs the grammatical form of the 'present' (or its equivalent), he [or she] situates the event contemporaneously with the instance of discourse that utters it. It is evident that this present, in so far as it is a function of discourse, cannot be localized into one particular division of chronicle time because it encompasses all of them but appeals to none of them. The speaker situates as 'present' everything implicated by virtue of the linguistic form he [or she] employs. This present is reinvented each time a human being speaks because it is, literally, a new moment, yet to be lived. This is, once again, an original property of language, so particular that it warrants the search for a distinct term to designate linguistic time and separate it from other notions with which it can be confused" (73–74) (my translation); see also note 38 in chapter 1.

21. Throughout *Time and Narrative*, Ricoeur expresses his indebtedness to H-G. Gadamer [see especially Gadamer, *Truth and Method*, trans. and ed. Garrett Barden and John Cumming (New York: Seabury Press, 1975)] with regard to what constitutes interpretation and "the fusion of horizons" (*Horizontverschmelzung*); see Ricoeur, TN1 70, 77; TN3 158.

22. Émile Benveniste, *Problèmes de linguistique générale, II* 70–71; (my translation).

23. Martin Heidegger, *Being and Time*, trans. J. Macquarrie and E. Robinson (Oxford: Basil Blackwell, 1978), 446, his emphasis.

24. The term *Gegenüber* is not Ricoeur's but borrowed from Karl Heussi's, in *Die Krisis des Historismus;* see Ricoeur, TN3 305, n.1. Ricoeur further adapts the distinction between representing something to oneself in the sense of "standing for" (*vertreten*) something and representing something to oneself in the sense of giving oneself a mental image of some absent external thing (*sich vorstellen*). The trace left by the past exercises a function of taking-the-place-of, of standing-for. This function characterizes the indirect reference proper to knowledge through traces and distinguishes it from every other referential mode of history in relation to the past. Subsequently, Ricoeur states, "it is only by means of an endless rectification of our configurations that we form the idea of the past as an inexhaustible resource" (TN3 305).

25. See Ricoeur's various essays in *Hermeneutics and the Human Sciences.*

26. For further discussion of what Ricoeur calls "the real" and problems with reference see Mark Muldoon, *On Ricoeur* (Belmont, California: Wadsworth, 2002), 61ff.

27. Owing to Ricoeur's analysis of *idem*-identity and *ipse*-identity, I will forego the traditional distinction between "persons and personal identity" and "self and selfhood" and interchangeably use the terms "narrative identity" and "narrative self." I take both terms to embrace embodiment, including fictional persons. In both *Time and Narrative* and *Oneself as Another,* Ricoeur explicitly borrows the Merleau-Pontyean notion of "I can" to express the lived body's ability to act. For Ricoeur, the lived body is a hinge-point between my own powers to act and the things that belong to the world order. It is the intermediary between action and agent and serves as a "propaedeutic to the question of selfhood" and the identification of "who" is responsible for his or her actions; see OA 111–13.

28. Paul Ricoeur, *The Philosophy of Paul Ricoeur,* ed. Lewis Edwin Hahn (Chicago: Open Court, 1995), 47.

29. Paul Trainor, in "Autobiography as Philosophical Argument: Socrates, Descartes, and Collingwood," *Thought* 63 (1988), states: "In reliving a subject's life, readers must understand the subject's relationship to others, and in recreating in their own minds the thoughts, feelings, and actions of the narrator, readers may actualize their own capacities to think, feel, and act in new ways" (394). To act in new ways means that we have to reinterpret a previous horizon of possibilities and options within a temporal framework. When we decide to change our own course of action, routine, and goals, then a new temporal framework is engendered. What changes, however, may not be an itemized agenda but a worldview, a sense of temporal passage, or our relationship to a perceived end-time that decisively changes our relationship to others, a value system, material goods, and career choices.

30. See Émile Benveniste, *Problems in General Linguistics,* trans. Elizabeth Meek (Coral Gables, Florida: University of Miami Press, 1971), 223–27. While Benveniste's works are very decisive in linking subjectivity, identity, and language together, they ultimately belie a residual foundationalism with regard to the "positing" of the subject being construed as its "constitution." See the criticism of C. O. Schrag,

in *Communicative Praxis and the Space of Subjectivity* (Bloomington: Indiana University Press, 1986), 124, n. 11.

31. See Paul Ricoeur, "Narrative Identity," *Philosophy Today* 35 (1991): 73–81.

32. See the various references already cited in note 19 of the Introduction as well as Roy Schafer, "Narration in the Psychoanalytical Dialogue," *On Narrative,* ed. W. J. T. Mitchell (Chicago: University of Chicago Press, 1981); Alisdaire McIntyre, *After Virtue,* 2nd ed. (Notre Dame, Indiana: University of Notre Dame Press, 1984), 204–25; Donald Spence, *Narrative Truth and Historical Truth: Meaning and Interpretation in Psychoanalysis* (New York: W. W. Norton and Co., 1984); Charles Taylor, "Self-Interpreting Animals," in *Human Agency and Language: Philosophical Papers I* (Cambridge: Cambridge University Press, 1985), 45–76; David Carr, *Time, Narrative, History* (Bloomington: Indiana University Press, 1986); Theodore Sarbin, ed., *Narrative Psychology* (New York: Praeger, 1986).

33. Barbara Hardy, "Towards a Poetics of Fiction: 3) An Approach through Narrative," *Novel* 2 (1968): 5.

34. See Ricoeur, *Freud and Philosophy,* 32ff.

35. Ricoeur, "Narrative Identity," 73.

36. A contemporary example of this reductionism is found in Gilles Deleuze and Felix Guattari, *Anti-Oedipus: Capitalism and Schizophrenia* (New York: Viking Press, 1977), when they state that "the subject — produced as a residuum alongside the machine, as an appendix, or as a spare part adjacent to the machine — passes through all the degrees of the circle, and passes from one circle to another. The subject by itself is not at the center, which is occupied by a machine, but on the periphery, with no fixed identity, forever, decentered, defined by the states through which it passes" (20).

Notes to Chapter 5

1. Ricoeur, "Existence and Hermeneutics," *The Conflict of Interpretations: Essays in Hermeneutics,* ed. Don Ihde (Evanston: Northwestern University Press, 1974), 19.

2. Ibid., 21.

3. Paul Ricoeur "Freedom in the Light of Hope," in *The Conflict of Interpretations,* 411.

4. Ricoeur, "Existence and Hermeneutics," in *The Conflict of Interpretations,* 22.

5. Paul Ricoeur, *The Rule of Metaphor: Multi-disciplinary Studies in the Creation of Meaning in Language,* trans. R. Czerny, K. McLaughlin, and J. Costello (Toronto: University of Toronto Press, 1977).

6. Albert Camus, *The Myth of Sisphus,* trans. Justin O'Brien (New York: Vintage Books, 1955), 13, 38, 8.

7. Ibid., 43, 11.

8. Ibid., 41–47.

9. Richard Rorty, *Philosophy and the Mirror of Nature* (Princeton, New Jersey: Princeton University Press, 1979), 155ff.

10. Camus, *The Myth of Sisyphus*, 4.

11. I'm employing the term "substantialism" as defined by Risieri Frondizi, in *The Nature of the Self: A Functional Interpretation* (Carbondale: Southern Illinois University Press, 1970). Frondizi states: "What I mean by substantialist prejudice is the presupposition that the existence of a phenomenon, activity, quality, etc., presupposes the existence of a substance as a substratum the supports it. This prejudice brings with it the implicit presupposition that there can be no activity without subject, no thought — in the Cartesian sense — without a thinking self" (10, n. 1). Frondizi goes on to say that substantialism allows one to conceive of the self after the fashion of a physical reality which brings it closer to the attitude of common sense, which maintains that "seeing is believing." One of the primary characteristics of the substantialist position, in regard to the self, is the question of immutability. "Perhaps fearing lest the empirical examination of the self dissolve into nothingness that which they most desire to preserve, they postulate the existence of a substantial, immutable nucleus that is completely unaffected by the modifications that might be brought about by the most violent changes in our inner life" (131).

12. For a discussion of the wide implications of narrative understanding in terms of ethics and justice see the final chapter in Mark S. Muldoon, *On Ricoeur* (Belmont, California: Wadsworth, 2002).

13. Risieri Frondizi, *The Nature of the Self*, 117.

14. See Paul Ricoeur, *Freedom and Nature: The Voluntary and the Involuntary*, trans. E. V. Kohak (Evanston, Illinois: Northwestern University Press, 1966), 69.

15. Ibid., 161.

16. Ibid., 69, 162.

17. See Mark Muldoon, "Ricoeur and Merleau-Ponty on Narrative Identity," *American Catholic Philosophical Quarterly* 71 (1997): 35–52.

18. Paul Ricoeur, "History as Narrative and Practice," *Philosophy Today* 29 (1985): 214.

19. Elsewhere in the *Phenomenology of Perception*, Merleau-Ponty will state that, ". . . I have the impression that it [time] is the mobile entity itself which changes its position, and which effects the passage from one instant or one position to another" (276, n. 1).

20. Paul Ricoeur, *History and Truth*, trans. Charles Kelbley (Evanston: Northwestern University Press, 1965), 309; my emphasis.

21. Paul Ricoeur, *Husserl: An Analysis of His Phenomenology*, trans. E. Ballard and L. Embree (Evanston: Northwestern University Press, 1967), 210.

22. The qualification is purposely made to reinforce the statements at the end of chapter 3 that, in the course of his philosophical career, Merleau-Ponty's thought certainly evolved, and his later thought does not defend many of the positions he held as author of the *Phenomenology of Perception*.

23. While Merleau-Ponty's argument that understanding embodiment is central to any philosophical reflection, his description of that embodiment is open

for various interpretations. The numerous works of Paul Fraisse, for example, describe at length how we structure the lived present based on the coordination of movement by organizing rhythms in a particular environment. Much of this has to do with the fact that we are bioacoustical beings drawn forth by the aural ambience in our vital milieu; see Paul Fraisse, *The Psychology of Time* (New York: Harper & Row, 1963); Paul Fraisse, *Psychologie du rythme* (Paris: Presses Universitaires de France, 1974); and Paul Fraisse, "Time and Rhythm Perception," in *Handbook of Perception,* ed. Edward C. Carterette and Morton P. Friedman (New York Academic Press, 1978), 203–54. As well, for a challenge to the primacy Merleau-Ponty gives to the lived present see the third essay "Duration and Evolution," in Keith Ansell-Pearson, *Philosophy and the Adventure of the Virtual: Bergson and the Time of Life* (London: Routledge, 2002).

24. Shaun Gallagher, "Introduction: The Hermeneutics of Ambiguity," in *Merleau-Ponty, Hermeneutics and Postmodernism,* ed. Thomas W. Busch and Shaun Gallagher (Albany, New York: State University of New York, 1992), 3.

25. Richard Taylor, "Time and Life's Meaning," *Review of Metaphysics* 40 (1987): 682.

26. Ibid., 676.

27. It is far outside the purview of this work to detail the various ways our lives become narrativized. As a conscious effort, it can be exercised through daily journals, memoirs, novels, short stories, creative nonfiction and even highly rationalistic works such as academic papers and tomes. For others, it may be oral stories told to grandchildren, nieces, and nephews that are passed from one generation to the next; for others, in a less conscious mode, it may be allegiance to religious narratives or the cultural myth of nationalism. For an interesting insight into the unreliability of identity, memory, and personal narratives, see Maureen Murdock, *Unreliable Truths: On Memoir and Memory* (New York: Seal Press, 2003).

28. This formulation is taken from "the Big Book" of *Alcoholics Anonymous* (A.A.). There is perhaps no better example of a contemporary organization that explicitly understands the continual process of reconfiguration with regard to identity over time; see *Alcoholics Anonymous: The Story of How Many Thousands of Men and Women Have Recovered from Alcoholism,* 3rd ed. (New York: Alcoholics Anonymous World Services, 1976), 58.

29. Friedrich Nietzsche, *Human, All Too Human,* trans. Marion Faber and Stephen Lehmann (Lincoln: University of Nebraska Press, 1984), §513. For modern summary arguments of this nature see William Earle, "Philosophy as Autobiography," in *Public Sorrows and Private Pleasures* (Bloomington: Indiana University Press, 1976); Paul Trainor, "Autobiography as Philosophical Argument: Socrates, Descartes and Collingwood," *Thought* 63 (1988): 378–96; Harry Settanni, *Five Philosophers: How Their Lives Influenced Their Thought* (Lanham, Maryland: University Press of America, 1992).

30. Julia Kristeva, *Hannah Arendt: Life is a Narrative,* trans. Frank Collins (Toronto: University of Toronto Press, 2001), 4.

31. Hannah Arendt, *The Human Condition* (Chicago: University of Chicago Press, 1958), 97.

32. Like Arendt, Ricoeur has also written passionately on politics and the role of narrative; for a summary see Bernard Dauenhauer, *Paul Ricoeur: The Promise and Risk of Politics* (Boston: Rowman & Littlefield, Inc., 1998). Perhaps the most accessible works to enter into Ricoeur's thinking on justice, politics, and narrative are Paul Ricoeur, *The Just,* trans. David Pellauer (Chicago: The University of Chicago Press, 2000) and *Le Juste II* (Paris: Éditions du Seuil, 2001).

33. Ricoeur recognized a conceptual gap in both *Time and Narrative* and *Oneself as Another* concerning the role of memory. To this end he published *Memory, History, Forgetting,* trans. Kathleen Blamey and David Pellauer (Chicago: The University of Chicago Press, 2004). Central to this work is "a just political memory." This formulation of memory attempts to seek a balance between an "official" collective memory that is often ideologically motivated and the testimony of individuals who may have died but whose stories echo in the memory of those still alive, as well as in texts and documents. For Ricoeur we must all be on guard against "official memory" that so often plays with "too much history here, and too much forgetting there."

34. Kristeva, *Hannah Arendt,* 45.

35. Arendt, *The Human Condition,* 324.

36. Eyal Chowers "The Marriage of Time and Identity: Kant, Benjamin and the Nation State," *Philosophy and Social Criticism* 25, no. 3 (1999): 57–80; see also Damon A. Young, "The Mortal Blessings of Narrative: Death, Poetry, and the Beginnings of Cultural Change," *Philosophy Today* 45, no. 3/4 (2001): 275–85.

37. Eyal Chowers "The Marriage of Time and Identity: Kant," 58.

Bibliography

Alcoholics Anonymous: The Story of How Many Thousands of Men and Women Have Recovered from Alcoholism. 3rd ed. New York: Alcoholics Anonymous World Services, 1976.

Adamson, Gregory Dale. *Philosophy in the Age of Science and Capital.* London: Continuum Press, 2002.

Al-Saji, Alia. "Merleau-Ponty and Bergson: Bodies Expression and Temporalities in the 'Flesh.'" *Philosophy Today* 45 (2001): 110–23.

Antliff, Mark. *Inventing Bergson: Cultural Politics and the Parisian Avant-Garde.* Princeton: Princeton University Press, 1993.

Anton, Corey. *Selfhood and Authenticity.* Albany: State University of New York Press, 2001.

Ansell-Pearson, Keith. *Philosophy and the Adventure of the Virtual: Bergson and the Time of Life.* London: Routledge, 2002.

Arbib, Michael and Mary Hesse. *The Construction of Reality.* Cambridge: Cambridge University Press, 1986.

Arendt, Hannah. *The Human Condition.* Chicago: University of Chicago Press, 1958.

Aristotle. "Physics," in *The Complete Works of Aristotle.* Ed. Jonathan Barnes. Trans. R. P. Hardie and R. K. Gaye. Vol. 1. Princeton: Princeton University Press, 1984.

———. *Aristotle's Poetics.* Trans. James Hutton. New York: W. W. Norton & Company, 1982.

Atkins, Kim. "Ricoeur's 'Human Time' as a Response to the Problem of Closure in Heideggerian Temporality." *Philosophy Today* 44 (2000): 108–22.

Augustine. *Confessions.* Trans. R. S. Pine-Coffin. Middlesex, England: Penguin Books, 1964.

Baert, Patrick, ed. *Time in Contemporary Intellectual Thought.* Amsterdam: Elsevier, 2000.

Bannan, John F. *The Philosophy of Merleau-Ponty.* New York: Harcourt Brace, 1967.

Benveniste, Émile. *Problèmes de linguistique générale, II.* Paris: Éditions Gallimard, 1974.

————. *Problems in General Linguistics.* Trans. Elizabeth Meek. Coral Gables, Florida: University of Miami Press, 1971.

Bergson, Henri. *Mélanges.* Ed. André Robinet. Paris: Presses Universitaires de France, 1972.

————. "The Problem of the Personality." *Les études bergsoniennes* 7 (1966): 15–24.

————. *Duration and Simultaneity: with Reference to Einstein's Theory.* Trans. Leon Jacobson. New York: Bobbs-Merrill Co. Inc., 1965.

————. *Laughter: An Essay on the Meaning of the Comic.* Trans. C. Brereton and F. Rothwell. London: MacMillan & Co. Ltd., 1911.

Borradori, Giovanna. "The Temporalization of Difference: Reflections on Deleuze's Interpretation of Bergson," *Continental Philosophy Review,* 34 (2001): 11.

Bouchindhomme, Christian and Rainer Rochlitz, eds. *Temps et récit de Paul Ricoeur en débat.* Paris: Les Éditions du Cerf, 1990.

Bourgeois, Patrick L. and Frank Schalow. *Traces of Understanding: A Profile of Heidegger's and Ricoeur's Hermeneutics.* Amsterdam: Rodopi, 1990.

Brockelman, Paul. *Time and Self: Phenomenological Explorations.* AAR Studies in Religion 39. New York: The Crossroad Publishing Company and Scholars Press, 1985.

Burgers, Antoon. "De Houding van Bergson en Merleau-Ponty t.o.v. de Wetenschappen." *Tijdschrift voor Filosofie* 27 (1965): 262–97.

Burke, Patrick and Jan Van der Veken, eds. *Merleau-Ponty in Contemporary Perspective.* Dordrecht: Kluwer Academic Publishers, 1993.

Burwick, Fredrick and Paul Douglass, eds. *The Crisis in Modernism: Bergson and the Vitalist Controversy.* Cambridge: Cambridge University Press, 1992.

Busch, Thomas W. and Shaun Gallagher. eds. *Merleau-Ponty, Hermeneutics, and Postmodernism*. Albany: State University of New York, 1992.

Camus, Albert. *The Myth of Sisphus*. Trans. Justin O'Brien. New York: Vintage Books, 1955.

Capek, Milic. *Bergson and Modern Physics; A Reinterpretation and Re-evaluation*. Vol. 7, Boston Studies in the Philosophy of Science. Boston: D. Reidel Publishing Co., 1971.

———. *The Philosophical Impact of Contemporary Physics*. New York: D. Van Nostrand, 1961.

Carr, David. *Time, Narrative, and History*. Bloomington: Indiana University Press, 1986.

Carterette, Edward C. and Morton P. Friedman, eds. *Handbook of Perception*. New York Academic Press, 1978.

Casey, Edward S. "Habitual Body and Memory in Merleau-Ponty." *Man and World* 17 (1984): 279–97.

Chamberlain, Jane. "Thinking Ricoeur's Husserl in *Time and Narrative*." *Minerva – An Internet Journal of Philosophy* 2 (1998): December 2002 http://www.ul.ie/~philos/vol2/husserl.html.

Chowers, Eyal. "The Marriage of Time and Identity: Kant, Benjamin and the Nation State." *Philosophy and Social Criticism* 25 (1999): 57–80.

Collingwood, Robin G. *The Idea of History*. Ed. T. M. Knox. Oxford: Oxford University Press, 1946.

Craig, Edward J., "Philosophy and Philosophies." *Philosophy* 58 (1983): 189–201.

Dauenhauer, Bernard. *Paul Ricoeur: The Promise and Risk of Politics*. Boston: Rowman & Littlefield, Inc., 1998.

de Beauvoir, Simone. *She Came to Stay*. Cleveland: The World Publishing Co., 1954.

Deleuze, Gilles. *Cinema 2: The Time-Image*. Trans. Hugh Tomlinson and Robert Galeta. Minneapolis: University of Minnesota Press, 1989.

———. *Cinema 1: The Movement-Image*. Trans. Hugh Tomlinson and Barbara Habberjam. Minneapolis: University of Minnesota Press, 1986.

———. *Bergsonism*. Trans. Hugh Tomlinson and Barbara Habberjam. New York: Zone Books, 1988.

Deleuze, Gilles and Felix Guattari. *Anti-Oedipus: Capitalism and Schizophrenia*. New York: Viking Press, 1977.

Derrida, Jacques. *Margins of Philosophy*. Trans. Alan Bass. New York: University of Chicago Press, 1982.

Descombes, Vincent. *Objects of All Sorts: A Philosophical Grammar*. Baltimore: John Hopkins University Press, 1987.

de Waelhens, Alphonse. *Une Philosophie de l'ambiguité: L'existentialisme de M. Merleau-Ponty*. Louvain: Publications Universitaires de Louvain, 1951.

Diels, Hermann. *Ancilla to the Pre-Socratic Philosophers*. Trans. K. Freeman. Cambridge, Mass.: Harvard University Press, 1977.

Dillon, Martin C., ed. *Merleau-Ponty Vivant*. Albany: State University of New York Press, 1991.

———. *Merleau-Ponty's Ontology*. Bloomington: Indiana University Press, 1988.

———. "Apriority in Kant and Merleau-Ponty." *Kant-Studien* 78 (1987): 403–23.

Douglass, Paul. *Bergson, Eliot, and American Literature*. Lexington: University Press of Kentucky, 1986.

Duric, Robin. "Creativity and Life." *Review of Metaphysics* 56 (2002): 357–84.

During, Elie. "'A History of Problems': Bergson and the French Epistemological Tradition." *Journal of the British Society for Phenomenology* 35 (2004): 4–23.

Earle, William. *Public Sorrows and Private Pleasures*. Bloomington: Indiana University Press, 1976.

Einstein, Albert. *Relativity: The Special and the General Theory*. Trans. Robert W. Lawson. New York: Bonanza Books, 1961.

Evans, Fred and Leonard Lawlor, eds. *Chiasms: Merleau-Ponty's Notion of Flesh*. Albany: State University of New York Press, 2000.

Faye, Jan, Uwe Scheffler, and Max Urche, *Perspectives on Time*. Dordrecht: Kluwer Academic Publishers, 1997.

Flew, Antony. *David Hume: Philosopher of Moral Science*. Oxford: Basil Blackwell, 1986.

Fraisse, Paul. *Psychologie du rythme*. Paris: Presses Universitaires de France, 1974.

———. *The Psychology of Time*. New York: Harper & Row, 1963.

Fraser, J. T., ed. *The Voices of Time: A Cooperative Survey of Man's Views of Time as Expressed by the Sciences and by the Humanities*. New York: George Braziller, 1966.

Fraser, J. T., and Nathaniel Lawrence, eds. *The Study of Time II*. New York: Springer-Verlag, 1975.

Fraser, J. T. *Time as Conflict: A Scientific and Humanistic Study*. Basel: Birkhauser Verlag, 1978.

Fressin, Augustin. *La Perception Chez Bergson et Chez Merleau-Ponty*. Paris: Société d'Édition d'Enseignement Supérieur, 1967.

Friedman, Robert M. "The Formation of Merleau-Ponty's Philosophy." *Philosophy Today* 17 (1973): 272–79.

Frondizi, Risieri. *The Nature of the Self: A Functional Interpretation*. Carbondale: Southern Illinois University Press, 1970.

Gadamer, Hans-Georg. *Truth and Method*. Ed. and trans. Garrett Barden and John Cumming. New York: Seabury Press, 1975.

Galilei, Galileo. *Galileo Galilei: Two New Sciences*. Trans. S. Drake. Madison, Wisconsin: University of Wisconsin Press, 1974.

Gallagher, Shaun. *The Inordinance of Time*. Evanston: Northwestern University Press, 1998.

Gallois, Philippe and Gérard Forzy, eds. *Bergson et les Neurosciences*. Lille: Institut Synthelabo pour les progrès de la connaisance, 1997.

Garrett, Brian. *Personal Identity and Self-Consciousness*. London: Routledge, 1998.

Geraets, Theodore. *Vers une nouvelle philosophie transcendantale; La genèse de la philosophie de Maurice Merleau-Ponty jusqu'à la Phénoménologie de la perception*. Phaenomenologica 39. La Haye: Martinus Nijhoff, 1971.

Gilead, Amihud. "Teleological Time: A Variation on a Kantian Theme." *Review of Metaphysics* 38 (1985): 529–62.

Gottlieb, Anthony. *The Dream of Reason: A History of Philosophy from the Greeks to the Renaissance*. Harmondsworth: Penguin Books, 2000.

Griffin, David R., ed. *Physics and the Ultimate Significance of Time*. New York: State University of New York Press, 1986.

Grogin, R. C. *The Bergsonian Controversy in France 1900–1914*. Calgary, Alberta: The University of Calgary Press, 1988.

Gunter, Pete A. Y., ed. and trans. *Bergson and the Evolution of Physics*. Knoxville: The University of Tennessee Press, 1969.

Gutting, Gary. *French Philosophy in the Twentieth Century.* Cambridge: University of Cambridge Press, 2001.

Hahn, Lewis Edwin. *The Philosophy of Paul Ricoeur.* Chicago: Open Court, 1995.

Hanna, Thomas, ed. *The Bergsonian Heritage.* New York: Columbia University Press, 1962.

Hardy, Barbara. "Towards a Poetics of Fiction: 3) An Approach through Narrative." *Novel* 2 (1968): 5–14.

Heidegger, Martin. *Being and Time.* Trans. John Macquarrie and Edward Robinson. Oxford: Basil Blackwell, 1978.

———. *Poetry, Language, Thought.* Trans. Albert Hofstadter. New York: Harper & Row Publishers, 1975.

Hesnard, Angelo. *L'Oeuvre de Freud et son importance pour le monde moderne.* Paris: Payot, 1960.

Hinchman, Lewis P, and Sandra K. Hinchman, eds. *Memory, Identity, Community: The Idea of Narrative in the Human Sciences.* Albany: State University of New York Press, 1997.

Hoeller, Keith, ed. *Merleau-Ponty and Psychology.* Atlantic Highlands, New Jersey: Humanities Press, 1993.

Hume, David. *A Treatise of Human Nature.* Ed. L. A. Selby-Bigge. Oxford: The Clarendon Press, 1978.

Husserl, Edmund. *Edmund Husserl: Texte zur Phänomenologie des inneren Zeitbewusstseins* (1893–1917). Ed. Rudolph Bernet. Hamburg: Meiner, 1985.

———. "Logische Untersuchungen, Zweiter Band: Untersuchungen zur Phänomenologie und Theorie der Erkenntnis." *Husserliana.* Volume 19/1. Ed. Ursula Panzer. The Hague: Martinus Nijhoff Publishers, 1984.

———. *The Crisis of European Sciences and Transcendental Phenomenology.* Trans. David Carr. Evanston, Illinois: Northwestern University Press, 1970.

———. "Zur Phänomenologie des inneren Zeitbewusstseins (1893–1917)." *Husserliana.* Vol. 10. Ed. R. Boehm. The Hague: Martinus Nijhoff, 1966.

———. *The Phenomenology of Internal Time-Consciousness.* Trans. James S. Churchill. Bloomington: Indiana University Press, 1964.

———. *Cartesian Meditations: An Introduction to Phenomenology.* Trans. Dorion Cairns. The Hague: Martinus Nijhoff, 1960.

Joy, Morny. *Paul Ricoeur and Narrative: Context and Contestation.* Calgary University Press, 1997.

Kant, Immanuel. *Critique of Pure Reason.* Ed. and trans. Norman Kemp Smith. New York: St. Martin's Press, 1965.

Kellogg Wood, Douglas. *Men Against Time: Nicolas Berdyaev, T. S. Eliot, Aldous Huxley, C. G. Jung.* Lawrence: University Press of Kansas, 1982.

Kemp Smith, Norman. *A Commentary to Kant's 'Critique of Pure Reason.'* 2nd ed. London: Macmillan & Co., Ltd., 1930.

Kerby, Anthony. *Narrative and the Self.* Bloomington: Indiana University Press, 1991.

Kierkegaard, Søren. *Repetition: An Essay in Experimental Psychology.* Trans. Walter Lowrie. Princeton: Princeton University Press, 1946.

Kolakowski, Lezek. *Bergson.* Oxford: Oxford University Press, 1985.

Kristeva, Julia. *Hannah Arendt: Life is a Narrative.* Trans. Frank Collins. Toronto: University of Toronto Press, 2001.

Kroes, Peter. "Physics and the Flow of Time." Pt. 2 of *Nature, Time, and History.* Nijmegen Studies in the Philosophy of Nature and Science 4. Nijmegen: Catholic University of Nijmegen, 1985.

Lacey, Alan R. *Bergson.* London: Routlege, 1989.

Langer, Monika. *Merleau-Ponty's Phenomenology of Perception: A Guide and Commentary.* Tallahassee: The Florida State University Press, 1989.

Langer, Susanne K., ed. *Reflections on Art: A Source Book of Writings by Artists, Critics and Philosophers.* Baltimore: John Hopkins Press, 1958.

Lawlor, Leonard. *The Challenge of Bergsonism: Phenomenology, Ontology, Ethics.* London: Continuum Press, 2003.

Lewis, Hywell D. *The Elusive Self.* Philadelphia: The Westminister Press, 1982.

Lloyd, Genevieve. *Being in Time: Selves and Narrators in Philosophy and Literature.* London: Routledge, 1993.

Loptson, Peter. *Reality: Fundamental Topics in Metaphysics.* Toronto: University of Toronto Press, 2001.

Lovejoy, Arthur O. *The Reason, the Understanding, and Time.* Baltimore: John Hopkins Press, 1961.

Madison, Gary B. *The Hermeneutics of Postmodernity.* Bloomington: Indiana University Press, 1988.

————. *The Phenomenology of Merleau-Ponty*. Athens: Ohio University Press, 1981.

Maritain, Jacques. *Bergsonian Philosophy and Thomism*. Trans. Mabelle L. Andison. New York: Philosophical Library, 1955.

Maxwell, Donald. *The Abacus and the Rainbow: Bergson, Proust and the Digital-Analogic Opposition*. New York: Peter Lang, 1999.

McIntyre, Alisdaire. *After Virtue*. 2nd ed. Notre Dame: University of Notre Dame Press, 1984.

Mensch, James R. *Ethics and Selfhood: Alterity and the Phenomenology of Obligation*. Albany: State University of New York Press, 2003.

Merleau-Ponty, Maurice. *The Incarnate Subject: Malebranche, Biran and Bergson on the Union of Body and Soul*. Eds. Andrew Bjelland Jr. and Patrick Burke. New York: Humanities Press, 2001.

————. *The Prose of the World*. Ed. Claude Lefort. Trans. John O'Neill. Evanston, Illinois: Northwestern University Press, 1973.

————. *Nature: Course Notes from the Collège de France*. Trans. Robert Vallier. Evanston, Illinois: Northwestern University Press, 2003.

Mitchell, W. J. T., ed. *On Narrative*. Chicago: University of Chicago Press, 1981.

Muldoon, Mark. *On Ricoeur*. Belmont, California: Wadsworth, 2002.

————. "Reading, Imagination and Interpretation: A Ricoeurian Response." *International Philosophical Quarterly* 40 (2000): 69–83.

————. "Ricoeur and Merleau-Ponty on Narrative Identity." *American Catholic Philosophical Quarterly* 71 (1997): 35–52.

Mullarkey, John. *Bergson and Philosophy*. South Bend, Indiana: University of Notre Dame Press, 2000.

————, ed. *The New Bergson*. Manchester: Manchester University Press, 1999.

Murdock, Maureen. *Unreliable Truths: On Memoir and Memory*. New York: Seal Press, 2003.

Newton, Isaac. *Sir Isaac Newton's Mathematical Principles of Natural Philosophy and His System of the World*. Ed. Florian Cajori. Trans. Andrew Motte. Berkeley: University of California Press, 1966.

Nietzsche, Friedrich. *Human, All Too Human*. Trans. Marion Faber and Stephen Lehmann. Lincoln: University of Nebraska Press, 1984.

Noppen, Jean-Pierre, Sabine De Knop and Renée Jongen, eds. *Metaphor:*

A Bibliography of Post-1970 Publications. Vol. 17, *Amsterdam Studies in Theory and History of Linguistic Science.* Amsterdam: John Benjamen Publishers, 1985.

Noxon, James. *Hume's Philosophical Development; A Study of His Methods.* Oxford: The Clarendon Press, 1975.

Olkowski, Dorothea. *Gilles Deleuze and the Ruin of Representation.* Berkeley: The University of California Press, 1999.

Papanicolaou, Andrew C. and Pete A. Y. Gunter, eds. *Bergson and Modern Thought: Towards a Unified Science.* Vol. 3, *Models of Scientific Thought.* New York: Harwood Academic Publishers, 1988.

Parotte, Wolf and René Dirven, eds. *The Ubiquity of Metaphor.* Vol. 4, *Amsterdam Studies in Theory and History of Linguistic Science.* Amsterdam: John Benjamen Publishers, 1985.

Phillips, Christopher. *Socrates Café: A Fresh Taste of Philosophy.* New York: W. W. Norton & Co., 2001.

Pilkington, Anthony E. *Bergson and His Influence: A Reassessment.* Cambridge: Cambridge University Press, 1976.

Plato, *Timaeus.* Trans. Desmond Lee. Baltimore: Penguin Books, 1965.

Polkinghorne, Donald. *Narrative Knowing and the Human Sciences.* Albany: State University of New York Press, 1988.

Priest, Stephen. *Merleau-Ponty.* London: Routledge, 1998.

Prigogine, Ilya and Isabelle Stengers. *Order Out of Chaos: Man's New Dialogue with Nature.* London: W. Heinemann, 1984.

Prigogine, Ilya. *From Being to Becoming: Time and Complexity in the Physical Sciences.* San Francisco: W. H. Freeman & Co., 1980.

Protevi, John. "'Inventio' and the Unsurpassable Metaphor: Ricoeur's Treatment of Augustine's Time Meditation. *Philosophy Today* 43 (1999): 86–94.

Quinn, John M. "The Concept of Time in St. Augustine," in *Studies in Philosophy and the History of Philosophy.* Vol. 4. Ed. John K. Ryan. Washington, D.C.: The Catholic University of America Press, 1969.

Quirk, Thomas. *Bergson and American Culture: The Worlds of Willa Cather and Wallace Stevens.* Chapel Hill: University of North Carolina Press, 1990.

Rabil, Albert. *Merleau-Ponty: Existentialist of the Social World.* London: Columbia University Press, 1967.

Ricoeur, Paul. *Le Juste II*. Paris: Éditions du Seuil, 2001.

———. *The Just*. Trans. David Pellauer. Chicago: The University of Chicago Press, 2000.

———. *Memory, History, Forgetting*. Trans. Kathleen Blamey and David Pellauer. Chicago: The University of Chicago Press, 2004.

———. "Narrative Identity." *Philosophy Today* 35 (1991): 73–81.

———. "History as Narrative and Practice." Interview by Peter Kemp. *Philosophy Today* 29 (1985): 212–25.

———. "The Power of Speech: Science and Poetry." *Philosophy Today* 29 (1985): 59–70.

———. "Narrative Time." *Critical Inquiry* 7 (1980): 169–90.

———. "The Human Experience of Time and Narrative." *Research in Phenomenology* 9 (1979): 17–35.

———. Introduction to *Time and the Philosophies*. UNESCO. London: The Benham Press, 1977.

———. *The Rule of Metaphor: Multi-disciplinary Studies in the Creation of Meaning in Language*. Trans. Robert Czerny. Toronto: University of Toronto Press, 1977.

———. *Interpretation Theory: Discourse and the Surplus of Meaning*. Fort Worth: The Texas Christian University Press, 1976.

———. *The Conflict of Interpretations*. Ed. Don Ihde. Evanston: Northwestern University Press, 1974.

———. *Freud and Philosophy: An Essay in Interpretation*. Trans. Denis Savage. London: Yale University Press, 1970.

———. *Husserl: An Analysis of His Phenomenology*. Trans. Edward Ballard and Lester Embree. Evanston: Northwestern University Press, 1967.

———. *History and Truth*. Trans. Charles Kelbley. Evanston: Northwestern University Press, 1965.

———. *Freedom and Nature: The Voluntary and the Involuntary*. Trans. Erazim Kohak. Evanston: Northwestern University Press, 1966.

———. *Fallible Man; Philosophy of the Will*. Trans. Charles Kelbley. Chicago: Henry Regnery Company, 1965.

———. "Hommage à Merleau-Ponty." *Esprit*, 296 (1961): 1115–120.

Rorty, Richard. *Philosophy and the Mirror of Nature*. Princeton, New Jersey: Princeton University Press, 1979.

Rosenthal, Sandra. *Time, Continuity and Indeterminacy: A Pragmatic Engagement with Contemporary Perspectives.* Albany: State University of New York Press, 2000.

Rötzer, Florian. *Conversations with French Philosophers.* Trans. Gary E. Aylesworth. Atlantic Highlands, New Jersey: Humanities Press, 1995.

Sarbin, Theodore, ed. *Narrative Psychology.* New York: Praeger, 1986.

Scharfstein, Ben-Ami. "Bergson and Merleau-Ponty: A Preliminary Comparison." *The Journal of Philosophy* 52 (1955): 380–86.

Schechtman, Marya. *The Constitution of Selves.* London: Cornell University Press, 1996.

Schrag, Calvin O. *Communicative Praxis and the Space of Subjectivity.* Bloomington: Indiana University Press, 1986.

Sellars, Wilfrid, ed. *Basic Issues in the Philosophy of Time.* La Salle, Illinois: Open Court, 1971.

Sertillanges, Antonin-Gilbert D. *Avec Henri Bergson.* Paris: Librairie Gallimard, 1941.

Settanni, Harry. *Five Philosophers: How Their Lives Influenced Their Thought.* Lanham, Maryland: University Press of America, 1992.

Sheen, Fulton J. *God and Intelligence.* Louvain: Université Catholique de Louvain, 1925.

Sherover, Charles. *Heidegger, Kant and Time.* Bloomington: Indiana University Press, 1971.

Shestov, Lev. *Job's Balance.* Trans. Camilla Coventry and C. A. Macartney. Athens: Ohio University Press, 1975.

Shoemaker, Sydney and Richard Swinburne. *Personal Identity.* Oxford: Basil Blackwell, 1984.

Smith, C. U. M. *The Problem of Life: An Essay in the Origins of Biological Thought.* London: Macmillan Press Ltd., 1976.

Soulez, Philippe and Frédéric Worms. *Bergson, Une vie.* Paris: Flammarion, 1997.

Spence, Donald. *Narrative Truth and Historical Truth: Meaning and Interpretation in Psychoanalysis.* New York: W. W. Norton and Co., 1984.

Spencer, Herbert. *The Works of Herbert Spencer.* Osnabrück: Otto Zeller, 1966.

Stancati, Claudia, Donata Chirico and Federica Vercillo, eds. *Henri Bergson: esprit et langage.* Liège, Belgium: Pierre Mardaga, 2001.

Taylor, Charles. *The Ethics of Authenticity.* Cambridge: Harvard University Press, 1992.

———. *Sources of the Self: The Making of the Modern Identity.* Cambridge: Harvard University Press, 1989.

———. *Human Agency and Language: Philosophical Papers I.* Cambridge: Cambridge University Press, 1985.

Taylor, Richard. "Time and Life's Meaning." *Review of Metaphysics* 40 (1987): 675–86.

Teichmann, Roger. *The Concept of Time.* London: MacMillan Press, 1995.

Trainor, Paul. "Autobiography as Philosophical Argument: Socrates, Descartes, and Collingwood." *Thought* 63 (1988): 378–96.

Turetzky, Philip. *Time.* London: Routledge, 1998.

Venema, Henry. *Identifying Selfhood: Imagination, Narrative and Hermeneutics in the Thought of Paul Ricoeur.* Albany: State University of New York Press, 2000.

Vergote, Antoine. *In Search of a Philosophical Anthropology.* Trans. Mark Muldoon. Amsterdam\Leuven: Rodopi and Leuven University Press, 1996.

Wall, John, William Schweiker and David W. Hall. *Paul Ricoeur and Contemporary Moral Thought.* New York: Routledge, 2002.

Weil, Simone. *Lectures in Philosophy.* Trans. Hugh Price. Cambridge: The Cambridge University Press, 1978.

Whitrow, Gerald J. *Time in History: Views of Time from Prehistory to the Present Day.* Oxford: Oxford University Press, 1988.

Yasuo, Yuasa. *The Body: Toward an Eastern Mind-Body Theory.* Trans. Nagatomo Shigenori and Thomas P. Kasulis. Ed. Thomas P. Kasulis. Albany, New York: State University of New York Press, 1987.

Young, Damon A. "The Mortal Blessings of Narrative: Death, Poetry, and the Beginnings of Cultural Change," *Philosophy Today.* 45 (2001): 275–85.

Index

action, 183–85, 189–91
ambiguity, 141–43, 156, 161, 172, 243
anognosia, 132, 134
aporias of time: ambiguity versus, 243; in Aristotle, 36–39; in Augustine, 31–36; in Bergson, 93–95, 181; in Camus, 235; in Heidegger, 50–59; in Husserl, 39–43; in Kant, 44–50; in Merleau-Ponty, 143–44, 181; poetic resolution of, 188, 210, 225, 227, 229, 237; Ricoeur on, 50–59, 198, 225–27, 236, 243; trace and, 201
archives, 200
Arendt, Hannah, 252–53
Aristotle, 36–39, 187–89, 227, 230, 252
Augustine, Saint, 32–37, 97, 179, 187, 199, 211, 227, 252

Beauvoir, Simone de, 165–68
behavior, 127–28
Benveniste, Émile, 198, 217, 277n20
Bergson, Henry, 67–118; and consciousness, 74–75, 89–92, 94–96; and duration, 70, 74, 79–95, 107, 238–41; and freedom, 70, 73, 88–92, 98–100, 115–17, 240; ideal resolution in, 211; influence of, 67–68; and intensity, 76–79; and intuition, 74–75, 92–94, 96, 107, 238; and language, 98, 102–7, 110, 112, 242; and meaning, 117–18; and memory, 87,

89–90, 113, 116, 267n27; Merleau-Ponty and, 119–22; methodology of, 72–75; and narrative, 108–15, 241–42; and perception, 85–88; philosophical context of, 8, 69–73; Ricoeur and, 240–41; and self, 96–115, 228, 232; and time, 69–70, 73, 97, 179–80 (*see also* and duration)
body: Bergsonian concept of, 84–88, 120–21; body schema, 138; habit, 134, 137; lived, 153, 246–48; Merleau-Pontyean concept of, 120–21, 132–45, 150–51, 174–75, 243–44, 246–48; phenomenal, 150–52
Boutroux, Émile, 69
Bréhier, Émile, 168, 247
Brockelman, Paul, 10–11

calendars, 198–200
Camus, Albert, 235–36
Care, 52–54
Carr, David, 10–11
catharsis, 209
causality, 81–82, 92
change: conceptualizing, 229–32; consciousness and, 80, 97; duration as, 81
character: fictional, 215; moral, 219–20
Claudel, Paul, 176
Confessions (Augustine), 252
consciousness: Bergsonian concept of, 74–75, 89–92, 94–96; causality not applicable to, 81–82, 92; and